Sating
the Preta

Lily Scot

COVER ILLUSTRATION

From the twelfth century Scroll of the Hungry Ghosts, national treasure of Japan exhibited at the Kyoto National Museum.

The scroll illustrates the world of the hungry ghosts, one of the six realms of Buddhism. Hungry ghosts are also known by their Sanskrit name *preta*.

Copyright © 2013 Lily Scot
All rights reserved.
ISBN-13: 978-0615818429
LCCN: 2013942255

DEDICATION

I could not have written this book without the
influence of these three dear people

Ellen

For her support and guidance through the
labyrinth of my history

Manuel

For showing me the way in

Honor

For helping me tell the story

CONTENTS

Lily Scot

PREFACE

In our increasingly anxious society, all of us are vulnerable to Complex Post-Traumatic Stress Disorder (Complex PTSD) as more of us experience psychological trauma first and second hand. For most of us, these are not horrendous headline-creating incidents. They are subtle moments of terror first felt by us in childhood that open us to risk and further emotional abuse in adulthood. Out of this complex trauma we learn reactions and behaviors we use in a psychotic merry-go-round of avoiding or confronting new terrors – Complex PTSD. Too many of us are the product of complex trauma, and too many others its unwitting cause.

Trauma is too quickly labeled as rape, beatings, torture, restraint and captivity. I think most trauma is far less shocking than these severe incidents. It's emotional manipulation, verbal assault, sexual harassment and molestation, intimidation, workplace abuse, and other non-violent trauma too tolerated by society. I do not mean to downplay severe trauma, but instead aim to raise consciousness about the diverse expressions of non-violent abuse that too many condone as discipline or corrective behavior change presumed to be needed by children, spouses, coworkers or employees.

Abuse of all kinds is not okay. What can be most traumatizing is terror of what might come;

what has been threatened or insinuated. The fear of the abusive person now sitting quietly in another room is worse than the reality of their actively abusive presence before us. Trauma is rarely delivered by crazed international terrorists, untreated mentally ill people run amok or pedophiles on the lam. These are myths we create to silence the fact that most abuse occurs in the course of victims' daily lives and is perpetrated not by strangers, but by those they are raised to trust.

I didn't even know I'd been emotionally abused until diagnosed with Complex PTSD late in life. If I'd known my very painful feelings were a treatable consequence of psychological trauma that wasn't my fault, I'd have found relief and led a healthier life at a younger age. I wrote *Sating the Preta* hoping young women and men experiencing feelings such as extreme anxiety and depression would relate to my story and seek help sooner.

I've tried to illustrate the development and characteristics of Complex PTSD through a personal story I hope translates the disorder into a problem that can be understood and treated rather than the unrelieved craziness that victims feel and loved ones witness. My intention is to help others set themselves more comfortably on a journey toward recovery, one perhaps similar to the transformation I experienced.

This story is also intended to suggest that in these troubled times we all become more accepting of each other and more insightful, forgiving and kinder in our judgment of what motivates those we meet. Their behavior may just be a reflection of the tremendous chaos fermenting in the soul from influences over which they had no control.

1950

The watercolor portrait of our house in Berlin was painted by an itinerant artist soon after the war, my mother giving the man only a few German marks for an afternoon spent detailing the features of our beautiful home. A quiet, peaceful picture, the light yellow house is surrounded by tall thin trees with dark green leafy branches. Ivy creeps up the walls nearing the shutters of the windows through which can be glimpsed shadowy signs of life. Lovely purple and red flowers grace the walkway next to which is a white baby carriage outside the kitchen window with me asleep in it, as I'd been when the painter happened by.

For many years I've looked at this painting, imagining my small self in that carriage, thinking how much innocence was lost so early and wishing I could return to that moment, to the comfort of that summer day. There has been much beauty and goodness in my life, but had I known then the degree of hunger and thirst for human connection I'd come to feel many decades later, the stillness and silence of that day would have been broken by the shrillness of a baby crying.

Faith, hope and years of support by wise counsel did lead me to find self-understanding and solace.

I would learn to sate the desire for human connectedness I craved without seeking approval from outside myself. I would learn how to dispel the shame I had for my past for I wasn't at fault. And I would learn how to protect myself and assure a better outcome for my life. But it would take time as well as courage and a great maturing of insight.

My father was posted in Berlin at the end of World War II as a lieutenant colonel in the army working with the German army's High Command on redirecting the wartime propaganda machine for peacetime use by creating newsreels, radio programs and newspaper articles to help the citizenry adapt to changing conditions. Having graduated from divinity school, he'd begun the war as a military chaplain and in time was promoted to military attaché in Beirut, Lebanon, in the army's G-2 intelligence division, handling reconnaissance missions in the Middle East. I still have his small black Beretta pistol and a handful of diplomatic passports, the expressions in the photos becoming increasingly dour over his years of stress and uncertainty.

My mother joined him after a transatlantic call reunited them in marriage, ending a divorce that had come early in their relationship. Her father, a Presbyterian minister, conducted the ceremony over the phone, her mother at his side, while she and my father reaffirmed their vows.

Our house in Berlin had been my father's best attempt at nesting, creating a home he hoped could compensate somewhat for their years of separation while he'd been overseas and the hurt he caused my mother by asking for a divorce, returning her to her parents' care, an unhappy outcome for a young woman hopeful for a secure future with a loving husband in a society that demanded marriage for women.

He'd been too afraid of marriage at a young age and too desirous of more worldly experiences as those he'd known before marriage and before the war when freely motorcycling through Europe as a graduate student first in Germany and then in Scotland, arriving there safely as the ominous chords of the prelude to war played across the continent. He'd written his father at the family farm in Linden, North Carolina to reassure them all that, contrary to rumor, no German bombs were blasting the shores of the Firth of Fourth, not far from where he rented a room.

During the war, while Mom sat home repairing her devastated young adulthood, Dad was privy to the Beirut high life, still a comfortable enough distance from the war arena. He was a very handsome young man. There is a black and white photograph of him dressed in his formal white uniform and brimmed cap, a stark contrast to his black hair and smooth, tanned face. His eyes are very clear and his trimmed moustache nicely frames a smile. He was as dashing in this portrait as any movie poster of Errol Flynn, and, in fact, there was a resemblance.

He was no less a figure when he decided, at war's end, that he was ready to commit to family life. I was born a year after their remarriage, a child's birth sealing their troth and signaling their new beginning. I imagine Mom's bulging stomach also informed any possible competition of her reinstatement as woman of the house. Other old, creased, black and white photos of Dad in Berlin show him in the company of dapper fellow officers and well-dressed, sophisticated women with stylish hats and long cigarette holders, Dad looking rakish in dark double-breasted suits, holding a cocktail or fingering a fedora hat.

Not long after I was born, my parents traveled a great deal, trying to reclaim their romance in private, strengthen their vows and rebuild a still fragile relationship. Dad escorted Mom through North Africa and the Middle East, our home later laden with treasures from these trips, including stones my father collected and labeled with the names of places from which they were gathered including ochre colored stones from Jerusalem, a chunk of the bombed Reichstag and tiles from Hitler's fireplace in his Eagle's Nest retreat in Berchtesgaden. For decades we had a hollow but very heavy metal bust of Hitler that sat in our basement.

I was left with Elzebet, our German housekeeper. I've seen one picture of her holding me, doting on me, in the garden behind the Berlin house. I was told she was a very gentle woman who mothered me as if I were her own. She was a pleasant looking, middle-aged woman with soft brown hair pinned in the style of the day, smiling at whoever took the picture.

After our stay in Berlin, when I was six months old, we sailed back across the Atlantic on The Queen Mary, newly refitted after retiring from her war years as a troopship. I remember nothing of the journey, of course, nothing of the well-appointed stateroom, our things packed in the leather-strapped and brass, buckle-bound wood steamer trunks I still have, elegant dinners with the captain and evening strolls on the ship's deck about which I've only been told. The trip tore me from Elzebet, and I must have mourned her sudden absence alongside confusion I might have felt about my often absent mother.

Our new home was in Arlington, Virginia, just outside Washington, D.C. where Dad had been promoted to work at the State Department under Secretary of State Dean Rusk. I later learned that our few years there weren't easy. Mom said Dad was unhappy at his job, feeling insecure about such an elite position though he'd excelled as an officer and a diplomat in the years he'd spent in Beirut and Berlin.

She said he was terrified of being with such very powerful men, thinking he didn't qualify for their company. It was also the 1950s and the early, snapping winds of the Cold War had arrived – a fearful time for everyone. The war was over, but Communism was the new enemy. Few, including my Dad, felt prepared for this tense, secretive time.

Mom wasn't comfortable with the formal role she played as a Washington wife. She hated the stiff hats, white gloves and starchy looking smiles she wore; her uniform of stately grace protectively hiding her frailties. I learned later how unconfident she felt, it taking years to outgrow her dormouse childhood. She never considered herself pretty and spent her married life worrying that Dad would leave her, she once said, for some more glamorous Heddy Lamar type. She could only see her plain brown hair and simple figure and felt she faded away behind the glasses she wore all her life. She had what was called "good features," especially her long, shapely legs. She was a graceful woman, quiet and sensitive.

Mom labored over parties held at our house for Dad's associates and their upper crust wives. I was three years old at one of these parties, wearing a scratchy outfit and sitting on a swing in our back yard, watching Mom spooning out salads at a buffet table for a group of women in brightly colored dresses and hats. There was her unhappy smile, lips stretched over her teeth as she did her best to be pleasant and welcoming. She'd been cross with me, telling me to go sit on the swing where I'd be out of the way. I felt sorry for her.

I wandered out to the goldfish tank in front of our house. I can still feel my chest pressing against the rubber rim of the pond and clearly see the fat orange fish slipping away suddenly when I reached into the cool water and touched it, its scales glistening in the hot summer sun. Dad had followed me there, and I remember him laughing. I looked way up at him standing in the bright sunlight and surprised myself with a giddy burst of sound.

I was no taller than his knee, my body round as a ball with big pink cheeks, green eyes and blond hair. He went so high up it looked like he could reach the blinding white and silver clouds in the dark blue sky and brush them away with his fingers. He slowly leaned down, his big smiling face coming closer to mine, grabbed me by my middle and lifted me up. A breeze passed as I glided up, my body spreading out in the moist air, his hands connecting me to his body like a branch to a tree. Flying above his head, my arms and legs reached in all directions, the fish in the tank now a small thing far below.

Then I seemed to float softly down as he swept me into his rocking arms. I felt so safe gazing into the swirling light color of his hazel eyes. He gently put me back down on the ground and I can remember my wobble as I lumbered forward, the ground looking as if it was tilting in front of me – the beginning of a long, stumbling journey, years later walking more steadily towards resolution and fulfillment still to come.

ඉඉඉඉඉඉ

I loved the Pioneer Room in kindergarten. Every Friday afternoon we'd run through the halls to get there and once through the door our frantic pace slowed, giggles and shouts stopped and the wonderment began.

Each child quietly donned an apron and a hat, these transforming garments waiting for us on wall pegs just inside the door. In this room, teachers took seats in one corner, observing the action without interfering unless needed. Boys and girls would slowly resume whatever project consumed their attention the week before. Instruction was minimal. Everything was waiting in its place until all the little hands picked up sewing, took out baking things, began sanding edges of newly cut wooden breadboards, picked up sling-shots to "hunt game" for dinner, carded and spun wool and cut patterns for clothes. Working without competitive incident, each of us became absorbed in our part of the pioneer day; each a small citizen in this community of helpful friends.

Rug weaving on the huge loom was what delighted me most. Each week I'd complete another two or so inches of the geometric Navaho pattern I'd chosen. Sitting on the wood bench, I'd place my feet firmly on the loom pedals as if sitting down at a piano to play. I knew just where I'd left off.

Picking up the shuttlecock of blue yarn, I pushed it left through the two layers of string stretching out in front of me towards the shaft bars at the center of the loom and then tamped the beater to tighten the weave. Switching two of the foot pedals to shift the treadles and change the angle of the strings, I returned the shuttlecock through the loom to the right, the weave secured. Two rows of blue yarn; then the white. I again switched foot pedals and sent the white yarn shuttlecock through the loom, the pattern changing slightly, advancing the diamond shapes. The process mesmerized me, narrowing my concentration until the sounds ceased around me and all I could hear was my breath lengthening into a soft, meditative snore.

Going to the Pioneer Room was a regularly anticipated journey into a safe and comfortable place. It was always exactly the same, except for the slow progress everyone was making. It was a child's world unaffected by anything more threatening than the imaginations of my friends. Even the boys enjoyed the pretend games and got caught up in the practices of family life. In the Pioneer Room, these schoolyard hooligans became responsible men with the job of protecting their homesteads while the girls worked earnestly to meet the hardships of prairie life. Girls who an hour ago had been witchy little snitches became considerate and respectful stoics on entering this room full of trials of mastery over conditions of imagined drought and wildfires, wind storms and invasions by war-loving Indians. You could lose your scalp in this room if you weren't careful. But we were vigilantly mindful of the terrible possibilities, while we pretended to store jams for the winter and sew thick cloth into vests for our brave hunting husbands.

Banging pots roused me from my weaving. A few girls in the kitchen were putting baking things away, signaling the close of the hour as all of us prepared to leave the room for another day. Boys garrulously returned from the hunt, proudly handing over their imagined game to the welcoming homemakers. I complied by finishing a row and neatly lining up my weaving materials. Walking to the front of the room, removing my apron and cap and hanging them back on a hook, everything seemed rightly and simply ordered.

It was time to leave school. A December day, the air was quite cold but the afternoon sun warmed my face as I shuffled along the sidewalk listening to the sound of my boots crunching in the deep snow. Nice houses and old trees lined the street in this pleasant Illinois neighborhood, a suburb of Chicago. We'd moved here when Dad found a minister's job at the Presbyterian Church. He'd chosen to leave the State Department and return to his earlier calling, having finished seminary school and taken his first congregation before joining the army.

Other than the abstract fear of Communism, the 1950s in post-war and post-depression America offered most people some long needed contentment: Families together, Dad at work, Mom in the kitchen, kids in school, and democracy moving forward. This was especially true in towns like this where mostly well-off families lived. Adults worked hard at keeping turmoil out of their lives and from their children. For all I knew, the whole country was a comfortable and compassionate place where in winter all children skated on ice ponds and ran home to drink hot chocolate in front of warm ovens cooking the evening pot roast.

Christmas was coming. As I neared home I thought of all the decorations my mother put up throughout the house. Not a corner was spared. She hung a large red bow with sleigh bells on the inside of the front door, the outside wreath visible through its window. She wrapped garlands and twinkly lights around the stair banister, filled the fireplace mantle with red and green candles and sprigs of balsam and spread special table runners everywhere on which she'd carefully placed treasured mementos of past Christmases. She'd even made a miniature winter scene as a centerpiece for the dining table. In the middle, small figures skated on a mirror surrounded by wads of cotton snow. Little fir trees dotted a landscape of billowy hills down which ceramic children sledded past tiny wooden houses and a church with a delightful stained glass window.

"Stop," shouted a boy. I hadn't noticed him as I walked along in my holiday reverie. He was tall and huge and stepped into the path to block my way. "Stand over there," he commanded, pointing to a spot on the sidewalk. I looked up at his immense round head in its plaid wool cap, stood still and didn't breathe. "Now!" he bellowed. I raced to where he pointed, my legs stiff in my snowsuit. "Ha, ha!" he shouted as soon as I got there, ramming his fist into my chest, pushing the air out of my lungs. He knew the spot was slippery ice covered with a dusting of snow. My feet shot out from under me, and I slammed down hard on the pavement. My back hit first and then my head seemed to crack as it smashed hard on the ice, tears filling my eyes and blurring the sight of him hovering over me, the red of his jacket shifting against the blue sky above his pale laughing face, fleshy pink lips quivering in mirth. He pointed a slush-covered finger at me and ran, still laughing, towards the nearby house. I tried to sit up, but a ball of packed snow hit my forehead and I was knocked back again, knowing full well he'd thrown it.

I lay there, my back and head aching, watching the grey, yellow and white of the clouds blend together through the lens of my tears. I took a deep breath, but as I filled my lungs I felt pain where he'd punched me. A distant car horn broke the quiet. No one was around, and I felt as if I'd been marooned on a strange ice planet. Cold seeped into my legs.

After some time, I rolled over, picked myself up, wiped my eyes and brushed the snow off my pants. Grabbing my lunch box, I headed home. Building anger kept pace with my steps, and my face started to burn. Soon I was marching, my feet stabbing the ground. "What a mean boy," I said out loud to myself. "He tricked me. Why?"

I flung open the front door of our house and raced into the living room. "Mom!" I yelled, and then looked into the kitchen. No answer. The only sound was the barking of my collie dog, wriggling excitedly at my return home. I picked up the phone and dialed the operator as I'd been told to do in an emergency. After hearing a short explanation for the call and learning that my mother wasn't yet home, the operator pleasantly cautioned me to wait for the arrival of the policeman she'd called. Assuring the operator I'd wait, I hung up the phone and went to stand by the window where I had a good view of the boy's house.

My normally pale and freckled face was flushed. *How could he be that awful,* I thought. I kicked off my boots and yanked off my wet snowsuit and knitted hat and threw them on the floor, my long blond curls falling around my shoulders. I jumped up on a chair, and pressed my nose to the window, hoping the boy would reappear so I could glare at him.

The doorbell rang and I ran to the door. I could see the policeman out the little side window panes, opened the door and let him in, the sleigh bells clanging loudly.

"Well hello there," the man said, looking nice in his blue uniform. "Are you Lily?" he asked, stepping into the hall.

"Yes, I am," I said proudly. "I'm the one who called for help. A boy knocked me down. I know where he lives."

"Is that so," the policeman said, kneeling down. "Is this your dog?" he asked, the collie coming to my side. I nodded. "Mind if I give him a gumdrop?"

"That's okay," I said.

The policeman took out a small brown bag, reached in and pulled out a few candies, giving one to the collie and another to me.

"Are you hurt?" he asked kindly.

"I hit my head on the sidewalk. It's alright now. It just hurt for a minute. I had a hat on."

"Mind if I take a look?"

"No," I said, indicating where I'd fallen. The policeman gently parted my hair and looked at my scalp.

"I don't see any injury. I'll bet you're mad though, huh?"

"Yes. He shouldn't be so mean," I scowled.

"No, he shouldn't," the man said. "Perhaps I'll have a talk with his mother. You said you know where he lives?"

"Yes," I said, racing to the window and pointing. "He lives in that green and white house over there."

"The one with the car in the driveway?"

"Yes. He's older than me. And big. He has brown hair."

The front door opened, a whoosh of cold air rippling the pine bough garland on the stairs. My mother came rushing in, clutching a heavy bag of groceries which she put down on the hall table.

"Lily! What's happened?" she asked, hurrying over. "I saw your car," she said, looking with concern at the policeman.

"She's fine," he said, smiling gently. "It seems she had a bit of a run-in with a boy down the street and called the operator for help. She fell and has a bum on her head you should keep an eye on. She's quite a little lady, your daughter," he chuckled. She was just showing me the boy's house. I'll go over and have a talk with his mother. Not to worry," he said, looking at me. "I don't think he'll bother you again. And if he does, just give us a call. You know where to find us!"

"Well thank you for coming over," my mother said. "I got caught in line at the supermarket. I'm so glad you came."

"Not a problem." He smiled and let himself out the front door.

"I'm sorry I wasn't here when you got home, Lily. I'll make you some cocoa, would that be nice?" she said, hanging up her long wool coat and hat in the hall closet.

"Yeah, okay." Picking up the grocery bag, she left for the kitchen, her full skirt swinging as she walked. I wanted her to stop, come back and hold me, just letting me be safe with her softness around me. I wanted her to ask me how I felt and ask more about what happened. But she didn't. And I couldn't ask, couldn't say anything. I just watched her put the groceries away.

Whenever I was sick, my mother would stroke my arm or face with her long fingers. She was there with cocoa or soup, a washcloth or pillow. She made me comfortable, but never comforted me as much as I wanted. She did the things mothers were supposed to do. I knew she loved me, but a closeness was missing – a mother's passion, like that of a feral cat for its young.

I turned away from her, went to the window and watched the policeman drive to the boy's house. After knocking at the door, he was let in by the mother. Some moments later he left, driving slowly in the narrow lanes made by tires through the snow. A plow appeared on the street, shoveling dirty mounds of slush onto the sidewalk where I'd fallen. A streetlight came on, casting yellow sparkles on the snow.

♋♋♋♋♋

Winters were frigid in the Midwest back then. To a five-year-old, a venture to frozen Lake Michigan was even more austere; something like visiting the ice. But for a few years, Dad and I would annually go on a late afternoon.

Arriving this winter at the lake, the bright sun hovered low; spreading an orange curtain over a bleak horizon, tired from a day's work and ready to make its descent. Evening winds grew stronger in the darkening sky, pressing themselves against the heavy, bluish clouds, pushing them slowly east. It was a wind you could hear as it swooshed by, slapping your cheek with its icy hand.

We approached the lake's edge with me carried high on Dad's shoulders, his six-foot frame towering above the ground. I was exhilarated by the fear of falling, though I trusted Dad and felt secure with his big hands holding my legs firmly against his chest.

There was really no lake's edge to be seen as we walked from deep snow onto ice which rose into waves seemingly frozen before hitting the shore. Every year we'd slowly ascend them, higher and higher onto white, crunchy cliffs. Here and there you could see through holes in the ice down into swirling black water beneath. Again the fear would come with its companion of raw thrill.

"Maybe we shouldn't go so far, Dad?" I warily offered as we made our way on the ice.

"No, we're fine," he said. "I've got you. And don't we want to try and catch the moon?" This was a favorite game in all seasons. We'd chase the moon as it rose, trying to grab it to take home and hide for ourselves, bringing it out and savoring the warmth and light of its friendly face when we needed it.

This fattening moon had risen to our left and Dad headed over the ice towards it, reaching out his hand. "I've almost got it!" He spoke gruffly like a character in one of his stories. "Come here you old moon," he called out, snatching at it. "I'm going to get you this time." He reached his arm out further, swinging at it over and over again, tipping us dangerously near the ice precipice.

I played along and stretched my arm out towards his, our fingers finding the bright yellow light, but not quite able to grasp it. "Come on moon!" I shouted, and then laughed. "You almost had it, Dad!"

He stopped his advance and reached out as far as he could, me shifting my weight to keep balanced on his shoulders. "I think I can just reach some of its light," he said, straining and curling his fingers as if to bring light into his palm. "Yes! I've got some," he said triumphantly as he turned his head up to see me and brought his hand to my face, pretending to bathe it with moonlight. "There, the moon's grace is in your bright eyes," he said, smiling at me looking down at him.

"Maybe I can get some more." He reached out again, curling his fingers towards the now silvery rays which had moved higher in the sky. "No luck. It's moved just too far out for us to reach it," he huffed, resigning to our failure. "We'll just try again next time."

"Here's some of my moonlight," I said, rubbing his cheek. "I have more than enough for both of us." The moon proudly held its place in the sky, its glow brightening. The sun was sliding below the horizon, its glow diffusing. We were silent for a time.

"Listen carefully," he whispered.

I closed my eyes and concentrated on hearing the lake. The swirling water below made a deep, rushing sound, the tide unmindful of the ice above it, its mission unimpeded by season. The ice groaned and with Dad standing still I could also feel a slight rise and fall of the ice shelf on which we were perched. The more I listened, the more groaning I heard; the ice like the heaving shoulders of someone grieving.

I opened my eyes but kept my hearing focused. The sun had sunk into the lake, leaving darkness except for the ethereal brightness of the crater-dappled moon, its glow now casting a broad, even light. Stars had emerged and the lake became astoundingly beautiful. I felt like the masthead on a great sailing ship far from harbor. But my ship slowly turned and carefully headed back down the white cliffs to the deep snow and out the path to the parking lot where we'd left our car.

"Mom's probably wondering when we'll be back for dinner," he said. I hugged his neck and burrowed my face in his hair. He pulled his thick coat around my legs to warm them and gave them a gentle squeeze. Looking back at the lake and the moon, I gave a goodnight smile.

Our Dodge was the only car in the parking lot. We slid onto the cold leather seats and Dad started the car to let it warm up a bit. "Boy, it sure does get cold fast once that sun goes down." He leaned over towards me quickly and I knew what was coming. "But I know where it's nice and warm," he said, laughing as he burrowed his face into my shoulder, kissing my bare neck and making munching sounds.

I pulled away and looked at the floor. "Dad, please," I said weakly. The enjoyment of being on the lake vanished. My feet and hands were numb. The blowing air from the car heater wasn't warm yet and the seat felt hard. I slid closer to the door and away from Dad. He was always doing that and I really hated it. My neck stiffened and my stomach tightened; my breathing shallow.

He headed the car out of the lot and started for home. "Oh, you know I just have to get some of that nice piggy meat now and then."

❦❦❦❦❦

Clutching the small birthday present to my chest, I hopped up the steps to the front door of my friend's house, waving goodbye to my mother who smiled and turned to walk down the street toward home. Louise home. Louise was a new girl in first grade that fall and had just moved in, one block from where I lived. I rang the bell and nervously looked down at my feet. In the hurry to get to the party, Mom had mismatched my socks; one red, the other yellow. The red one had fallen down and was bunched around the strap of my shiny black leather shoe. I bent over to pull it back up, the lace on my new slip scratching against my thigh. When I stood up, my underpants shifted uncomfortably. I wanted to tug them down, but the front door opened. My friend's beaming smile greeted me, a sparkling party hat set in the curls of her brown hair.

"Hi, Lily. You're the last one. I wouldn't let Daddy start the party 'til you got here!"

"Sorry," I said, handing her the present.

"Thanks! I'll put it with the others. Come on." She skipped down the short, dark uncarpeted hall to the living room.

I followed her, hearing the other girls before I saw them nestled together on the couch. They were all giggling and chatting excitedly. I knew most of them, but they looked so different in their party dresses and paper hats. It wasn't the same as seeing them in their play clothes climbing around the branches of the chestnut tree on the corner where we often gathered.

The girls brought color to the sparsely furnished and dreary room. Though Louise and her father were new to the house, there were no boxes to hint at any unpacked knick knacks. The shelves held no books or photographs. The most character came from the pile of presents on the table and a cluster of party balloons. I knew that Louise's mother had left them the year before for some reason. *Maybe that's why it's so barren in here*, I thought.

"Sit next to me!" squealed the tiniest of the little girls. I dropped into the space made for me on the one big armchair in the room.

From the kitchen came the animated voice of Louise's father. "Who wants to be the first to pin the tail on the donkey," he said, entering the room and passing out drink cups and soda.

"I do, I do," yelled one of the girls, jumping up. She eagerly accepted the blindfold, a handkerchief he tied loosely around her head.

I watched the girls get spun dizzy by the father, a short man with dark hair and thick-rimmed glasses. Each wobbled in turn towards the wall, pins in outstretched hands, feeling for the paper donkey. All the girls screamed in shrill crescendos when the tails were pinned on its nose, ears, legs and everywhere else wrong.

Soon it was my turn. I stared at the donkey's rear end, determined to remember the spot even when twirled. I stood perfectly still, but excited, while the blindfold was tied. The father spun me, his hands on my waist, turning me faster and faster. It seemed a long time before he stopped. When he did, I ran towards what I hoped was the wall, slammed into it and stuck in the pin. Pulling off the blindfold, I saw I had missed the donkey altogether. The other girls were hysterical. I laughed too, but dizzily slid down into a corner of the couch.

For the next hour, Louise's father entertained the party guests with games until we were tired and out of breath, collapsing onto the living room floor and furniture. "Anybody still hungry?" he asked, heading for the kitchen.

"We want cake, we want cake," the girls chanted.

The father returned with a white frosted cake, a huge number six surrounded by lit candles. I was almost six years old myself. We sang the birthday song, reaching a screeching pitch by the end, and it wasn't long before the room was strewn with paper plates and crumbs. Louise then opened her presents, the girls oohing with pleasure at each new gift. Soon, amidst the colorful debris of wrapping paper, exhausted girls spread themselves across the floor, bits of frosting stuck on their hair and clothes. Some started exploring the watercolor and charcoal pencil sets. Louise and a friend played with a beautiful new Breyer horse, a perfectly scaled model horse outfitted with full riding tackle. Other girls played with the Betsy McCall doll, named for the original paper dolls in McCall's ladies magazine, dressed in one of her many outfits.

Mothers eventually arrived to take their worn-out children home to baths and naps. Louise politely saw them off, thanking them for a fun time. "You don't have to leave yet do you?" Louise asked me, pleading. "You live close by and Dad said it's okay."

"Okay," I said; eager to stay. Finally only I was left, Mom not having come yet.

"Let's play a game," shouted Louise, animated with newly charged energy. "Daddy, what can we do now?"

"How about a game of hide-and-seek?" he suggested, as he wadded up wrapping paper in the living room and stuffed it into a rubbish bin. "I'll play with you to make it more fun."

"That's great," Louise agreed. "You two hide first. I'll count to 20."

Louise pounced on the sofa, buried her head of

brown curls in the pillows and began to count. "One-one hundred, two-one hundred …"

I surveyed the room. I thought I might just fit behind the TV on the table and scurried over to it, squeezing myself in the narrow space behind it.

"Twelve-one-hundred … thirteen-one-hundred," continued Louise.

From my hiding spot I could see her father standing quietly for a moment and then walking out to the hall.

"Nineteen-one-hundred … twenty. Ready or not, here I come," Louise squealed as she raced around the room looking under tables and behind doors. "I know you're here!" She raced into the kitchen, and I could hear the opening and slamming of pantry doors. Bursting out of the kitchen through another door into the hall, I heard the rattle of the tall hat rack and umbrella stand. "I found you, Daddy!" Louise screamed.

After running through another room off the hallway, Louise came to the living room, pacing wildly about. "Aha!" she announced. I flattened myself against the cardboard backing of the TV, breathing ancient dust into my nose, but her jabbing fingers had reached behind the set and found my shoulder. "I got you!"

Her father and I each took our turns as seekers, the exploration expanding into upstairs rooms. I found Louise soon enough, the visible edge of her blue party dress giving away her position under a bed, but it took forever to find her father on the basement landing. On my turn to hide from him, he kept narrowly missing me hiding in the laundry basket, but eventually threw open the lid and grabbed me, laughing and tickling my stomach.

We decided to play one more round of the game with Louise as seeker. As she began counting, her father smiled, put his finger to his lips and whispered, "Why don't we hide together? I know where she'll never find us." I eagerly agreed and followed him out of the living room on tiptoes.

He opened the hall closet and motioned for me to follow him in. I did so and found the closet much deeper than I imagined, his portly frame pushing to the rear of the space behind what seemed like miles of coats. I tripped over boots and shoes, stumbling forward. Then he stopped moving and I bumped into him as he turned to face me.

"We have to keep very quiet," he said, "and not move at all."

"Okay," I giggled, obediently falling silent and still.

Ages passed. I could hear Louise off in other rooms calling out to us. The closet became hot and stuffy. The coats were bulky.

Her search finally brought Louise to the closet. She flung open the door and began pummeling the coats at the front. "You must be in here," she shouted. Her father's hand softly covered my mouth, assuring my silence. As he did this he moved closer and pressed himself against me.

Louise's hands found nothing and she left, huffing her disappointment. Her footsteps retreated down the hall.

More time passed with an occasional muted sound of a door slamming. It was getting hard to breathe, though he'd taken his hand away. The fur coat in front of me became stifling and itchy to my face. I could hear his breath getting heavier. His body began pressing harder into me, jamming me against the fur coat. His breathing got hoarse and rough sounds were coming from his throat. He pushed me again and again into the fur coat, making me stumble forward. Something hard began sliding up and down my back, rhythmically pushing. It scared me. He let out a sudden strange rasping sound. *Maybe he's hurt himself*, I first thought. But then from his soft moans I instantly knew what he'd done, children having remarkable intuition about such things.

I plowed through the coats, wedging my arms in front of me, stomping into shoes and boxes. I felt for the closet door handle, turned and pushed it with all my strength, running out into the hall, out into the air.

"There you are!" Louise shrieked.

Light was streaming through the window panes in the front door. I raced to throw it open, ran down the steps and loped across the yard. The whole world seemed to slow down as I ran. I could watch my feet taking each step, as if it was someone else's body. I saw I'd left my shoes behind. The grassy ground and then black asphalt pavement were intensely clear to me. I scanned the street to cross it, the red, gold and yellow leaves blurring across the trees. I saw the curb pass slowly under me as I sprang over it, the ground turning from soft to hard. It was more than quiet; I heard absolutely nothing. It was as if I was deaf but with really good eyesight. I could see the slightly open back door of my house down the street. I focused on it getting larger until I saw my hand reaching out to grab the doorframe to go through and inside. Looking down as my foot slammed silently on the doorstep, I saw my now filthy mismatched socks, feeling ashamed and worried that Mom would be mad. My knees bobbed up and down as I dashed up the back stairs to my room, closing the door behind me, still with no sound.

I stood in the center of my room. My breathing seemed to stop. The late afternoon light pouring into the room was blinding. I felt weightless, as if I was lifting off the floor, and I wondered if I was dying.

Air gushed out of me in a hot stream. Lungs empty, I sucked in a new breath and held it tightly, my heart pounding. The slowness of motion stopped, time passage became normal again. Sound returned and I could hear my breath releasing from my chest.

Still panicked, I looked down at the back of my legs, sure to see blood. There wasn't any. *Where had it gone?* I thought. *There must be blood.* I pulled down my underpants. No blood. Fear flooded me and I wanted help.

Opening my door, I ran down the hall and headed quietly down the front stairs to the living room where I knew my parents would be. Mom was sitting in her blue padded swivel rocking chair reading a book. Dad sat nearby in his worn leather armchair, reading the newspaper. I seemed to float over to Mom and stop suddenly, staring straight at her, arms pinned to my sides, my back stiff, my face taught with fright.

"Why honey," she said, when she noticed me. "Home from the party already?"

I stood rigidly still, waiting for her to realize everything that had happened. *She had to know. She'll do something. She'll help me*, I thought.

"Did you have fun?" she asked. "Are you hungry?"

She didn't know. How could she not know? Something's wrong, I thought. *Did I look like I'd had a good time? Why didn't she see that? Why hadn't she come to get me from the party?*

I couldn't talk about what happened. Not to her. Not to Dad. I didn't know how to tell them and they wouldn't understand. They might even blame me.

It seemed as if a glass box was around me, its surface gleaming. I could hear Mom talking but her voice sounded muffled, like it would if I heard her through a window. I felt if I were to speak I wouldn't be heard either.

"How about you change your party dress and I'll make us all some chicken and dumplings for dinner. Would that be nice?" she said, rising from her chair, her voice still muffled by the glass walls of my box. But then, she said, "Where are your shoes, Lily?" and it suddenly sounded very clear.

She towered above me, her long-fingered hands smoothing down her dress, her face seeming so far away. I was more scared and alone than ever. *I've done something very wrong,* I thought. I felt as if I was fading, almost invisible. I looked in her eyes, but they didn't seem to be really looking at me.

She can't even see me, I thought. *I'm alone and now I'll always be alone.*

I opened my mouth to cry out, but vomited instead.

"Oh my, too much cake I guess," she said.

It seemed I had two choices: I could let myself keep fading and die, or, I could save myself. I turned to go up to my room, looked down and saw my feet in dirty socks next to the vomit. I watched as my feet started to move, first the red foot, then the yellow.

Red. Yellow. Up the stairs. Red. Yellow. I was choosing to save myself. No one else ever would now. The first thing to do was change my socks. Then I'd know what to do next.

I'd later understand how much my childhood changed then. Wonderment would persist with its belief in a spirited world of gnomes, ensouled stuffed animals and goodness incarnated annually as Santa. But a loss of trust had seared deep hurt into me and from then on, any time I felt manipulated or threatened, I instinctively guarded myself, unable to stop new fear from rekindling the smoldering flesh surrounding that pain. I'd try to call out for understanding from inside, but the sound would be muffled or unheard and I'd again feel invisible. Then the urgency to save myself would reemerge, and I often became defensive and argumentative, even enraged, unable to control my reactions. Fight or flight. I felt an enormous shame that escalated and compounded over time, keeping vigilant from its home deep within me while the remnants of my self-esteem searched desperately for grace and healing.

∾∾∾∾∾∾

Resilient as any child, the passing years brought new discoveries as I looked for ways to become safely visible again. We moved to a new house across town reserved for the minister's family. It was on a street with tall, old trees and big lawns. There were lots of kids in the neighborhood and I made friends.

By age nine I'd become enraptured with possibility. It was my Renaissance. I learned to play the flute, read lots of novels and wrote short stories.

My room was an adventure. The walls were covered with *National Geographic* maps of countries and continents, maps of the ocean floor and the planets that I read about. *Jupiter is the largest planet.* I made models of the planets, using Styrofoam balls of varying sizes, their exteriors molded with flour paste mountains and valleys and carefully painted according to the colors shown in their pictures. *Mars is the red planet.* Toothpicks connected Saturn's rings and joined the moons to their planets. Gobs of sticky paste covered my fingers and got in my hair. Acrylic fumes curled up my nose. I often caught myself softly snoring, my mind completely absorbed in the work. My planets could move on circles of string I'd attached around the room near the ceiling, and I could reposition them at will, standing on a chair. I was master of my little universe.

The planets got me interested in geology. I had a rock collection and spent hours testing and identifying them with chemicals from a kit, subjecting my specimens to brutal climate conditions from an ice bag or a hair dryer to verify their hardiness or witness small transformations. I loved mica best. It was other-worldly, its smooth blackness and shine like something mysterious we'd find on the moon when we got there. I just knew it.

Less interesting rocks became fodder for my mouse cage. I had two white mice that mated and produced tiny round, pink babies that looked like pencil erasers, but were soft and warm. I caught a wild brown mouse from the woodpile, carefully carrying its shaking little body inside and dropping it into the cage, thinking they could all be friends. I felt dreadful watching it run around in panic looking for an exit, finally let it escape into a small box I held in the cage for transport back to the woodpile.

The woodpile was my outdoor refuge behind the garage where no one could watch me in my cabin in the wild. I was a lone pioneer woman and snuck dry goods and supplies out of the house to use: A bowl, little dishes, a cup, a few utensils, a hand towel, an apple corer and cookie cutters. I'd sit on my tree stump and pretend to peel potatoes for soup, simmering my supper in a large pot over an imagined fire, singing pieces of songs: *Mamma, mamma crow, fly up to the mountain.* The woodpile smelled dank and wonderful. *Mamma, mamma crow, fly up so high.* Mom had made a long cotton skirt and an apron for me to wear and I'd sit braiding my hair, the sun warming me. *Mamma, mamma crow, fly up to the mountain.* Soon I'd drift into daydreams about prairie life. *What do you see as you pass by?*

Across the street, my friend and I created an entire frontier town out of paths through the trees on the hill next to her home. We had a post office, general store, doctor's office and a church. Our small houses neighbored each other, of course. We'd visit for tea and sandwiches that magically appeared, our fantasies not interrupted by her mother's quiet visit. Then pulling our wagons through town, we'd do our errands, picking up imagined bolts of cloth and dropping off pretend knives for sharpening, running here and there in our busy day. We'd stop and chat with almost visible shopkeepers, telling the butcher *You should've seen old Wilcox's face when our cow Blarney wandered into his vegetable garden.* Through the day my friend and I seemed to blend together, our thoughts moving freely between us, our friendship a sanctuary.

Mom would call me to dinner from across the street and I'd run home to find her tuna casserole steaming on the dining table out on the screened-in porch of our house. She always covered the casserole with crunchy potato chips. *And for dessert, we have fruit Jell-O,* Mom would usually say, putting the dessert bowl on the table, topping the bright green mass with whipped cream. I loved our dinners on the porch, the evening breeze passing through, making us comfortable and happy. We'd talk and laugh about silly stuff. In 1959 anything seemed possible. Except for the vague threat of a Martian or Communist invasion, it was safe in our world.

After dinner I'd play with the neighborhood kids. Hide-and-seek games would go on forever, quiet darkness interrupted by shrieks and laughter as seekers found hiders and we'd come together for a new game, maybe capture the flag or a water balloon fight. On really hot, sweaty nights the bursting balloons felt incredibly good, our clothes saturated with cold water, screams of *I'll get you for that!* and squeals of delight rising out of our bodies with the escaping heat.

Eventually we'd all be called home again. I'd go upstairs where Mom would be running my bath. I'd soak clean in the bubbly water, dry off and put on just-washed cotton pajamas.

Once back downstairs I'd throw myself onto Dad's lap for a story he'd read or just make up. We'd fit comfortably together in his plush armchair. Mom would sit reading, knitting or sewing in her blue padded swivel rocking chair.

The room was furnished with antiques from

Mom's family. Claw-footed Queen Anne tables, oval gilt mirrors, a blue velvet setee, and a straight-backed chair with a beautiful needlepoint seat cushion made by my grandmother. A tall, hand carved wooden statue of some German saint would travel with us from home to home as we moved, eventually ending up with me as I had a fondness for the fellow, perhaps because Mom always patted his head and talked to him when she dusted. We also had one of the first television sets and would watch *Rawhide* or *Kraft Theater*. But programming was sparse back then and most nights I'd listen to one of Dad's stories. His favorite that became an ongoing series was *Green Monkey Island*.

One hot summer day while Jimmy green monkey was exploring, he found a piece of glass on the beach, Dad began one night. *It was the size of Jimmy's hand with smooth, rounded edges. He'd never seen anything like it. Why, you could see clear through it. Not sure what to make of it, he put it in his pocket and walked on.*

Further along, Dad continued, *Jimmy green monkey saw another piece of glass. He ran to it and found that it was also smooth and nice to hold and through it he could see the plants and rocks on the beach.*

I snuggled deeper into Dad's arms and he held me close. I loved the feel of his flannel shirts, especially this red and blue plaid one. Its fuzziness was so soft on my face and its folds cradled my head against his shoulder. I felt like I was sinking right into him.

Excited by his find, Jimmy green monkey hopped and skipped home to show off his discovery. He ran into Old Fitch green monkey closing up his banana store. 'See my new invention?' Jimmy called out.

Why I say, that's quite unusual, my young friend.

'You find a way to harden water? What're you going to do with it?' Old Fitch asked, perplexed but amused.

Don't know,' answered Jimmy. 'Something spectacular though!' 'And on down the road Jimmy went. He found his Dad, Farmer Hairy green monkey, coming in from his orchard of Macadamia trees.

'Dad, Dad!' shouted Jimmy. 'Come see what I found on the beach!' Farmer Hairy looked through the glass.

'Well that's like nothing I ever laid my eyes on before. You should show that to Grey Beard green monkey. He'd know what it is if anybody does."

I laid my arm out on Dad's leg and, knowing what I wanted, he began tickling it with long strokes of his fingers. It felt so good. Mom looked over at us and smiled, leaning her head back on her chair to listen as Dad continued the story.

Jimmy ran up into their tree house and out onto his branch, which forked into smaller branches that cradled him when he slept. He hid among the broad leaves and held up his two pieces of glass for further inspection, placing them side by side and moving them closer and farther apart. Then he held them one in front of the other and moved them back and forth. He turned them around and held them up again. And then a very strange thing happened.

I looked up into Dad's soft hazel eyes and he into my blue ones, while he paused and smiled. I noticed that grey hair was beginning to mix with black just back of his temples.

"What ... what happened?" I said, my mouth dropping open a little.

Well, when Jimmy green monkey held the two pieces of glass one in front of the other at a very specific distance, Dad continued, *the objects on the other side were larger, a lot larger than how they normally looked without the glass. Jimmy almost fell out of the tree he was so excited*

The next day Jimmy built a long tube out of a thick, hollow reed into which he placed the two pieces of glass at just the right distance from each other. When he finished, he triumphantly held up the tube to see if he'd gotten it right. Yes! The pieces were set perfectly. Looking through the tube, anything he saw was huge! A macadamia nut looked like a boulder; an insect, a dinosaur; a twig, a big tree branch. It was amazing. If he turned the glass at the end of the tube back and forth he could focus on objects at different distances. He couldn't believe he'd made it work. He named it his viewing-tube.

Jimmy green monkey ran to the beach and aimed the viewing-tube at the horizon, shifting the glass one way and then the other. And what do you think he saw?

Again, Dad paused and looked at me.

"What, what?" I almost squealed.

Jimmy green monkey saw … a brown dot that with a twist of the glass became another island when it was focused! No one had ever known of any other island besides theirs. He almost stopped breathing. Not trusting what he'd seen, he looked again. There it still was.

I was fighting my drowsiness, being very content in Dad's lap. I picked up one of Mom's hairbrushes, which she kept in her reading basket by the chair for occasional primping. I gave it to Dad, who started brushing my hair, drawing it slowly through my long curls. There was no feeling as good as this.

He could make out the trees on the island, Dad said, without interrupting the story. *He could see small hills and thickets of what looked like the brambles on his own island. He kept panning back and forth across the island and then saw something move! He twisted the glass just a tiny bit further and it came into view. And do you know what it was?*

"What, what?" I gasped.

Jimmy green monkey saw … another monkey. But it wasn't a green monkey. No, it was … a pink monkey. And it was a girl pink monkey, with long curly fur. Jimmy almost dropped the viewing-tube, his jaw falling open in shock. This couldn't be, he thought to himself. Unsure, he looked again. But there she was; the most beautiful girl monkey he'd ever seen. For a moment, it seemed like she looked right at Jimmy, who completely froze, staring at her. And then she walked away and out of sight. Jimmy went home in a stupor. Without saying more than 'good night' to his Mom or Dad, he climbed to his branch, nestled the viewing-tube safely in the leaves and dropped off to sleep, thinking about pink monkeys and long curly fur.

Dad smiled and gave me a crushing bear hug signaling the end of the story for now.

"No, no, you can't stop now!" I protested.

"Well it's time for all little monkeys to get to sleep," he said, tickling my tummy until I laughed hard.

"Okay, okay," I said, "but this story better go on tomorrow night."

Picking me up in his arms to carry me to bed he said, "Well certainly. I need to know what happens too, you know."

"Good night, sweetheart," my mother called from her chair.

Dad carried me up the stairs into my room and tossed me on my bed. I crawled under the clean sheets and snuggled my pillows and my stuffed rabbit. He sat down in the chair next to my bed and lit a cigarette. Leaving the light off, he began moving his red -glowing cigarette in circles, making patterns as moving it quickly caused the red glow to streak through the air. He drew a long oval and said it was Jimmy green monkey's island. He showed me Jimmy's family tree, using up and down motions the cigarette and he drew where his branch was. And that was all I saw because my eyes slowly closed as I fell fast asleep.

Many years later in reading Dad's memoir of his boyhood, I learned that it was his father who had invented Green Monkey Island. *This stern disciplinarian*, as Dad referred to him in his memoir, *who was inclined to paddle his children through life like a canoe*, also had a gift of whimsy and many nights around the fire he'd regale his children with these highly imaginative stories, a "thousand-and-one-nights" tale with versions for any number of characters and circumstances. Perhaps that's what inspired Dad's later writings, his sermons, to be full of stories, especially Christ's parables, drawing his attentive parishioners around the warming fire of his soliloquy, passing on wisdom, sparking the tinder of human understanding.

1960

The plane drifted through the cloud-layered sky like a slow moving ship. Dad had given me the window seat and my nose was pressed to the glass, taking in the dreamy sight. The clouds were the huge, vertical kind and we glided between their silver towers. Below were flatter expanses of clouds and it looked as if you could leap off the wing onto their soft cushions, lying down to feel the warming sun. Years later, Mom would say that whenever she was flying through clouds she'd picture my grandparents resting on them and smiling at her as she passed.

We were taking this trip because Grandma had died. Mom and Dad always tried to spare me pain and grief so Mom had gone to the funeral, while Dad and I left for Hawaii, far away from the sadness so Mom could freely mourn.

Grandma's death was accidental. Like many women of her generation, she didn't know how to drive and when the parked car she was in started to slide down the hill, she panicked. Not knowing one pedal from the other she opened the door and tried to roll out and away from the car. But she didn't make it. The car rolled over her and she was crushed, later dying from internal injuries. As Grandpa had parked the car, he was never able to free himself of the belief her death was his fault, which of course it wasn't. I missed Grandma very much. When Dad and I got back from our trip, Grandpa would come to live with us, which I thought would be nice. He was now so old and though he was never tall he'd shrunk to almost my height. He had a glass eye from an accidental slip of a dentist's drill. I didn't know how a sweet man like Grandpa could have tolerated such pain, and I always winced when he looked at me with his unmoving eye. I was glad I'd now be able to sit with him to watch his Yankees play on television and maybe help him smile.

After hours of flying, snacks, naps and, it seemed, a hundred games of rock-paper-scissors with Dad, we landed in Honolulu. The warm and very moist air was like nothing I'd ever felt before. The trip to the hotel was short, but I took in all the sights of this city that seemed as big as Chicago, our neighboring city at home. Palm trees were everywhere and looked just like Dad had described, only there were so many kinds of them. Big bright flowers with funny tongues stood out from dark green bushes and the sidewalks were dusted with sand.

The hotel was many stories tall and had a private courtyard with a huge swimming pool. Our room was on the fourth floor. As soon as we unpacked, I wanted to go swimming. Dad obliged me, we changed our clothes and headed down the quiet hall on thick, elegant carpets to the back stairs and out through the glass doors to a suddenly noisy courtyard full of people.

For a long time I swam and dove and swam some more. Exhausted, I floated on my back, staring up at the blowing fronds of the towering palm trees circling the pool.

Eventually I made friends with another girl, also age 10. "Let's play tea," I suggested.

"Is that a game?" she asked.

"Yes," I said, explaining we'd both take deep breaths, sink to the bottom of the shallow end and pretend to pour and drink tea like fine ladies.

"That sounds fun," she said, and we began our descent. We struggled to stay on the pool floor drinking our "tea" with pinkies raised, but soon had to burst to the surface, alternately laughing and sucking in air. We did this many times, all with slight variations. But by early afternoon she had to leave with her parents and I was alone again.

I decided to explore the deep end and try diving to the bottom; always a challenging feat. Snaking my way through the flailing limbs of noisy swimmers, I reached the end, took in a deep breath and dove way down, enjoying how much quieter it got. I could see something on the bottom, but it was blurry in the bright rays of sunlight shifting in the undulating water down to the blue pool floor. After repeated dives using stronger kicks I saw it was a child's plastic key ring. I tried to reach it, my muscles straining, but it was too far down and my lungs couldn't hold enough air. I floated to the surface, feeling the water pressing on my body. *I'd love to be a fish*, I thought, *wrapped in warm salt water, sliding along gentle currents, feeling free.*

On one dive I saw what seemed to be a window in the side of the pool. *That's weird*, I thought. I swam closer and peered in, pressing my hands against the glass to shut out the light to see inside.

A crowded row of men sat at a bar facing the window, drinking, gesturing and joking to each other in the dark room. I shot to the surface for more air, and on the return dive I saw notes taped to the window with words on them. I swam closer. The words were written backwards so that anyone in the pool could read them.

A woman dove into the pool, her long graceful body trailed by bubbles. The men all turned to watch her. She was a beautiful blond woman in a red bikini. The men pointed animatedly to the notes on the window, but she didn't see the men or the notes and swam away. The men silently roared their disappointment through gaping mouths, tossing swizzle sticks at the window.

I dove again and swam up to the notes. Now I could make them out. One said: *Take it all off.* Another read: *Don't be shy. Show us what you've got!*

I focused further into the room and saw that the men at the end of the bar were all looking at me. They were laughing. One held his hands on his chest as if holding breasts and rocked in a jesting way. The men laughed again and then looked back at me.

I bolted upward, coughing water out of my lungs as I broke the surface. I treaded water awkwardly; wanting to kick at the men I was sure could just reach up, grab my feet and pull me down through the window. I thrashed my way to the pool ladder, hoisted myself up and ran back on wobbly legs to our lounge chairs.

Dad wasn't there. I twisted back and forth straining to look for him. I was cold and I felt naked in my bathing suit. I was sure that people looking in my direction were staring at me and talking about how they'd seen me act in front of those men. I wanted Dad to help me. But what would I say? I felt ashamed. It was my fault and he'd be ashamed of me, too.

Grabbing the hotel towel and wrapping it around me, I curled into a shivering ball and dropped onto the chair. Hot, stinging tears soaked the towel. I covered my eyes and shut out the light. The sounds around the pool weren't friendly anymore. Everything sounded shrill. I wanted to go home.

I fell asleep and sometime later Dad shook my shoulder and I woke up, feeling dazed and unsure of where I was.

"Oh my little princess, you're quite sunburned," I heard him say. "We'd better get you back to the room. It's getting late anyway."

I roused myself slowly, opening my eyes and glancing around. The memory of the men in the bar came right back to me, but it was like a confusing dream, the men's faces swirling underwater and then fading away like a passing thought.

The pool seemed different. Not many people were there and the uncluttered lounge chairs were pulled into neat rows. Strings of twinkling lights circled the palm trees and colorfully lit lanterns swayed in the open windows of the café.

I sat up and looked at Dad, still in his swimming trunks, but now wearing a large shirt covered with huge orange flowers, petals blaring like trumpets out of a dark blue background, the same funny tongues sticking out that I'd seen on the plants outside.

"I've got to get a picture of that sunburn!" he said. "Stand over there by those geraniums on the ledge." Dad was always taking pictures of me and I hated it. "I don't want to, Dad. I'm tired."

"Oh, just one picture? C'mon. It'll be quick." I

slowly gave in and walked sullenly to the ledge, standing there without expression. "Please give a smile," he begged. A weak smile crossed my face. "Okay, now just pull one of those beautiful flowers closer to your face and turn your head a little." This was what I hated most – him posing me whether I wanted to or not. I grabbed the flower and pressed it to my cheek, the smile stuck on my face. "That's nice!" He finally took the picture and let me go.

I bundled up my things, and we left the pool. As we passed the lounge, I wanted to ask Dad if we could look for the bar with the window into the pool, but no words came. What could I say that he'd believe? A ball of muscle gained weight around my stomach and I said nothing.

Back in our room, Dad had me take a shower. The hot water he ran stung my sunburn. I made it cooler and soaped myself, letting the water run over my body to rinse me clean. A washcloth would only hurt. Climbing out of the huge shower, I was cold in the bare, white-tiled room. My legs shook. A towel would feel rough so I grabbed the thick, too long bathrobe the hotel provided and wrapped myself tightly in it.

"Come out so I can take a look at that sunburn," Dad said from the bedroom. I left the bathroom and stood in front of him, the heat of the sunburn coming back to my skin and chafing against the terrycloth robe. "Lay down on the bed, Hon." I rolled onto the covers and pressed my face into the pillow. He carefully pulled the big bathrobe from me, like unwrapping a precious vase. I felt awkward as he did this, but the stinging burn distracted me.

"That's a bad burn," he said. "Mom gave me

some first aid cream to bring just in case this happened. I'll get it and we'll fix you right up."

In a few moments I felt his weight sink down on the bed and his hand putting icy cold cream on my back. He rubbed in big circles, spreading the cream further and further. He rubbed the cream down onto my thighs, tracing where the edges of my bathing suit had been. I got nervous. My stomach shifted upward and a bad taste came into my mouth.

His hands were pressing into me. I was afraid his fingers would push through my skin and sticky, hot blood would ooze out of me. Suddenly I found myself back in the closet with Louise's father pushing on me. Pushing and pushing, rhythmically like Dad's hands on my thighs. My face pressed into the pillow and I felt suffocated by the memory of the fur coat and the smell of animal hide. My breathing slowed and it seemed my lungs were collapsing.

He isn't trying to hurt me, I thought, sucking in a deep breath. He rubbed too near my chest and I squirmed away. I didn't want him touching me there. I wanted to trust him, but I was afraid to. *If Louise's father could ... could Dad?*

I saw the taunting eyes of the men in the window glaring at me, and I imagined I was drawn through the glass as it dissolved, the pool water flooding into the bar and washing me up against their gruff, smiling faces, hands gripping me, the men tossing me back and forth in a game of catch through water now heavy and thick, their laughter a low growl traveling slowly through the water swirling around me.

When Dad stopped, tears came, along with sadness deeper than I'd ever felt, worse than a friend moving away. I started drifting off, like the plane we'd taken passing into a towering, bright yellow and white cloud.

"There," he said softly, covering me lightly with a sheet. "That should do it. You just lie here now and let this lotion sink in while I shower. Then we'll both get ready for dinner."

He bent down and nuzzled his mouth into my hair, my ears and down onto my neck. "It's a good thing your piggy meat didn't get too burned," he said, making his munching sounds and kissing my neck again. I floated deeper into the dimmer, wispy center of the cloud, his voice receding.

When he got off the bed, air seeped quietly back into my lungs. I lay still for a while after he left to shower, but my skin turned prickly and cold from the lotion. I rolled off the bed, wrapping the bathrobe around me as I went to my suitcase and pulled out a dress for dinner. My skin hurt when I pulled on my underwear and the dress. Its straps dug into my burned shoulders. I searched for another dress and found one with broader straps. Raising it above my head to pull it on, the skin on my shoulders still felt tight, but I got the dress on. Then I coarsely brushed my damp hair and put on sandals.

I went into the living room of the hotel suite. It was small, but had a couch, table and chair. I sat gingerly on the chair, my hands folded on my lap and waited, not hungry at all.

Dad eventually came out of the bedroom, dressed and ready for dinner. "All set?" he asked. Silently I followed him out to the hall and into an elevator full of people excitedly talking. I was glad for the noise. On the way to the restaurant we passed a room full of boisterous people. A waitress walked by with a tray of clinking glasses. I peered in and recognized the bar with the window into the pool, the pool lights shimmering though the dark water now that it was evening. A man seated at the corner of the bar caught my eye. He smiled and winked at me. I froze, watching cigarette smoke pass over his craggy face. Then I bolted ahead to meet up with Dad waiting at the restaurant door.

For many years I was terrorized by a recurring dream of walking along a beach in the dark, only a full moon lighting the rolling waves as they hit the hard, wet sand. A small sound, starting like the far away growl of an angry dog, gradually gained volume and became the loud beckoning of a throng of men chasing me. In each dream I'd run down the beach, faster and faster, trying to gain distance on the men holding blazing torches, the closest of them reaching out to grab my ankles. Some wore floppy hats, some had thick beards and all had dark, ragged clothes. Their faces were huge and ruddy with bulging eyes shining in the red and yellow torch light. As they got closer and louder, they'd shout at me to slow down, but I'd run faster, my long legs striding hard and just as the lead man swooped out his hand to grab my foot, I'd hit enough momentum to rise into the air as his hand swept under me, my toes pushing off the sand, a heavy weight dropping from my body as I glided upward into the sky, being pulled safely forward by a silver flute that appeared in my hands, my fingers holding tightly onto the keys. I'd soar weightlessly towards the stars, the men becoming blinking specs on the ground far below. In each dream I'd anticipate the immense relief, exhilaration tingling in a wave up my spine. My flight would crest and slow, the flute guiding me through the warm darkness, the twinkling stars my protective companions. Over years of the repeating dream, the terror would so blissfully dissipate that the sight of the men became briefer and the flight longer until my dream-self would more easily fall to sleep on a drifting bed of thick clouds.

꙾꙾꙾꙾꙾꙾

Growing up as a preacher's kid had its own set of rules. Most people expected me to be different from other kids – that I'd be pleasant, cooperative and selfless at all times. I had friends whose parents used me as a role model, never failing to point out some positive quality they were sure I had, true or not. I felt I couldn't let them down and tried to appear even-tempered and polite as if my genetic code had an extra morality strand, something to keep me directed toward perfection. It was a responsibility of the family of a man who'd been called to spread God's word, though my own parents never made me feel that way. I don't remember them ever disciplining me.

I had a few good friends and was well enough liked. But I was cautious among the adults and tried to not stand out too much, which was hard since I always sensed I was being viewed by someone in church on Sundays. Sometimes I'd get next to Dad in the receiving line after the service but pretend I wasn't there, hiding behind his billowing black clerical robe as he reached to shake another hand, his draped arm flowing in front of me, red velvet stripes on his robe softly brushing my face. But there'd usually be someone who'd remark on what a darling, beautiful little child I was. I became quiet and shy, not wanting to disappoint anyone.

The liberalism of the early 1960s inspired Dad to use the pulpit for contemporary messages, especially then to combat racism and encourage his congregation to take up the cause of civil rights for blacks everywhere. Dad was more interested in social justice than the scriptures, although his extensive education allowed him to quickly find any passage, including the parables he often used to communicate his beliefs. I listened to many sermons of his I didn't really understand, but always loved Dad for the rigorous advise he gave his attentive flock about the issues of the day. Meek as he might have been in many situations, he was a bold orator in his pulpit. He enjoyed an authority difficult to achieve in most occupations. I was proud to be his daughter.

Liberal politics may have helped Dad, as well as Mom, lead much of the congregation's community outreach, but nothing ever changed the very insular culture of the Christian church. I always felt part of a sacred mystery quite separate from reality. For me, the church was a safe place and I was comfortable by myself in the sanctuary, sometimes lying down in a pew to stare at the vaulted ceiling or out the beautiful stained glass windows, feeling not alone but in the company of the loving spirits and old souls who I knew lived there. I felt privileged to share in its silent intimacy and loved to wander through the choir loft, sit in the elaborately carved wood chairs of the chancel, or walk up into Dad's pulpit and look out, imagining the resonating sounds of people filling the pews during service, their echoing coughs and the rustling of their church programs. Dad even let me play the organ and once we blared Chopsticks together out of the powerful organ pipes, Dad laughing and saying we'd get him fired if any of the Deacons were around. Sometimes I'd go with him up the many flights of steep metal stairs in the immense bell tower at Noon to be almost deafened but thrilled by the great clanging of the monstrous carillon bells sounding out the hour.

Mom was a minister's daughter, too, her father one in a line of Scottish Presbyterian pastors. He was a gentle, caring and intelligent man who was held to an older and even higher moral standard expected of "men of god" by churchgoers in congregations of his time.

Mom felt the same limitations I did growing up in the church, describing herself in childhood as a wallflower. Back then, and especially in a minister's family, parents didn't talk with their children about problems or fears. Stoicism and self-sacrifice were expected. Care was given to others outside the family. Her parents had been missionaries living in Manila in the Philippines where families had real problems. In places like Easton, Pennsylvania and New Hartford, New York where Mom grew up, American life was good in the early 1900s. You followed a few basic rules and everything would be fine.

She showed me a photograph of herself at about eight years old wearing a plaid dress with an absurdly large bow on her head. "I think my mother put it there just to dress up my unruly hair and plain face," she told me. I felt sad for her, but she just shrugged her shoulders. "That's how it was and I accepted it," she said. She'd learned to accept many things without speaking her mind. Until later.

Grandma was much different than Mom. A well-respected community pillar, she was easy to compare to Eleanor Roosevelt. With graying hair pinned close to her head and wearing one of her flowered dresses, she looked very much like the former first lady, a belt barely cinching her solid girth, her impressive bust held up by her stiff posture. She was a strong square-faced woman who took care of the weakest in the congregation, always making sure everyone had enough to eat and clothes to wear. She organized constant fundraisers, raffles and rummage sales to see to the needy at all times of the year. I still have her cavernous silver-plated coffee urn, the miles of gold-threaded tablecloths and stacks of linen napkins used at church socials. I remember her always speaking with confidence, her voice as strident as my grandfather's when in his pulpit, though he was so docile otherwise.

My strongest memory of my grandparents was staying with them during one of Mom and Dad's long trips when I was small. It was Christmas and I liked to plug in the tree lights during the day since the tree looked gloomy to me otherwise. But that made Grandma angry about wasting electricity and she'd get down on hands and knees to crawl under the tree to pull out the plug. Her flowered dress would shift around on her broad rump as she squeezed herself under the lowest branches, grunting and grousing with extreme displeasure. On one day when this was happening, I looked over at Grandpa sitting in his favorite armchair, a big grin spreading over his face. He caught me looking at him, and we stifled our laughs with our hands, his glass eye motionless as the good eye bounced between Grandma and me, the lights on the tree flickering on and off as she yanked at the plug.

Mom loved her mother, but said she always felt lesser than this great mass of a woman, as Grandma seemed to me. From Mom's stories, I always thought she didn't feel very close to her mother either, a connection apparently not made during all Grandma's busy days handling her end of her husband's ministry. Grandma tended to Mom's needs like she cared for the sick and lonely, making sure she lived well but perhaps not offering all the motherly attention Mom might have appreciated. I came to understand how this relationship had extended into the one between she and I. Mom was treated the same way by her mother as she treated me.

There was the one time when Mom confronted her mother. It seemed she enjoyed telling me about it.

"I was a teenager at the time," Mom began. "I'd seen your Grandma on Saturday nights sitting in the parlor holding hands and talking quietly with some man I didn't know. Grandpa would be in his church office, working on his sermon for the next day. I thought he knew about these," she hesitated, "these trysts, and he allowed them to take place, discreetly removing himself from the house." She paused and then held up a finger to accentuate her point. "And then, I got so mad at Grandma for her deceit that the next time she berated me for some foolish mishap of mine, I lashed out at her about her secret man," she said, wagging her finger as if still admonishing Grandma. "I never saw the man again." She relished speaking of her brilliant success in speaking her mind to this maternal fortress who, as I heard the story, I pictured like a balloon in a Macy's Thanksgiving Day

Parade, a stout woman in a floral dress and sturdy shoes looming over my tiny street-bound mother with a grimace in her square face, a small veiled hat fixed to her head.

Mom's eventual migration as a young adult to a small Presbyterian college in Pennsylvania opened up new ground for her. Her happiest stories are from this time. She excelled in basketball. I was shocked to see a photo of her in a gym suit, palming a ball and readying herself for a three-point basket. She also rode horses and often went riding with her first and only love before meeting Dad. She looked more radiant in those years than at any other time, a spirit of freedom glistening on her smooth face.

After college she worked as a librarian in Manhattan. "I rode the train from our home in Pleasantville down into the city to work," she told me. "I got to meet new people and I learned about things happening outside of our little church community. I was a sophisticated commuter all right," she said, triumphantly. "After work I'd walk back to the station through Central Park, crossing the bridge over the lake. It was always lit at night by the beautiful globed lampposts that I think are still there."

She made it sound like a movie set from that era. When I was grown this was a dangerous place in the park and it was hard to imagine my delicate mother walking there alone. Of course, she had a protective independence to be proud of back then. No longer a wallflower, she'd blossomed into a graceful, but strong woman with exuberant promise, a strand of her mother's moxie woven into her self-will. It'd be years before she'd feel this way again, marriage and raising a child a diversion from what she might have otherwise created for herself. That was the choice for women those days – home and family or a trying and usually unsuccessful effort at self-fulfillment, even if Katherine Hepburn made it look so easy. Most married women denied their courage in the same way they'd hung their wedding dresses in plastic sheathing in the back of their closets; an aspiration best left to memory.

Dad's childhood was spent on a sprawling peanut farm in North Carolina. The family lived at Sunnyside, a large home surrounded by an expansive oak grove, orchards and gardens, animal pastures and big peanut fields. The house had a detached kitchen, a huge barn and a smokehouse. His father was a stern, domineering Calvinist. I never met him since he died before I was born, but it was said he wasn't always a nice man, being brutish to his gentle wife and quick to take any of his four often misbehaving boys out behind the barn for a whipping with a tough leather strap. Dad's mother was a subdued woman marrying into her husband's proud, aristocratic and clannish family; descendants of the Scotch-Irish immigrants who had settled along Little River and Cape Fear. When Dad's father, one of twelve children, inherited the land from his father, the "old parson," he was largely instrumental in founding the town by donating sizeable land from the plantation for a railroad station, a school and a church.

Dad was the third of six children. He competed with his brothers to get noticed by their father, seeking his attention by telling jokes at family meals, taking a cue from his father's love of storytelling, his softer side. As this worked well in getting a laugh out of him, he nurtured this talent, embellishing it with avid reading.

Joining the ministry later was largely his father's decision, as one of his sons had to become a minister, another a lawyer, another a teacher, and the last a businessman, as was customary in those days. For the two girls, one became an elementary teacher like her mother had been and the other, the rebel, left the south and became a high fashion model in New York, certainly not so customary.

Dad used jokes and storytelling into adulthood, always needing to attract attention. He was a talker more than a listener, and he couldn't stand silence. I always thought he was uncomfortable around other people unless he had control of the conversation. He wasn't one for easy, close friendships, being more comfortable knowing people from a distance. It seemed Dad was most comfortable in the pulpit or as the raconteur at the head of any dinner table, confident only as long as people were interested or amused by him. Outside of his self-created limelight he was often timid. In his later years, we'd find a pint of grain alcohol under the kitchen sink, or a flask in his golf bag in the garage; evidence that courage was hard for him to come by.

He also didn't know how to be physically close, or he'd get too close and be cloying, rarely getting it right. It may be his father's distancing along with his own striving for attention that accounted for his not setting good boundaries with people, including me.

Once married, Mom and Dad struggled to find a comfortable love together, though their common passion for humanity and their travels to learn about the world brought them closer together. Still, he found loving her challenging, finally announcing on their fiftieth wedding anniversary that he'd discovered he really did love her. For those years he'd often exasperated her with his incessant need for approval and love. But after he died she missed him very much and wanted to join him. Fifty years is enough time to lose yourself in someone else.

All my grandparents died when I was young. I hardly knew Dad's mother. In a photo of her holding me as a baby she's looking at me warmly, a lovely smile set in a strong jaw, blond hair swept high on her head, and a broach pinned to the lace of her collar. I look like her.

My last memory of Mom's parents together was our visiting their home, right next to Grandpa's church with its wonderful red door. I remember sitting on the floor, my elbow propped on the straight-backed carved wood chair with Grandma's needlepoint seat covering, reading the newspaper comics in front of the black and white television with its grainy images of two men very important to the adults watching the broadcast. I listened hard, trying to understand why, knowing it was very grownup to talk about politics and which of these men would become president. You could tell they were rooting for the nice looking man with the thick, wavy hair. They were enjoying being together that day, even with Mom's only brother joking in his typical way, cheering for the other man on the screen, the one with the heavy eyebrows, his eyes darting back and forth in an unmoving head, which was funny to me.

Dad's relationship with his church ultimately changed. He was fired. The church was large and prosperous and the powers above Dad wanted it to not only remain that way, but increase. They felt the minister's role should include fundraising and although Dad tried it a bit through meetings with well-off church members, he found pitching the advantages of a wealthy church to be distasteful. He was, as he preferred to think, a man of the cloth and was sworn to a lack of worldly goods. His job was to communicate the scriptures and their application to everyday life, carry messages of faith to his parishioners, serve their spiritual needs and pray for their healing when ill or spiritual well-being on death – not to raise money. He and the church parted ways.

Our family was given an elaborate farewell dinner with lengthy speeches praising Dad, a framed portrait of the church with some nice words about Dad in fancy script, a large silver bowl and an engraved chalice. Our family sat on the dais feeling awkward. I knew my parents well enough to recognize their strained faces. Mom's lips were stretched tightly across her closed mouth, her eyes drawn into a squint behind her glasses. It looked as if her mouth were to open it would spew bile. Dad showed a kind acceptance, but there was no light in his eyes and his mouth was almost slack, the corners forced into a weak smile. I was slumped in my chair staring at the blue dinner cloth with white satin edges.

I knew how angry they both were. I'd heard them talking late at night in bed about how no minister should be asked to be its businessman, that others should do that work. It made me angry to know how hurt they were. The congregation loved Dad and his good reputation had brought many new people into the church.

In the weeks that followed, Mom became more resigned to leaving the job and the town behind. She never liked having problems hang around, preferring life to be more clean and comfortable. "*Well, that's behind us now*" she'd say when something unpleasant was finished or resolved, as though no other problems would present themselves. Life was happier in black and white; grey was unbearable for her. For a long time into my adulthood, I found living with uncertainty just as hard. I wanted bad things to end. Eventually I realized there was no white or black and that grey was a reasonable color. Grey was predictable and ever-present. No seeking the unattainable or fearing an apocalypse. Cruising in vagueness can be sedating. You just do your best.

A few months later we moved to a more progressive town in New Jersey, a suburb of New York City. I hated leaving my friends, but was happy for Dad. He was a lot better off and looked confident. I was proud to see him in the pulpit again, gesturing to the people seated in the spacious sanctuary, his strong words echoing off the walls. Mom seemed to find the change uplifting, having more energy and looking for new things to do.

It wasn't long before I met a boy who lived at the end of our street. Timidly we got to know each other and eventually became each other's first romance. I can still smell the cologne on his pin-striped collar and the feel of his soft wool sweater as we slow-danced to the Shirelles's *Will You Still Love Me Tomorrow* and The Lettermen singing *The Way You Look Tonight*. We'd usually be some place where kids could be together but not alone like a sock-hop in the big decorated gym at school where teachers seemed to float by as we danced, or at a social in some carpeted church basement, soda and potato chips nearby and a couple of parents scattered on the old donated couch in the corner. Life was changing and so was I.

⊙⊙⊙⊙⊙⊙

All day at school I felt queasy. When a bad headache also started, I went to the school nurse who saw nothing wrong with me, but suggested I leave early, which I did. Mom came to get me and when we got home she made hot tea and loaded the living room couch with cushions and blankets for me to curl up in.

I lay there all afternoon, watching *Flying Leathernecks*, a World War II movie. I loved war movies, especially with airplanes. War was no reality to me and the movies made life seem exciting with people like John Wayne always great heroes. Sometimes I went with friends to Elvis Presley movies and science fiction thrillers at the theater downtown where they showed cartoons and newsreels before the movies. But on a sick day at home, there was nothing better than a war story.

After the tea and grilled cheese sandwich and John Wayne's flying stunts, my stomach still ached. My underpants felt stuck to me and when I pulled at them to look I saw blood. I ran to the toilet and sat there horrified. This was something I'd long dreaded and hoped to be older than twelve when it came. Growing up was okay, but I hated being a girl and becoming a woman scared me. I didn't like thinking about it or even using the word "woman." I couldn't explain it, but I felt ashamed. Everyone would see me differently now. I'd be visible, men would stare at me and I couldn't do anything about it. Miserable, I put my head on my knees, closed my eyes and cried, glad for the darkness.

"Lily?" Mom called through the bathroom door. "You've been in there a long time."

I blew my nose, took a deep breath and opened the door for her, holding out my underpants like a dead animal I'd found under the sink.

"Oh, I see," she said, her voice softening. "Well, I thought this time might be coming, so I prepared for it." She reached into the linen cabinet and pulled out what I knew to be menstrual pads as I'd seen girls with them at school. What was unfamiliar was the elastic contraption that I guessed held the pads in place. She showed me how it all worked, being both practical and kind.

"So you're a woman, now," she announced with a big smile. I burst into tears again. "It'll take some getting used to, I know," she reassured me. "It can feel confusing, but you're on the verge of lots of exciting times. Being a woman these days isn't like what it used to be."

I didn't know how to tell her how I really felt, excitement not being part of it.

Being a woman was different for my mother. She was happy to reach a time when women were coming into new freedoms. Her own life had been spent playing unwanted roles and having little voice in situations important to her. Dad could preach from the pulpit at full volume if he wanted to, calling on the faithful to be good Christians. Mom had a support role as his wife, one that hadn't allowed her opinion much public expression.

These days though, social norms had changed and

being an outspoken woman was acceptable thanks to Betty Friedan and a few other pioneering feminists. Mom would find her voice and come to speak often about issues that concerned her. She drove the Red Cross van, taking people to medical appointments or on errands. She became president of the board of the local YWCA and used that platform to advance new ideals for women. She became more like her own mother after five decades of feeling less than ordinary. Enduring public scrutiny when Dad was fired had brought out her strengths, long hidden behind his career.

She was coming into her own and liked the change. In a few years she'd be marching on Washington to protest a war and working for social justice; a resounding echo to my father's scowling, barely veiled political rants to pews of listeners, some in agreement, some not. But he was a theologian and had all the scholarly references he needed to prove that violence, hatred and fear mongering were not tenets of Christianity.

For me, becoming a woman was terrifying, not liberating. I didn't want to become sexual, to have breasts, to be seen and be watched. Down deep where memories hold emotions hostage, I already suspected what I was in for and becoming a woman felt like a punitive sentence; a strain on me for the rest of my life. The image came to me of the bikini-clad blond in the pool in Hawaii, the men in the window gawking at her, their silent mouths opening and closing like bulge-eyed puffer fish.

"I just don't feel like that, Mom," I blurted out, running into my room and throwing myself on my bed, heaving in sobs again. "I don't want to grow up. I don't want to have to be like ... that."

"You'll get used to it, honey" she said casually, handing me a pair of pajamas she'd pulled from the dresser. "We all do."

"Well I won't," I said defiantly, punching my arm into my pajama top. "I never will. I'll hate it." I was angry at Mom for not understanding, for not hearing me.

I grabbed my stuffed rabbit off the bed and stomped downstairs, the menstrual pad feeling like an alien thing between my legs. I curled up again on the couch, burrowed my head in the cushions and watched *Sea Hunt* until I began to get sleepy, dimly aware that Mom had sat down beside me to smooth my cheek with the long fingers of her warm, slender hand. I loved her, but thought she'd never completely know me. I snuggled close to her and laid my head on her lap, letting her brush my tears away as I drifted off to sleep.

ᏕᏕᏕᏕᏕ

Compressed into a tight ball on the thick cushion of a wicker chair, I was lost in the early 1600s, reading Longfellow's story of *Evangeline*, the Acadian maiden in search of her true love after the British expelled the French from Nova Scotia. Deeply engrossed in her travels along the Mississippi, I imagined myself one step behind hers, shadowing her as if I'd run into her if she stopped moving. I badly wanted to be the modest and pure Evangeline; to have a simple, passionate mission and be adventuring on that river, hearing its sounds and feeling its currents pulling the boat along as water churned over the wheel, owls hooting in the darkness, quietly moving toward someplace called Louisiana. She was apprehensive, but serene and focused on her destiny. She was admirable.

For me, it was the waning of my Renaissance, of adventuring through knowledge and discovery without regard to the future. Now, officially a young woman, I was headed on what I deemed was a forced march toward a destination I had no interest in – me growing up. It was my first year of high school and I was so afraid of starting school I thought I'd throw up, worrying about people not liking me.

Once I'd been in school a while, I started relaxing around classmates who seemed to like me enough, but gave me no special attention either, my making no close friends. I liked math and history classes, and French was great. Learning a new language was hard, but satisfying. I memorized a French poem about a fox and recited it for the ladies at a meeting of the local French Society. Mom was there. I remember her seated in the front row, smiling proudly. It was a very long poem and as I started the last stanza I sensed the audience was impatient for the recitation to finally end, Mom sharing looks and smiles with the other women. But I loved saying it, moving my mouth in such different ways than English to make the sounds; squeezing my cheeks and lips together, curling my tongue and rolling sounds against the back of my throat.

For one project, I made a five foot-long replica of an area in Paris starting from the Arc de Triumphe monument down the broad avenue of the Champs-Elysses to the Place de la Concorde monument, the

Tuilleries gardens and the Louvre museum at the other end. For weeks it was a great place to play, my imagination slowly delineating this fantastic world through crafting materials.

The monuments and museum were made out of clay, and I'd carefully carved images in their sculptured exterior wall panels with toothpicks, including faces on tiny robed figures and even carving one man on a rearing stallion. The gardens I made of miniscule crepe flowers, and I'd put more in flower boxes along the street with little trees used for architectural models. The gardens also had clay statues and a large urn, along with benches I made from strips of balsa wood and a lake made with a mirror surrounded by green felt for grass, inspired by the cotton-surrounded lakes of Mom's winter centerpieces. There were balsa wood storefronts along the street for special shops and movie theaters, cafes and restaurants. Each was painted with designs and colors I looked up in books. Toy cars moved along the road and small dollhouse people filled the sidewalks.

I'd walked miles over town and back home going to the craft shop, the toy store and the library. The shop owners and the librarian all knew what I was working on and helped me find the things I needed. As I walked I'd take special notice of the trees, the flowers in the park and the look of the shops downtown. It was all research for my model and I loved walking along in the warm sun, carrying my bag of carefully purchased supplies.

By the time I finished it, I'd acquainted myself with some of the dollhouse people, who had names, imagined family members and personal histories. A pair of lovers strolled the gardens, a mother and daughter shopped on the avenue, an older woman headed toward the museum, and two boys played with a boat on the lake.

I'd spent all my time on the model working completely alone. I'd liked it that way, not having to worry about what anyone else thought. Only my parents had seen it, and they thought it was great. I was used to doing things by myself and spent a lot of time on school work, only seeing other kids at school or the occasional party or sleepover. I'd learned to entertain myself or just enjoy being quiet and pensive.

When my mother and I took the model to the classroom at school, we carried in its three large pieces separately. My French teacher exclaimed over the first piece containing the Arc de Triumphe and didn't know what to say when we brought in the other two huge pieces of the replica. It was clearly more than she expected for the project and, as it turned out, more than any of the other students had done. I felt self-conscious about it the next day when my classmates saw it. They were all quiet about it at first. I knew my actions now had social consequences.

The teacher asked me to explain what all the buildings and monuments were, which I did as the kids crowded around the model. They began to enjoy it and asked if they could move the cars up and down the avenue and play with the doll figures. It was fun watching them, and I was glad they liked what I'd worked so hard to build.

One student wasn't so thrilled. She stopped me in the stairwell after school, blocking my descent, and waited until no one else but her best friend was around to turn and blast me angrily. She was one of the blackest, toughest kids in the school, a muscular athlete who excelled at all sports. When we played baseball she'd smash balls over into the soccer field. I had lousy eyesight and couldn't hit at all and was usually asked to run, which I was good at, while someone else hit. When we played field hockey she was one of the girls who'd try to slice into other girls shins, like mine, with her stick. I learned to avoid her, thwacking the ball to advance it to a teammate on the other side of the field when I saw her charging me. There was no maneuvering around this girl.

That day she was so mad I could barely get what she was saying she jived so fast, waving her arms threateningly and calling me "bitch." But I heard enough to understand her problem. I was white and she saw me as privileged, though she didn't know much about me. But that didn't matter to her. Watching me in French class was enough, I guess. There I suppose I may have looked to her like I had some advantages. My aunt, Dad's sister, was in Paris much of that time modeling for Vogue; something I'd said in class. It could be that sort of thing made me stand out in this girl's mind. But the Champs-Elysee model had apparently done it. She hated me. "You wanna take this fight outside?" she challenged me.

It was as if I had the basketball and she was glaring at me with rage as she got positioned to strike. I'd become her target even if she was maybe angry at something or someone else she couldn't fight. There'd been major race riots that year, especially in Alabama, over desegregation in the schools, black voting power and every other civil right they lacked. We'd talked about it in history class, where she and I were also classmates. I'd said I liked having diversity in school. *I don't need no whitey for a friend,* was part of her rant on the stairs that day. On a day later in November, I'd see how the black girls cried, their anguish deeper than anyone else's. But not this girl. She didn't cry. She was angry, the Kennedy assassination just one more horrific defeat in the battle that was sharing her life.

I stood looking at her, my arms slack at my sides trying to imagine fighting this girl. She'd kill me with one punch. I had no idea how to fight. The best I could do if she came at me was some blocking move I'd learned on the basketball court. Besides, I had no interest in fighting her. She hadn't done anything to me. Hitting her in the head wasn't going to make her like me anymore. I believed in non-violence, like Dr. King said.

Her confrontation was so direct and physical I wasn't even angered by it. My anger always came from getting my feelings hurt and twisted, not this. So I tried using reason with her, which I'd learned I was good at. It was like debating; quickly maneuvering around your opponent and advancing your ideas far enough ahead to where they couldn't touch them – a kind of mental field hockey game.

"I'm not into fighting," I said. "I have no reason to fight you. But I'm sorry for anything I've done to make you so mad."

She was silent then; confused looking. Her friend laughed, grabbing the girl's elbow and pulling her outside. The girl shook her head in exasperation and stomped out the door, mumbling a phrase that had no meaning to me. Her friend looked back, smiled and nodded. I had the feeling she approved of me. Only then did I notice I was hardly breathing, my chest readied for impact, my arms now tensed. I took a breath as they left.

The girl was nice to me after that. And her friend would smile and occasionally punch me playfully in the shoulder saying something like *Hey, girl* in appraising recognition of my existence. I'd smile back. Maybe they liked my toughness as something they could relate to. I hadn't seen it in myself before and it became something I was proud of; something I'd need. It gave me an edge where I'd had no good boundary with others before.

I learned in those years how to not stand out or get any favored treatment from teachers. I dialed down my appearance and intelligence so I'd be more acceptable to other kids. It made things easier. I wore sedate clothing in muted colors and tried to blend in. I spoke out enough in class to get good grades, but not overshadow anyone else. I learned to denigrate my accomplishments and play up others' successes.

Like everyone else my age, I wanted to fit in, to be liked, although by trying to be bland and not excel, to be the wallflower my mother had hated being, I failed to deepen and strengthen myself, leaving only my toughness on guard. Protectively cauterizing my development left me unskilled for adult demands later on. I'd end up relying too much on others to get my needs met as I couldn't do it on my own. Maneuvering that dependency into place became my skill and if it felt threatened I was learning defensiveness as a backup, later to be woven in with some aggressiveness when needed – the tools of my survival kit that I held onto for safety like gripping my flute as it pulled me into the night sky in my still recurring dream. Growing up a little crazy takes time and experimentation.

♋♋♋♋♋

For a fourteen-year-old, the marching band was great. I could care less about football, but being in the band made me part of something. We practiced hard during the week and gave our all to the weekend games. I loved it, never feeling more right than when we were in formation, marching from one position to another, my steps hitting just the right spot, coming to a stop at the right time, everyone in their right place. The kaleidoscopic patterns shifted in seemingly random directions with our sharply perpendicular and about-face turns, our maneuvers coming to momentary rests in circles changing into squares and then a star that would explode and come to rest again as the high school monogram before returning to our original block formation in which we'd march off the field, ending our half-time show. Like dancing to a Baroque fugue, our lines would merge and then disband only to return eventually to our comfortable beginning, our right places. It made me feel whole and sane – "coming round right" as the Shaker song said.

The music excited me – the drum cadences, blaring horns, bellowing tubas and the high pitched trills of my flute soaring over it all. It was fast paced, loud and all around me. As we marched, different instruments would pass by – a drum, a clarinet, a trombone, a tambourine. Sounds got louder or fainter as players moved closer or further away. It was like walking down a carnival midway through noisy hawkers of games of chance, the melodic calliope, the far off trumpeting of elephants and the jingling jewelry of belly dancers. The music's loudness and the changing sounds resounded through my body, my bones vibrating to the rhythms.

We played hard. Through Sousa marches, Broadway show tunes and old popular songs, we'd do our part to support our team and have each Saturday afternoon fit into every spectator's idea of great football. It was a nice day in a safe nation. I was part of that serenity and it felt good.

I even liked my uniform. The long navy blue pants with the white satin stripe down the outside seam fit well and the matching jacket was snug and comfortable. I liked the big shiny buttons and the white braiding on the shoulders that matched the long feather plume in my very military looking top hat. I wore white gloves, too. I hadn't worn gloves since Sunday school and I liked the feeling of formality and dignity they gave me. I liked the idea of wearing a uniform, of being like the others, short or tall, round or small. I could hide. No matter who said what or what happened, we all looked the same and were a part of the same band. There was camaraderie I couldn't find otherwise in my school. You could laugh at a joke you didn't even understand and it was okay. No one would give you that funny look like they knew you were just trying to fit in. You were already in.

Wearing the uniform also gave me an acceptable physical definition. I felt chastened by its authenticity. It gave me a break from worrying about what to wear and feeling I should compete with the swift changing fashion those days – the bright new colors, paisley patterns and weird materials, or daring clothes like see-through blouses pictured in magazines. Most girls were thrilled by the new looks and couldn't wait to buy clothes and experiment with their hair. Not me.

The cheerleaders were the most advanced. They'd show up at school in the very latest outfits with all the accessories, wearing fake eyelashes and pale pink lipstick and bouffant hair or maybe the new straighter styles from "swinging London." I envied how easily they flaunted themselves. I didn't feel that was something I was entitled to do. I might stand out, seem either egotistical or sluttish. I was different. At one band practice, the cheerleaders were also working on their routines. No one realized that when the band finished one formation and headed into another that our line of wind instruments would arc straight into the line of cheerleaders busy twirling their batons, flipping their hair and jumping around seductively in short-shorts. I was on the end of our line and as we neared them I angrily shouted *Move it girls!* It felt really good to scream at them, and they backed right off. I didn't know where this urge came from; it wasn't like me to yell at anyone. But I did know I envied their sexual comfort, while I felt cursed by a deep festering need to repent for sins I didn't even understand. It was wrong for me to be sexual and I hated them for what I assumed was their sustained chastity. They were better than I was. They could be sexual because they weren't sluts.

I was fine in plain shirtwaist dresses, dark colored A-line skirts and loose sweaters. That my stiff, cardboard lined band hat crushed my hair didn't bother me. I hated spending every night when I was dead tired from homework on rolling long hair onto ridiculously huge, spongy curlers just so I could have puffy hair in the morning like the other girls. In my uniform, I was anonymous. I was covered from head to toe and amounted to little more than a blue dot among others marching on the football field.

Every Saturday as we paraded through the goal posts toward the fifty-yard line at half-time, the cheering of the crowd reinforced our purpose. We straightened into our best postures and marched with knees raised high, falling into synchronous steps and counting our paces to the smart cadence of the drums, the complicated rhythms of the snares giving strength and definition to our moves. Reaching center field as we launched into diagonals, crisscrossing our lines to new formations, the crowds cheered our precision.

I had a huge crush on the trumpet player, the tallest boy in the band, lanky with longish blond hair. He wore glasses that gave him a secretive, intelligent look. And he had a great laugh, throwing back his head and letting it go.

I waited for weeks for him to talk to me, often positioning myself near the horn section before practice to make contact easier. We'd share glances, but it took forever for him to approach me. When he finally did, he asked me to be his date at the prom, only I was so flustered I misunderstood him and said something stupid instead of a simple *yes!* He ended up thinking I didn't want to go. By the time I figured it out and told him I'd not understood what he'd asked me and that I really wanted to go, he'd already asked someone else. I ended up going with another boy and the horn player and I spent the dance with undesirable dates knowing we could have gone together. He never asked me out after that, and I could never get up the nerve to talk to him again.

He and I also played in the school's orchestra like most of the band members. Joined by the string instruments, our repertoire greatly expanded from band music and I liked the more sedate melodies we learned. Our more demure demeanor in the orchestra, however, was no match for our bawdy, loud marching band, especially on bus trips to other schools when we broke into unprincipled chaos, throwing things and singing songs off the radio hit list that weren't among the approved band numbers, like screeching *I Wanna Hold Your Hand* at top volume. No, during orchestra the chaste chords of all the seasonal songs we played at winter and spring concerts bound our behavior and we all felt quite serious and very mature. Girls wore black skirts and white blouses; the boys in black pants, starched white shirts and skinny ties. I wore a thin, white cardigan over my blouse, tucked under my buttoned collar. Only some girls wore a little makeup and a few wore stockings during concerts.

All this music playing meant hours of practice. In my room at home, I'd practice every day after school before doing my homework. But for one of our concerts, even this amount of practice wasn't enough. My very dependable friend, the first flute player, wouldn't be there. That meant the flute solo was up to me. I was terrified, but there was no way out of it. Our orchestra leader saw my extreme hesitation to play it and offered to help me during study hours. An elderly and gentle man with a soft, gaunt face, he'd sit next to me patiently while I worked on the solo, a four-beat elevated run of notes giving a special finish to one movement in a sophisticated concerto. I'd start and stop, start and stop, sweat seeping through my sleeves.

"Try it more slowly at first," he advised, "Then work up to speed."

I played the notes very slowly. "Can't I just play it like that for the concert?" I pleaded.

"No," he said, smiling. "Don't worry. You'll get it."

After a couple of weeks, I was finally able to get through it, but still wished I didn't have to play it at all.

On the night of the concert I dreaded every moment before that concerto and hoped an earthquake would relieve me of this horrid responsibility. But no, we proceeded steadily through the holiday tunes, the concerto the last piece before intermission. As it began, my kindly orchestra leader raised his baton and smiled encouragement at me. Advancing through the sheet music, measure by measure, my nervousness built to a peak and the whirling in my stomach became unbearable. Just as I began to feel lightheaded and thought I'd pass out for sure, my solo part came. My fingers pinioned the keys on my flute and wouldn't move. I looked in terror at the orchestra leader standing right above me and at his long, disappointed face. My shame in that moment was only matched by relief that I didn't humiliate myself by starting and then failing to play the notes correctly. As it was, no one would even know the solo should have been there. Except me, except my teacher and except for all the years later when I'd remember that embarrassing moment.

The orchestra teacher suggested to my mother that I take music lessons outside of school to build my confidence. She set me up with a teacher and once a week drove me downtown to the office building where he gave lessons. She'd do errands or sit in the car reading a book while I practiced. The teacher's room was sparsely furnished, a space rented for the convenience of his students and for a single purpose. He was younger than most of my teachers in school and pleasant enough.

Each week for the longest time he had me practice my breathing. "Breathing is the most important part of playing any wind instrument," he'd say. And I'd practice filling the base of my lungs first, then pull in as much more air as they could handle, hold the breath and then let it out slowly to his count. Over and over we'd do this before I started playing my scales for that lesson. He gave me practice books to play at home; graduated lesson plans to help improve fingering skills. I'd play these drills until the droning sound must have driven my parents, and the neighbors, crazy. But no one complained and I kept on.

His emphasis on breathing exercises was insistent. He'd stand behind me at each weekly lesson, his hands on my shoulders. He was short, barely taller than me. "I should be able to feel your shoulders rising if you're taking in enough air," he'd say. Dutifully, I'd begin my long intake of breath, allowing my shoulders to raise his hands. "That's it," he'd encourage, "You're getting it now."

After a few weeks, it seemed these exercises were taking over the half-hour lessons. We never seemed to get around to what I'd practiced at home. He might have me play a few short melodies, but that was it. During one breathing lesson, he placed his palms against me, one on my back and the other on my upper stomach. Hands in position, he started his count. "Eight beats in," he said, then counted out the beats, "hold for eight," he continued, "and now eight beats out." My chest rose and fell with his counts, feeling like it might burst. "You're still not getting the air deep enough," he declared, his thumb pressing against my rib cage. "I need to feel the air hitting down here," he said, pressing harder. "Try again."

A familiar feeling came over me like I had whenever I knew Dad was about to go for my piggy-meat again – that squeamishness along my spine as I cringed and pressed my head into my shoulder so he couldn't get to my neck easily.

On what became my final flute lesson and breathing practice, the teacher's hand shifted into a subtle caress, his finger sliding into the open space between the buttons on my cardigan sweater, lightly tracing the bottom edge of my bra and then gingerly squeezing me. He continued counting. I stopped breathing altogether.

"I don't want to play," I said, abruptly pulling away, packing up my flute and leaving the room. He was silent and had turned his head away.

My mother waited in the car outside. I got in, closed the door with a slam and stared at the dashboard, not looking at her or saying anything.

"Is the lesson over already?" she asked.

"No," I said firmly, still not looking at her. "But I don't want to take lessons anymore." I thought it was obvious I was upset.

"Okay," she said quietly. She drove home without a word about it, and never questioned why I was so angry.

As we rode in silence I wondered what made some men think they could get away with doing things like feeling up girls in closets or flute lessons. That summer a man had even put his hand on my thigh on the bus I'd taken into New York City to meet my aunt for a Broadway show. I'd gotten up out of my seat and spent the whole ride standing in the aisle. Another time someone on a crowded subway had grabbed my rear end and I had to push myself through the packed riders to get away from him.

I never knew what to do and never felt I could say anything. These were adults. Children and young girls didn't tell on adults or criticize them. I always felt I'd done something wrong so it was my fault anyway. It was easier just to be quiet and hope nothing bad would happen again.

Weeks later at the end of October, I was walking home from school when a car pulled up beside me. I looked over and saw my flute teacher smiling at me through the window.

"Want to go for a ride?" he asked. "It's such a nice day. I thought I'd drive up to the overlook on the ridge. Want to come?"

I stared at the man, incredulous. I had no doubt what that ride had in store for me and I couldn't believe he thought I'd go along. I kept walking while his car cruised along and after several long moments he drove away.

I walked hard and straight to my favorite after-school diner, sat on my usual stool and was greeted by the same friendly waitress who was always there that time of day. "Same as always?" she asked.

I nodded; she smiled and turned to place my order. The sounds in the diner were familiar and comforting. It was crowded and everyone was talking. The October sun streamed through the window, making the shiny metal on the jukebox gleam. A record dropped and "All My Loving" began to play. The waitress brought over my tuna salad sandwich on white bread with potato chips and a lime rickey soda.

"You okay?" she asked, looking closely into my face. "You don't seem like yourself today. What's up?" She waited for my answer, wiping the counter with a cloth.

"Oh nothing," I said, smiling timidly. "Just a bad day at school, I guess."

"Well, we've all had those," she laughed. "Drink your soda and you'll forget all about it. I'll get you a refill if you don't," she said, and patted my hand.

ᏅᏅᏅᏅᏅᏅ

A boy often hung around at the end of band practice, sitting on the bleachers near where we kept our instrument cases at the football field. I'd watch him covertly and he'd keep a steady gaze on me, a cigarette dangling from his lip, a cap shading his face, propped by his elbow on one bleacher, a booted foot resting on another like a still from a James Dean movie. He was different from other kids I knew and certainly different from me. With his pomaded black hair and leather jacket he was one of the last greasers. He had friends with motorcycles and arrogant faces who sometimes cruised by to talk to him. But mostly he lounged on the bleachers alone. He intrigued me.

"What's your name," he asked one day after most all the band had left, his head cocked back with a sly grin.

"Lily," I replied after a slight pause, still packing my flute away and avoiding his direct look. He didn't answer right away. I turned towards him before he spoke again. His head tilted forward and his gaze shifted to a penetrating stare.

The modest Rose puts forth a thorn, the humble sheep a threatening horn, while the Lily white shall in love delight, nor a thorn nor a threat stain her beauty bright, he said. "My name's Vinnie."

Now it was my turn for a momentary silence. "I see," I managed. "And the name of your poet friend?"

"Just an old, dead guy," he said. "But not a bad poet." He moved closer and gave me a friendly smile. "Listen, I'd like to take you home or wherever you're going."

I wasn't sure what to make of him and whether I should say yes or not, but was curious. "Okay. I'm headed home. But we'll have to walk. My parents will flip if they see me on that bike. It's not far." I couldn't admit to him I was also afraid of his bike, though its badness did entice me.

"That's okay. I don't have another helmet anyway," he said, bounding off the bleachers. "I'll pick it up on my way back."

That walk home was one of many we'd take. He lived in another town neighboring the football field, so he didn't go to my school. He met me after almost every band practice, usually escorting me home, or at least it felt gentlemanly to me. For an Italian guy with slick-backed hair, he was certainly polite. At first he dropped me off home and left, greeting Mom when she was there, slowly waiting for my trust and an invitation inside.

One weekend he invited me to his house, a small brick one-family he lived in with his father, who usually wasn't there. He worked in construction and had long hours most of the year when it wasn't freezing. I met his father a few times when we'd all sit in the kitchen, the two of them sharing a couple of beers. He was an endearing, scraggly man often referring to events that happened *When your mother was here.* Then he'd collapse on the living room couch with the newspaper and fall asleep in the dim, somewhat shabby room that I imagined was probably much neater – when the mother was there.

We sat in Vinnie's small upstairs room where he showed me poems he'd written, his bookshelves lined with old classics like Blake and Keats, volumes of modern poetry and a large collection of beat poets including Ginsberg and Ferlinghetti. I told him how upset my English teacher got when, for our poetry project, I'd chosen a Ferlinghetti poem about two lovers too sunburned to embrace but longing for each other. I thought it was an exceptional poem, but her astonished response was to say: *I can't believe a nice young girl like you would read Ferlinghetti!* Instead, she made me use a poem by Richard Wilbur about fresh, clean white sheets hanging out to dry in the sunny breeze. Virginal stuff.

Vinnie laughed at that and shared some other, even more obscene poetry with me, introducing me to Ginsberg's *alcohol, cock and endless balls.* I listened to him read more of the poem while looking out his window, the outside dirt on the glass brightening somewhat by the sun shining through onto a thin faded yellow curtain, wispy threads handing from its hem. I could hardly relate any of my experience to the poem, but responded to its recognition of deep and disconcerting feelings, those of a new subculture of young people unafraid to explore their sensory lives in contrast to the yearning for normalcy and decency that dominated their parents' culture after the war.

Vinnie's poems were sad and often angry narratives on his growing up, his family's struggles and the loss of his mother to bone cancer. They were as grim as his surroundings in the uncared for house, the grimy street, the dark neighborhood bar a few doors away and the broken windows in the deserted factory nearby. But I understood his need to write down his thoughts and read others' poems that validated his experience. If he didn't, his hurt would do more harm. As it was, Vinnie liked to laugh and looked for reasons to do so. Sometimes they were dark reasons, but his humor and his poetry held him together. That and fast rides on his bike.

I went for more visits on the weekend with him that had to be masqueraded for my parents as times I spent doing homework at the library, shopping downtown or going to a movie. The lies steeped me in guilt, but I wasn't sure they'd approve of Vinnie. He at least visually presented himself as a hoodlum, or "hood" as the slang had it, and Mom had already eyed him suspiciously though nothing had been said.

The more time we spent together, the more intimate we got. Sitting close, Vinnie began feeling me up, but took it slow. It felt nice. He was the first boy I'd been this physically close to. Dancing with someone wasn't like this; this excited me deep in my body in ways I only knew through exploring myself alone. Feeling me up got to be what I'd heard girls call heavy petting in their whispered conversations in the bathroom at school between classes; knowing who'd done it and who hadn't was the titillating goal of these serendipitous get-togethers. As I stood at the sink and looked at them in the mirror, I'd watch the changing drama in their faces, lipstick and hairbrushes swooshing by me in great arcs of excited hand gestures as they prattled and primped. But I still wasn't sure about the limits of petting and their talk wasn't clear on that point. Was actually having intercourse still something only really loose girls did or were any of these girls or their targets of gossip doing that too? I didn't know them well enough to ask and just tried to sort it out from all the babble.

Now it was me at least doing the petting and it was getting heavier. I kept liking it and did little to stop Vinnie until the day he was tugging at my bra strap and broke it. The spell I was in also broke. I sat up in a sudden wave of modesty and asked him for a safety pin to fix it. I got shy and scared that we were moving too fast. I told him so and quickly left his house, not returning for a few weeks, insisting instead that he come to my house. When he used to walk me home from school, Mom's presence there put a brake on things.

"I haven't seen Vinnie in a while," she said, after he left one afternoon. "You two back together?" She busily picked up the living room where we'd been hanging out; she liked things tidy. As comfortable as it was to live in, the house always looked exactly the same, everything in its place. It was mysterious how she accomplished that.

"Yeah, sort of," I said, maintaining my lie about not having been seeing him.

"He doesn't stay long," she said, as more of an

inquiry than a statement.

"He has a job he goes to sometimes when they need him."

"Oh, really?" Her interest peaked. "What does he do?"

"Helps out at a garage. He's learning mechanics. He can almost rebuild a car engine," I told her.

"I see," she said, the word "*see*" drifting down to the carpet like a piece of the lint she was picking up that the vacuum had missed. "Well it's good he's making money."

"He writes poetry, too," I threw in.

"Does he? I'd love to read one of them sometime." She headed for the kitchen with a handful of lint and our soda glasses and chips bowl.

I could tell she wasn't keen on Vinnie, but was trying to be interested and supportive. Parenting then was so different from when she grew up. Advice books now talked about leniency and letting kids make their own decisions. Morality was getting looser and Mom was trying to go along with it. But it was hard for her having been raised strictly; she had strong boundaries. I don't think she knew exactly where the morality line had shifted. So she'd smile and try to act jovial when I could tell she was uncomfortable. Sometimes she'd do a little skip and hop as if to say either to me or to herself: *Everything's fine!*

She'd see Vinnie and me sitting close on the couch watching TV or occasionally she'd catch us petting. But she wouldn't say anything, gave no advice. It was like a "go ahead" signal to me. And if Dad was around he seemed oblivious to anything going on, though I think he was ignoring what he didn't know how to handle, leaving the details to Mom. I think I was ignoring what was going on, too. It was easier to just go along with Vinnie than resist and since no one was suggesting I do otherwise I just started sliding into him like water gushing through an open culvert. I had no boundaries set for me and no morality line. I sure wasn't making a decision for myself. I hadn't learned how to do that with sex. And I wasn't thinking to ask either. I wasn't even thinking, just responding. I didn't seem to have any thoughts or clear feelings, as if I'd left them in another room like an unfinished book casually left on a table.

By late fall, it was getting colder outside and the walk to my house from school was shorter than to Vinnie's and I just stayed home when he had to leave. Football games got played on fields dusted with snow. For band practice I wore gloves with the ends of the fingers cut off so I could still play my flute, its metal keys freezing to the touch. We wore thermal underwear and thick socks. Our practice drills got shorter and very snappy. Mostly we used marching formations we'd mastered in the warmer start of the season, especially those that kept us moving fast. It was thrilling; our young bodies took to it like king penguins marching across Antarctica.

It wasn't too long, though, before we began spending more of our time back at Vinnie's, at his urging. I was afraid of disappointing him, worried that he'd break up with me if I didn't go. We took to cuddling which turned to mauling each other under our sweaters, but over our underwear. In my case, after band practice, it was a lot of underwear. Vinnie's hand groped for the ribbed hem of my thermal shirt, slid underneath and found its way to my bra, a finger lightly tracing its bottom edge and then squeezing my breast, his thumb tracing my nipple as it hardened under the fabric. Eventually, my bra got unhooked. I just allowed it to happen, as if it wasn't really happening at all. It was so gradual that I didn't feel pressured. It was just as if I'd always had sex.

I was too young to know what was going on inside me, no wisdom instilled to guide me about my rights as a child. I didn't realize that, in a way, I *had* always had sex; sex with men, though, not boys. It wasn't a choice; I'd been sexualized in very subtle stages, the lesson being that pleasuring men was expected. No one told me differently.

I didn't understand then that my attraction to Vinnie was as a peer. I was being intimate with someone my own age and I didn't know how to handle it, but at least it made some sense, unlike anything I'd felt before. I wanted sex to feel normal; I wanted to *be* normal. What I would later come to know is that I didn't have that chance. I thought that to be loved and accepted I had to acquiesce to Vinnie, crossing no boundary on the way since there weren't any; my privacy having already been trespassed by men leaving muddy footprints.

I sometimes thought about Vinnie during the day. While classmates quietly discussed the Ottoman Empire, I'd gaze out the history class window at the snow falling against the dark afternoon as if it was the window in Vinnie's room. The day dream brought with it the feeling of his finger gliding toward my breast, although during one of these reveries it suddenly wasn't his hand at all, but belonged instead to my flute teacher. I shuddered at the old memory, the good feeling leaving me like I'd been hit in the head by an icicle falling outside the window.

As if puberty weren't enough, it was a confusing time for me in other ways. Sexual images were breaking into advertising with fewer restraints than ever; James Bond girls were multiplying in number and getting more undressed with each movie, and Mary Quant had produced the miniskirt and with it a longstanding change in women's fashion. This gradual stripping of women was behind what frightened me when I started menstruating. It was subliminal, but very effective. I was becoming prettier and I was afraid of getting a body like Ursula Andress. I was powerless over this transformation and terrified of having beauty expose me, removing any remnant of self-protection I'd managed by hiding in silence behind the thinning wall of childhood. It was during those days that the nightmare returned of men clawing at my ankles as I ran down the beach.

I didn't know how or who to trust since my trust had been violated. I was skeptical and distanced from people or over-trusting. There was no healthy middle ground. Since Vinnie was a friend my age, I wanted to trust him and allowed him the lead, hoping he better knew what was normal and right. I certainly didn't. When Vinnie's fingers started tracing the edge of my panties, I let it happen. When he unhooked my bra, I let it happen. I didn't think and I gradually shut down. Pleasure and shame mixed like hot chocolate pouring into white paint. I just lay there while he had sex with me; water through the culvert. No resistance, no questions. No thought of saying "no", no thought of getting pregnant. It was expected of me and Vinnie wouldn't love me if I didn't let him.

It was then I started flinching even more when

Dad touched me. We'd be watching TV on the couch and he'd rub my feet. It felt good, but not right. He'd pull my foot closer to him to make rubbing it easier for him, nothing more, but my heel would feel the flaccid bulge in his pants. I'd grab a pillow and put it under my foot. Or he'd try to kiss my neck again and I'd wedge his head between mine and my shoulder.

How about a picture of my princess? he'd keep asking, wanting *again* to pressure me into some ludicrous pose. One day I was standing, as I often did, on the floor register that brought heat up into our cold house from the furnace below. I'd usually do this after a bath, my robe billowing out from the rising heat, drying and warming my body underneath. I stood there combing the tangles out of my wet hair. Dad appeared with the camera, ready for a shot. "You look just like a duchess in her chambers," he said, the flash going off the instant I realized he was there.

"Dad, I didn't say you could take my picture," I said, reacting by storming up the stairs to my bedroom. "The least you could do is ask!" The picture came out with an expression of troubled surprise on my face. Not a duchess, but a pissed-off teenager in a bathrobe with stringy wet hair.

It was time for Dad to stop, but he couldn't do that. I'd later understand he felt no discomfort to signal that something was wrong. He hadn't grown up with boundaries either. He'd learned to pleasure his abusive father with humor and take the whippings when they came. He'd witnessed this man he was trying to love hurl verbal assaults at his gentle mother, the sweet-faced woman in the photographs I'd seen. No middle ground, no normalcy of physical attention. Little wonder he didn't know how to behave with me.

Mom didn't give him any clues either. She saw the neck-kissing and never commented on it. He was more physical with me than he was with her. I caught them one time coupling in their bed on a Sunday morning, with me walking silently out of the room so as not to disturb them. But other than that I rarely saw overt affection between them. Sucking on *my* neck was okay though.

I started to argue with Dad about anything. The subject didn't matter. He was insecure outside of his intellect and just needed to be right; wanted the last word. He'd sulk if anyone disagreed with him. I'd get so angry I'd throw it back at him.

We argued once about a radio. I'd pretzeled myself into an arm chair in what Mom called "the formal room" because of its more elegant furniture, and I was intensely focused on a textbook for school. Dad walked in carrying a radio in one hand, its plug in the other. He was quietly tiptoeing so as not to disturb me. I watched as he maneuvered his way around the writing desk, bending down to plug in the radio. He turned it on and tuned in a station, keeping the volume low as he fiddled with the dial. Finding the classical music station, he turned up the volume. Flute music streamed through the room while Dad tiptoed towards the hall. As soon as he got there, the music ended and an announcer came on to make a pitch for supporting the station.

"Dad, the music's nice, but I'm trying to concentrate on my reading."

"I just thought it was so quiet that you might like a little soft background music," he answered.

"Yes, thank you, but the announcer's on now and its distracting."

"Oh. Well, it's flute music and I thought my flutist would like to hear it."

"That's nice, Dad. Maybe another time. But right now they're soliciting donations and it's annoying. Can you please turn it off?"

"Oh, that'll end soon. There should be more of the concert soon."

"Dad, please," I said, adding emphasis.

"I'll just turn down the volume a little. That should help." He tiptoed to the radio and turned the dial.

"Dad, now it's even more annoying. Please turn it off?" I said with more insistence.

"I just want to make my Duchess happy." I'd never completely understood this occasional nickname other than his desire to put me on a pedestal of his own creation. He liked to serve me by providing luxuries like radio music or treats on a plate he'd bring and set beside me. Nice enough gestures, but his timing was often way off and his insistence on my enjoying these niceties got under my skin. It was his needs he was meeting, not mine; his need to be wanted and appreciated.

"I know, Dad."

"Maybe if I move the radio over here," he said, unplugging it and setting it on the far table, stretching the cord to the outlet in the hall.

"Really, Dad! It's okay. I don't want the radio." Now I was angry. Was it so difficult to just take it away? Yes, for him I guess it was.

"Oh, now I've made the Duchess mad. I'll just go away." He unplugged the radio again and tiptoed out into the hall. "You don't want my nice music."

"I just don't want any music right now, Dad.

Please understand." He disappeared around the wall, heading for the kitchen. Several minutes later he rounded the wall again, now carrying a small tray. Tiptoeing still, and without looking directly at me, he set the tray next to me on the window sill and quietly left the room. Slices of melon and ham alternated on a small platter, a strawberry gracing the center. I could hear flute music drifting in from the kitchen.

Eventually I couldn't even look him in the eye anymore. I loved him and I respected him for the educated, intelligent man he was, but I didn't always like him. He made other people feel responsible for his emotional needs which seemed insatiable. I had to distance myself from him and succeeded. Years later I was sorry he was so pained and had struggled hard with his own father for love that was never expressed. But I couldn't feel sorry for him at the time, just angry. I never told anyone about these feelings, even later when I was face to face with a psychiatrist who asked. I had no answer then for why it was this way. I couldn't even get close to thinking about it. That would take time, lots of time.

When Vinnie penetrated me the first time, it was as if I wasn't there. My body reacted, did the motions, felt sensations. But I wasn't there. I'd withdrawn into some batch of neurons where I was undetectable. That's how it was and how it stayed. I withdrew from him. The distancing was the flip side of over-trusting. He wrote a poem about me living in an ivory tower, unreachable.

Then he sent a friend of his, an older boy, to talk to me. I invited him into the house and he and I sat in the formal room with the antique furniture, across the open hall from the more comfortable living room where my parents sat watching the news with Huntley and Brinkley, not more than twelve feet away from us. The boy-man sat on the blue velvet setee in his leather jacket and shiny pants. I took the straight-backed carved wooden chair with my grandmother's needlepoint seat. He told me Vinnie had sent him to break up the relationship. Watching my mother's face across the hall engrossed in the broadcast, I asked him why. He told me Vinnie didn't like it that I'd agreed to sex so easily; said it was cheap of me and he didn't want to see me anymore. I don't even remember responding. The messenger just sort of drifted out of the house on his own cue.

After he left, I was surprised when Mom asked, "Is everything okay, Lily?" Amazingly, she'd noticed something might be wrong. But by then I was getting used to handling my private life on my own, and her input seemed rather tardy. Unlike some other girls I'd heard from at school who by our age were constantly fighting with their mothers about all things related to boys, I didn't have that conflict. Mom hadn't given me any reason to fight back, though I wished she had. "Yeah, Mom. Everything's fine."

♋♋♋♋♋

It was the "Summer of Love" as it became known after 100,000 hippies, mostly college students, gravitated to San Francisco, the vortex of the cultural revolution in 1967.

And there was Vietnam, where many other young men were going. The war was full tilt by then, waged nightly on TV through endless close-up images of stricken victims and bloodied soldiers, and waged also in secret, platoons of Special Forces making stealthy forays into Cambodia.

Race riots filled the streets of Newark and Detroit, black Americans hot and tired, ideas like "free love" and the "Age of Aquarius" not quite making it onto their agendas. Urban warfare spewed down the streets like the water jetting from open hydrants onto steaming pavement, anger hissing from anguished faces.

The news media was a daily slide show of these events, and I was aware of how other kids my age and older were contributing to the intensity happening around the country. But not me or kids I knew. We lived in a very progressive town, but I didn't know anyone getting drafted and I wasn't part of the small, local anti-establishment scene.

I graduated from high school that spring and had been accepted by Bard College in upstate New York. It was all I could do to just think about leaving home and being on my own on a campus. I wasn't ready for the 1960s and it was already heading toward the end of the decade. Far from being part of the counter-culture, I was still setting my hair, wearing a girdle and using menstrual pads. My first roommate in the freshman dorm would introduce me to tampons, pantyhose and loose, straight hair. For now, my clothes were still classic skirts and blouses and demure cotton slacks; not yet jeans and peasant blouses or tie-dyed tee-shirts and ankle length skirts made of Indian fabrics. My blond hair was getting very long and thick, I was much taller and my breasts had grown into a significant feature of what had become a beautiful young woman.

Going to college as this developing person scared me. It was happening too fast. I wasn't sure of myself at all and worried about being around older people. I was envious of kids who could hitchhike to the West Coast with nothing but a backpack and some vague notions about freedom.

My parents were more political than I was. Dad had been hired by a national consortium of churches with headquarters in Manhattan and had started traveling. When he wasn't working with churchmen overseas, a job which eventually took him around the world, he was working at the home office and active in protest movements.

Mom had gotten a job as a human services caseworker in Newark, not far down the interstate from where we lived, but right in the midst of social unrest. Her boss was a large black woman who bullied the staff. Mom was sent alone into overcrowded housing projects to interview women on welfare with too many kids and too few skills for a job. Usually, if the husband was still around, he'd have to hide in the closet when Mom came or the woman would lose her welfare if the department found out. Mom quickly saw up close how hopeless things were for most of these families and between that and her boss she didn't want the work. She was a minister's daughter and wife, not a street-pounding social worker battling impossible odds. That's when she started driving the Red Cross van and became president of the local YMCA. She also joined Dad in protests and political work through the local churches.

That last school year, Mom had taken me on trips to visit colleges. We had a surprisingly great time. I wasn't used to being alone with her for long stretches without Dad around. Just having her drive the car was new. She drove all over New England, taking me from one college interview to the next. Some were day trips, some were overnights. We were out in western New York somewhere when a blizzard hit. She drove through white-outs and over icy bridges, amazing me with an independence I'd never seen in her. On longer trips we went to restaurants, where I realized I'd never seen her order and pay for a meal. She was really quite a capable woman and I was sorry she acquiesced to Dad so much, although most women her age did the same. She had what Clarissa Pinkola Estes calls *the wild woman;* that instinctual and creative feminine soul. *The shadow that trots behind us is definitely four-footed,* Estes says in describing our wolf-self we're too civilized to release, to let run wild. When Mom pretended to be happy, I could see her wolf shadow prancing behind her. Years later she and Dad decided it best to leave their lakeside house to move into a retirement community for the assurance of nearby medical care. She told me that the night before they left she'd walked down among the tall cedar trees they'd planted years earlier as near twigs along the water's edge. Then she screamed out into the darkness – a deep howl from her wolf in its agony, her life slowly ending without her ever running wild.

At my college visits I was asked what my major would be. I said psychology, though I wasn't sure why or what that had to do with my future. I'd tell them I wanted to understand the mind and human behavior. What I really wanted to understand was my mind and behavior. I didn't think I was growing up right, but didn't know why. I thought I'd done things wrong. I wasn't chaste. I'd sinned. I was different from most girls and would suffer for it. So I'd study psychology and maybe there were clues there. Maybe I was fixable. What I didn't see then was the shadow that was also following me, four-footed and muscular; the unfixable wild woman on a dark path not entirely of her own choosing.

After all the visits, I decided Bard College best suited me. It was small and less frightening than other schools. It was also progressive; a hippie college. I was told it wasn't mainstream academia and I should be prepared for that. Well despite my appearance, I wasn't mainstream myself, so it looked like the place to be, though I wasn't sure I'd fit in there either. It also accepted me as a student. The Ivy League schools where my friends were going hadn't taken me anyway. No family money for future donations my parents had offered as an explanation.

Along with the rest of my fears about going to college, I had to separate from my boyfriend Sam, who I'd met senior year and who I've loved all my life. Sensitive, intelligent, savvy and honest, he was also handsome with a sweet smile and a tousle of brown hair that fell into bright and gentle eyes. He became president of the student council and chose me as his communications manager since I wasn't voted in as council secretary. My parents thought he was terrific.

He had lots of friends; I had few. His friends were hip, literate, interesting people. I struggled with feeling like one of them, never finding a comfortable spot, always a little jealous of his easy friendships. I worried I couldn't measure up and he'd lose interest in me. One of his friends was a confident, guitar-playing girl with long brown hair who smoked pot. I couldn't compete with that. I was afraid and withholding and becoming more subdued. Any personality I'd managed to develop was fast disappearing, fading into a blond stain on the air.

One day Sam completely surprised me by saying I was *living in an ivory tower*," using just the phrase Vinnie had in his poem. He was trying to help me understand why he'd gotten upset with me. I had to see that I did distance myself from him and everyone else. It was how I protected myself, but I must've been aloof sometimes, insensitive or flat out obnoxious. I criticized one of our friends for her perky hairstyle and her pixie-like way. I thought she was flirting with Sam so I got jealous and snippy. It was pathetic. I liked her and the other girls in our group, but felt I had something to hide and they didn't. Again the assumption of sustained chastity in other women, unlike myself. Relating to guys was easier.

I loved Sam, but I was way too needy; not so much clingy as fragile, as if I'd vanish if he walked away. He wasn't my other half, he was my whole. My dependence on him was unhealthy, but I didn't understand that then. It'd be many years later when I'd see its destructiveness and recognize the pattern in my relationships with men. Back then I just became endlessly quiet, all my curiosity and spirit held inside. I've never forgotten his gentleness and patience with me. He loved me despite myself.

I was happiest when we were alone, of course; when I had all his attention. We'd grab a thickly crocheted throw from the porch and amble down to the wide rope hammock hanging from a tree at the bottom of the flower garden. The blanket took off the chill of early fall afternoons while we cuddled in the hammock and talked about serious and silly things. Sam loved Pogo comic books and told me its latest stories. Snug against his soft shirt, I'd listen while watching the sun dappling through the deep green leaves on the ruddy-colored, gnarled branches above us. Bees buzzed in the garden and soft breezes passed by, carrying the scent of flowers. It wasn't hard to imagine Pogo relaxing with his pal Albert outside his tree house *smokin' seegars*. And then Sam and I would kiss, softly with open eyes, the sun sparkling in his, its light grazing his crooked smile as he'd pull slightly away and give me one of his *heh, heh, heh* Pogo laughs.

We spent the year together and eventually made love, once at my house and once at his. It was so different from being with Vinnie. Sam didn't expect sex. We loved each other and our affection and then sex was natural and tender. It made me less ashamed. He deserved being trusted and it felt good.

But the second time we had sex I got pregnant. I knew because I was throwing up.

I hated having to tell Sam. We spent days not sure what to do. Then standing on the front porch one evening, he said he'd be willing to get married and have the baby with me. I told him that wasn't possible. We were going to college and this would change our lives in ways we couldn't handle. We were kids ourselves and in no position to have a baby. Sam was relieved.

Telling my parents was unbelievably hard, but I needed their help. They weren't pleased. Certainly Mom wasn't. Dad was more quiet and thoughtful.

"How could you let this happen, Lily?" Mom

vented. She'd been making dinner when I made my announcement and was now wiping her hands raw with a dishtowel, pacing back and forth in the living room. "I always worried about you two down there in the hammock under that blanket. Darn, I should've said something!"

That would've been helpful, I thought. I was sorry she was so upset, though.

"It didn't happen in the hammock, Mom," I practically whispered. It'd happened on the living room couch, but I could hardly confess that the dirty act happened on a piece of our furniture. It made me feel a little less ashamed, though, that it hadn't happened in the hammock while she'd been watching from the kitchen window. *"Yuck."*

"When this is over I want to have a talk with you two," she fumed. I wondered what she'd say. Advising us about sex or condoms was certainly late in coming. "At least this didn't happen with that boy, Vinnie. I never trusted him. At least we liked Sam." Already Sam was in the past tense.

Mom finally seated herself in her familiar fretting position; one hand gripping an arm of her chair and a knuckle of the other hand pushing into her gritted teeth, while staring at the floor. She may have been angrier with herself than me.

I was angry with her for her reaction. I was almost grown. I was leaving home soon. How dare she choose now to finally say something and have it be chastising me for behavior she'd ignored and normal feelings she hadn't told me how to handle. She'd been ready with the menstrual pads, but not ready with any womanly advice about how to enjoy romance without sex or even how to not get pregnant if you did have sex. Now both of us were staring at the floor, my anger voiceless.

Dad finally broke the silence. "Let's try thinking about what we're going to do."

Most girls those days were having their babies and putting them up for adoption or having back alley abortions and often becoming sterile or dying from it. It was still a while before Roe vs. Wade legalized abortion in the U.S. and middle class girls like me sometimes had abortions in places like Puerto Rico, if they could afford it.

It all came together quickly. We made one visit to the gynecologist who lived down the street and who Mom and Dad knew would be discrete. The pregnancy confirmed, the doctor helped make arrangements. I don't remember the flight we took or the hotel where we stayed. My only memory is of the hospital and not much of that. Everything was put on urgent automatic. I also chose to forget things. It was a numbing time.

I do recall being with the doctor afterwards in the recovery room. He was a small, wiry Hispanic man and very kind. I was coming out of the anesthesia that seemed like a heavy, dense black hole in space that had sucked all my thoughts and feelings into and through it to some unknown place.

I knew I'd had an operation. He'd told us that, at three months, I was too far along for a "D and C."

"Was it a boy or a girl?" I slowly asked.

"You don't want to know that," he said, closing his eyes and nodding his head distraughtly back and forth. "It's best if you don't know," he said with finality.

"What did you do with it?"

Lily Scot

"No, no," he said. "You can't think about these things." He patted my shoulder, still nodding his head, and smiled sympathetically. A nurse came in to check my vital signs and the doctor quietly left. She took my hand to get my pulse. It felt good to be taken care of and I slumped back on the gurney letting the pillow cradle my head. The nurse draped a warm blanket over me, tucking it under my sides. I watched her putter about, feeling calmer with her nearby. She tidied up the space and rechecked the saline drip. Then she slipped out and pulled the curtain closed behind her. The ward was quiet with only hushed voices coming from the nurses' station down the hall. I tried to sleep, but couldn't.

A sadness deeper than I'd ever known rose through me as if emanating from the black hole of the anesthesia, like a faint rhythm in the universe pulsing through me. My feelings were coming back. And the crying began.

I knew the doctor was right and knowing details would make everything worse, but the loss was so strong. Adoption would have been one choice, but very difficult. Not knowing what happened to the baby, I'd spend my life feeling responsible. Chances are, a white baby with hazel eyes and soft brownish-blond hair would have been readily adopted by good parents. But letting go of caring for it would have been impossible for me. At least I had the right to choose. A few years later, the Supreme Court would decide this right belonged to all women.

Still, urgent and excruciating questions flooded my mind. *What would he have looked like? What would she have liked?* I've very often thought about the baby over the years, though I never regretted my decision.

It was a terrible choice, but one I had to make. I couldn't care for a child then. I didn't know enough to raise another person. Looking back now, I also understand that the same permanently smoldering burn deep in my gut would have caused harm to both of us. I was a child myself then. I needed to find my own way, not ruin someone else's life. Years later I'd give birth to another child and raise him well, loving him *more than all the numbers,* I constantly told him, (and still do), *more than all the stars in the universe, all the drops of water in the sea, and all the grains of sand on earth.*

Back then, though, I agonized about what the child would have been like. *Like me? Like Sam?* Or maybe some sweet combination of human potential that would have found its own way despite my frailties. I'll never know. And to never have touched that baby causes a sadness that will never go away.

After leaving the hospital, my father drove me up into the El Yunque rain forest and through the mountains, circling back to San Juan. We were silent most of the way. With the windows rolled down on the big Buick Riviera we rented, I could breathe in the mist and smell the woody scent of the endless trees covering the hills with immense, rich green leaves. I was so tired and leaned my head against the seat while Dad steered us around tight turns in the road as it wound up and down.

The steep hillsides were covered with crops of bananas and coffee. Occasionally we'd drive by a small house jutting off the hillside on narrow supporting posts. Children and chickens were everywhere and dark brown-faced women smiled when we waved to them as we passed. Men with leathery faces sat on stools in small roadside bars, drinking, smoking, talking and laughing together in the comfortable way of old friends who'd grown up together in this beautiful place.

"See the rainbow?" Dad asked. I followed his gaze and sure enough, there it was in the warm afternoon light. "Let's follow it," he said. "Maybe we can find the end with the pot of gold."

"I think that's just in Ireland, Dad," I said, teasing him along, "but let's go find out."

I loved and admired my father in that moment, one of the times I chose to put my anger with him on hold. When others were suffering was when he had great empathy and easily put his needs aside. He was a good minister. He couldn't heal his own old wounds, but he could help others. I think that's what inspired him, what maybe gave him moments of the inner peace he so anxiously sought. He knew I was still a child and had meant no trouble. I was also a responsible person; I just didn't know how to handle some parts of growing up. That day he touched what innocence was left in me and tried to bring me some peace; he let me know it was okay, that I could make mistakes and have time to grow up.

We drove for a long time, heading for the rainbow and as often as we were sure we could see where it touched the forest floor, its end, of course, never came. And that was fine.

The next day we all flew home. I was uncomfortable from the pain and the long row of stitches in my stomach. As we got into our seats I didn't want to buckle my seat belt. Mom was next to me and Dad was on the aisle. Mom asked the stewardess for a pillow, which she rested on my stomach while she gently pulled the seat belt over it and clasped it, leaving it loose. I pressed the pillow with my hand, and she covered my hand with hers, slowly stroking it with her long, graceful fingers. I leaned my head on her shoulder, closed my eyes and got drowsy. Mom and Dad were quietly talking. I heard Mom say, "Well, that's behind us now."

Sam spent the summer working for his father as his punishment for impregnating me, earning money to help pay for the abortion. He'd missed out on a cross-country road trip with his best friend, but was amazingly good about it. Before leaving for different colleges that fall we were loving, quiet and sad. We promised to see each other often, knowing nothing was certain. The hammock hung idle, barely visible through the yellowing leaves of its tree.

ᏬᏬᏬᏬᏬᏬ

I liked going to school at Bard, but was nervous as any freshman. That it was a small, rural college made it easier for me to be away from home. You can still walk from one end of campus to the other, though the college has many more buildings now. Back then it was near its original configuration with men's and women's dorms in old ivy-covered mansions overlooking the Hudson River, a small and exquisite chapel, charming faculty houses, one an octagon, stately academic halls and Stone Row, a row of impressive stone buildings used as freshman dorms. I lived in the only contemporary building at the time, the women's freshman dorm that was built in a swamp and rumored to be slowly sinking, although it's still there these many years later.

I had the usual freshman classes along with

psychology, my major. I studied hard and had a job at the library, doing what menial tasks I don't remember, but it compensated for the lowered tuition I'd been given. I hung out in my dorm and in the coffee shop and slowly met a few people, though it took hours of my sitting alone, terrified of talking to anyone. Meeting people was through their initiative and usually after they'd sat down at my table which held the only open chairs left in the place. In time, as a hanger-on to one of these groups, I got introduced to smoking pot and found myself getting driven down to Adolph's, the off-campus bar, for burgers and booze.

1968 was a good time to be at Bard. Bob Dylan sometimes came on campus from where he lived in Woodstock across the river. He ran the movie projector on Friday nights when crowds of stoned "freaks" filled Sottery Hall to cheer or hiss and boo at that week's film. Bob and I share a May birthdate so I hope he won't mind my mentioning his often getting into minor mischief on campus and having to do service by helping out the building and grounds crew around *Maggie's Farm*, as he called Bard, Margaret being the dean's first name at the time. And then there was that water pump outside of Adolph's that was broken *'cause the vandals took the handles*, or so the legend goes.

I got into politics then. It was impossible not to. Martin Luther and Bobby had both been shot that spring, race riots and student violence were everywhere, the My Lai massacre had happened in Vietnam, and CBS's *60 Minutes* first aired on television. Bard College was a small haven along the Hudson for stoners who talked politics far into the night.

During winter break, I was a psychology intern as a nurses' aide at a state psychiatric center outside of Manhattan. I worked in the children's ward. I brought in a roll of blank paper one day, taped it on a long wall and handed out crayons to the kids. They were untrusting at first, but soon became a raucous frenzy at the wall, colorful pictures covering the paper. Amazingly there were no fights. It was just really loud and almost out of control. Among the wild scribbling I could make out houses and trees, various male and female figures, some smiling and waving, some seeming to scream out of large round mouths, and a number of penises. Part of my job was to type up handwritten case histories of the children, and I knew the unpleasant experiences many of them came from, some at the hands of their own parents. Penises were no surprise.

There were children dual-diagnosed with psychiatric problems and mental retardation, as it was referred to at the time. They were in a different ward, but I'd read the case history of one of them who I wanted to meet. I asked a ward nurse I'd gotten to know pretty well, and she was willing to introduce me. She took me to a room with bare grey walls that was unused.

"Wait here," said the nurse. "I'll bring him to you."

I waited, feeling like an awkward spectator, but compelled to meet this client with a combination of psychology student interest and human curiosity.

The boy slowly entered the room, his direction towards me guided by a gentle push on his elbow by the nurse. I was quiet. He walked a few feet and stopped, hid head turning slowly from one side to the other.

As his medical history indicated, this four foot, five inch, 23 year-old young man had no eyes. If there were even sockets, they were completely obscured by skin, leaving no evidence of any optical structure. He had no eyes, simple as that. His skin was taut from forehead to nose and cheeks. X-rays had revealed the presence of something deep behind his face, but nothing conclusive. Surgery was not suggested.

"Hello," I said softly. His head localized to my voice. "How are you?" It was a stupid question from someone with no reference point whatsoever for how this young man might feel or how he was doing. I felt ludicrously inept at observing him, my psychology studies so far only reading and discussion.

His head tilted toward me, his non-eyes querying me apprehensively, though he was mute and couldn't express concern. He did seem resigned to being observed, as he'd experienced countless times with doctors and psychiatrists, but also seemed primed for flight if needed. Abandoning any pretense of professional observation, I gently touched his arm. His face riveted towards mine and he smiled. "It's nice to meet you," I said warmly, not knowing if he could even understand me. I heard his breathing deepen; relaxing into what I hoped was relief.

It was then I noticed the old scars from burns on his arms which I'd read in his record came from lit cigarettes, abuse occurring years earlier by staff at another institution. In seven years, evidence of abuse by caretakers would be made public and new laws made to assure humane treatment of these individuals once called morons and idiots.

"I should get him back to his ward soon," the

nurse said.

"Yes," I nodded, moving my hand down the boy's arm to find his, which I shook in parting. "Good-bye, Billy."

"Come with me, Billy," she said, guiding him out of the room. "It's time for lunch."

As he neared the door, Billy turned and gave me a big smile. I stood there, feeling deeply touched by something very powerful -- a moment of grace that made up for my certainly feeling more the idiot than he ever was.

I'd remember Billy forever. Meeting him and others eventually decided my career in helping people who couldn't help themselves. Along with the mentally ill and disabled would be others who'd been discriminated against and abused, especially older kids who'd been abandoned and women with young children who'd known terrifying domestic violence. I felt a kinship with them, even though my own circumstances were nowhere near so dire. It doesn't matter, I know now. The fear and anger you shelter, the shame growing densely at the root of your being – I came to understand that about myself and so could understand others better.

Back at school after the break, I was glad I'd signed up for a course in abnormal psychology. Along with trying to understand myself, I wanted to learn about the kids like those I'd met at the hospital; kids who'd grow up, their demons growing as fast and even stronger inside them than they were on the outside.

Of course I didn't study all the time and was soon riding back to Adolph's with whatever car full of people I'd gotten hooked up with on campus, still the overly quiet tag-along.

I met Cole on one of those trips. He was a junior, studying literature and creative writing. He was very tall and too thin, with black hair and blue eyes. *Black Irish* he called himself that evening after we separated ourselves from our friends hanging out at the bar. *Black Irish with some French and a dash of Cherokee,* he'd said. The Cherokee gene accounted for his high cheekbones. I imagined his ancestors traveling from Ireland to maybe Quebec and, like Evangeline, down the Mississippi River, some man betrothing an Indian maiden before traveling on. *I'm from the South, near New Orleans,* he told me.

Cole was shy and self-conscious, which I liked, along with his deeply penetrating, even hypnotic gaze and very apparent intelligence. He was striking, and I thought we'd probably end up more than friends.

We started dating, Cole picking me up at my dorm and taking me into Rhinebeck for dinner at Fosters Coach House Tavern, one of the alternatives to Adolph's for Bardians. The movie *2001: A Space Odyssey* was released that spring and Cole and I saw it over the river in Kingston. He was more moved by that film than any other we saw together, Cole's relationship with the universe having very intense meaning for him. Other times we'd hang out on campus smoking hash and walking through the formal gardens at Blithewood Mansion, the women's dorm overlooking the Hudson, or listening to the *Bad Rock Group* with senior students Don Fagen on piano, Walter Becker on guitar, and maybe Chevy Chase sitting in on drums. Yes, it was a good year to be at Bard.

It wasn't long before I regularly stayed with Cole

in his room at Ward Manor, the mansion housing upperclassmen. It was a great stone building with a broad terrace overlooking the property down to the river. Though the common rooms were very ornate with dark wood, long drapes and chandeliers, the men's rooms were small and sparse. Cole and I shared his single bed, our slim bodies just barely staying on the mattress.

My taking birth control pills removed the pregnancy worry, so sex was easier. We were very awkward though. He told me he hadn't had a lot of sex before and the sex I'd had wasn't enough for me to know what to do either. That a lot of shame was wedged in my sexual response didn't help. So exploring what would work for both of us wasn't easy. But we managed and eventually settled into a routine that worked well enough.

When summer came, I left for home and Cole went to see his family on the Florida gulf coast. I took it easy. When Dad got home from work I'd watch him putter around the garden, deftly hoeing weeds from around the masses of flowers. He always had his little sunny patch at the edge where he'd grow tomatoes and salad greens, and he loved to run melon vines along the back fence until it reached the shade of the densely overhanging tree with the hammock hung underneath.

On weekend afternoons when the sun was strong, Dad wore an enormous cone-shaped straw hat from a trip to China for his job, a pair of rugged sandals he'd gotten from some other country and an old pair of grey shorts with a worn brown belt. His aging torso sagged, but his back showed the muscles of a tall man who'd been pushing a wheelbarrow for many years.

Mom often joined Dad in the garden, tending to her petunias, zinnias and marigolds against backdrops of phlox, daisies and black-eyed Susans. Kneeling in her floral printed shirt and shorts, she disappeared among the towering plants.

Over the years, Mom and Dad had finally made good company for each other, silently maneuvering around the garden like butterflies circulating the brightly colored petals, always in tandem and never far from each other, now and then alighting on the same flower just like Mom and Dad finding a bit of conversation about the various plants. After so many years in a cocoon, their struggling marriage had emerged into something capable of short distance flights between tensions arising out of long buried resentments and worries.

I'd get drowsy watching their calm garden reverence, drifting into a nap on a blanket spread against the slope of the hill leading up to the house.

It was a small Queen Anne-style Victorian house. A round turret on one corner and a weathervane at its peak made it look like a tiny castle. The turret created a round alcove for every room on that corner and housed a round table off the living room, a round bed for my parents on the second floor and a small round attic space where I'd go to play my flute or daydream. This turret inspired Vinnie's poem about my reclusiveness in an ivory tower and Sam's similar comment on the day we sat on the porch swing. The huge foundation stones of the turret an arm's reach from us, Sam glanced at the tower as he politely complained about what I surmised were my trapped emotions and how I used love as a crutch.

The house was yellow with while trim surrounding the roof over the large porch furnished with white wicker chairs, a couch and table. It was a comfortable place on a summer day.

I passed through that languid summer, even enjoying my father's company except for the odd moments of unwanted physical contact, especially his neck kissing, though I'd still encourage him to brush my hair while I sat on the floor in front of him, or have him tickle my arms which I'd drape across his knee. As long as I initiated the boundary crossing it was okay with me, though I had no idea how strange this behavior would seem to an outsider. We were fully enmeshed, he and I, except when his neediness roused my anger, me trying to get control of our relationship on my own terms, which were fuzzy at best. I couldn't then see that his neediness was like mine that I think angered Tom.

Mom was witness to all this but never reacted, letting everything take its course. For the most part she would hum liturgical-sounding tunes and perform her little dance of acceptance and delight, only occasionally showing her own frustration with Dad's neediness and blurting out a short tirade, which sent him sulking to the bottom of the garden where he'd go to *eat worms,* as he'd say, knowing punishment was due, but seeking even more attention for his now distressed state.

But as summer passed, I started having disturbing feelings. I couldn't concentrate and had eerie sensations like my head was stretching far from my feet, and sounds seemed to reach me through a tunnel or as if vibrating through water. It was hard to make sense out of simple things and I'd get easily confused and then scared. I wasn't smoking any pot and wondered if I was having some kind of withdrawal symptoms. I decided to see our family doctor, without mentioning it to my parents. He couldn't determine any physical cause and sent me to a psychiatrist, who I saw for several visits.

It was this psychiatrist in his leather furnished, book-lined office who first asked about my relationship with Dad and for whom I had no answers or even clues and even felt squeamish talking about him though I didn't know why. I'd been reading Dostoevsky's *Crime and Punishment* and many of our counseling sessions centered around the character of Raskolnikov and how his self-torment is far worse than his crime of murder, leading him to obsessive delusions and moral degeneration. I wasn't sure, but the psychiatrist seemed to imply that Raskolnikov and I had secrets to share. The psychiatrist talking about the man's plight did make me realize I strongly empathized with his troubled existence. Self-loathing, immense shame and a clutching need for redemption did live quietly in me and I struggled to understand the crime I'd committed. Mostly, like Dostoevsky's protagonist, I searched for vindication, though I'd hardly murdered anyone. Roskolnikov certainly had it worse than me, though my moral degeneration was still in years to come. The psychiatrist diagnosed me with generalized anxiety and prescribed a combination of uppers and downers *to level me out,* he'd said.

I went back to school in the fall, but far from leveling out I started feeling even more unbalanced and confused. I couldn't follow what was happening in my classes and my grades began to drop. I took up again with Cole, but was more distant and quiet, trying to hide my disoriented state out of embarrassment. I tried explaining that something wrong was happening to me, but didn't know what it was or what to do about it. He was certainly sympathetic but couldn't do anything for me either. He'd sit with his fingers steepled, his vibrant blue eyes peering over the top of his thick, black rimmed glasses, nodding in attempted understanding, much like the psychiatrist I'd seen. I felt like a crazy child.

I went home at Christmas, grateful for some rest. One evening while standing at the upstairs bathroom sink, the left side of my body went limp and I fell on the floor. I couldn't speak or call for help, though fully conscious. It took a while, but I dragged myself with my right arm, pushing with my right leg out of the bathroom and across the hall, then down the stairs to the living room where Mom and Dad were reading. When they saw me, Dad swooped me off the floor into his chair, where I sat smiling dumbly, my left side limp. Mom asked me to put my index fingers together, but instead I put my right finger in my mouth. Horrified, they called the doctor who came and examined me and then sent me to the hospital for observation.

Later that night an amazingly intense pain started in the back of my brain and all I remember after pushing the call button for the nurse was a needle going in my arm. I'd had a stroke, a blood clot spending months traveling up my left leg into my brain where it came close to causing a hemorrhage.

Mom stayed by me the next few days, caring for me with a deeper concern than I'd felt from her before, having been told that if the clot had gone to my lungs I would've died. She discreetly left the room when Sam stopped by for a visit. I was surprised to see him as we'd hardly spoken since leaving for school. His concern was apparent.

He sat by my bed, running his hand under the covers to find mine. I was weak and exhausted and very glad to have him there. He smiled and we just looked at each other for a long time in the quiet of the room.

"I've been thinking," he said.

"Oh?"

"Would you like to get married?" He smiled. "I would."

I was stunned. Sam was a very independent young man with a wide open future full of possibility. That he was still willing to commit to spending his life with me was amazing. It took me a few minutes to answer.

"No, Sam, I can't. I've already told Cole I'd marry him. I'm sorry." For reasons I wouldn't understand for years, I was saying no. I'd become entranced by Cole, convinced that our future together would be incomparable to any other possibility, including life with Sam.

What I couldn't realize at the time was that Sam was too healthy for me. I don't think I'd have known how to live with someone as emotionally strong as he was. Cole and I were twisted together like a double helix of connections that fit perfectly, but were really unhealthy. We couldn't escape each other and had to either get better or grow more malignant together. No matter which, we had some destiny to get to. Nothing seemed to stop that.

Sam was very hurt and left quickly. Mom came

into the room a few minutes later.

"What happened to Sam?" she asked. "He passed me in the hall and looked upset. He hardly said good-bye."

"He proposed to me and I turned him down."

"Oh dear," she said slumping into the chair. "That's just so sad."

"I feel really awful. But I just can't. I'm committed to Cole, and I think we've got a real future together. Being with Sam just doesn't feel like the right thing to do somehow."

"Choices aren't always easy. I chose your Dad over another man who loved me."

"Really?" I'd never heard about this fellow.

"Oh yes. His name was Dirk. We were quite the item. But your Dad came along and grabbed my heart." She tilted her head and looked at me. "I didn't regret it, but on occasion I do wonder about Dirk. Those young loves are never forgotten."

"Well I've lost something very precious. I hope I don't regret it."

It was the first woman-to-woman talk I remember having with her and I welcomed it. I was almost grown and we could be more revealing to each other, I guessed. And I'd been through enough heavy stuff that warranted her attention. I hoped we could maybe fix what had kept us apart.

I thought again about Sam and a memory of visiting him working as a children's camp counselor. I was walking towards him on a path in the woods, summer heat baking the pine needles on the forest floor, sending up a strong scent of balsam as I looked into his gentle face. I've never smelled pine needles since without thinking of Sam and missing him very much.

The cause of my illness was soon determined, the physician telling us the stroke was from my using birth control pills, estrogen dosages of the pills being high back then. Once out of the hospital, I read articles published in British medical journals about studies proving an average of one in 300,000 women could die from taking these pills. Big Pharma in the U.S. had been in a rush to cash in on the large profits it expected from this very marketable contraceptive, despite the risks. My loss, their gain. A number of women had died and their families had sued, as did many women who'd survived. The company cleverly arranged a cap on lawsuits and I missed out. Though I wasn't paying a lot of attention to the women's movement raging around me, this personal incident made the mantra of *our bodies, ourselves* very sensible. But my feeling of powerlessness in those years wasn't so bolstered by anger that I felt any more called to activism for women's rights.

I also had to leave school, being told I needed time to recover. I couldn't imagine picking up my studies again anyway. Cole came back early from Florida when he heard what happened, and we decided to move off campus to a small house in Red Hook for that spring semester until he graduated. For weeks I had electroencephalograms at the local hospital to test my brain's electrical activity. After a while, they decided I was going to be fine. I don't remember a lot about that time other than it being a simpler hippie life of painting and cooking and photography. We may have had a cat. I'm not sure.

ﾃﾟﾃﾟﾃﾟﾃﾟﾃﾟ

From the small white frame house in Saugerties that Cole and I rented after he graduated, you could see the Hudson River through the trees that stepped gracefully down the long embankment towards the shore. It was late summer, the river hosting the many ships that silently coursed its deep channels, finding ports upstate.

Our wildly overgrown yard carried the scents of well-established wildflowers, neighboring lilac trees and honeysuckle bushes. Dense stands of Sumac trees joined conifer, beech and maple in a sweeping border around the huge yard that kept other houses out of view.

We weren't far from Woodstock and our nicely bucolic surroundings were more than miles away from the intensity of our time. Student protests against the Vietnam War made for a violent spring on many of the larger college campuses, though Bard was quiet. I was still pretty out of touch, trusting Bob, Gloria, Stokely and Abbie, among others, to carry the necessary messages.

For the moment, I was more engrossed in the comings and goings of the bugs in the grass where I lay protected by the yarrow and blue cornflower plants towering above me. I lifted my head a little and saw Cole dancing by the kitchen window to the new Cat Stevens album he was playing.

"You still got that joint?" Cole called from the window. "I know you're out there." I shot my arm up, the glint of the roach clip in the afternoon sun broadcasting my position. I heard the backdoor squeak open and I could tell when he was near by the soap bubbles he blew towards me that fell gently down, bursting their wet coolness on my face. He joined me, stretching his six foot, three inch body alongside mine. He sucked in a long toke and held it before turning to press his lips to mine, which opened and took in the hot smoke. A train whistle blew down by the river as I slowly exhaled.

"Want me to breathe for you?" Cole asked. This was one of our favorite things to do together.

"Sure." Closing my eyes, I lay still and let all the air out of my chest. His moustache brushed and parted my lips as he closed his mouth over mine and sent fresh air into me, filling my lungs, then sucking it back out again, repeating this in-and-out of air a few times. It was amazingly relaxing to let him take over this automatic task of my body. I returned the favor for him and then we lay there awhile next to each other, holding hands and feeling the weight of our bodies relaxing on the ground, softly matted with long grass and sweet smelling flowers.

Cole rolled over close to me and began softly tickling my face, which I loved. His fingers lightly moved down my neck and bare arm, still tickling. Then he slowly caressed my breast, bare underneath a thin cotton shirt which he unbuttoned and spread open, my skin feeling the warm sun as his tongue found the space between my breasts and ran down around my belly button, his fingers and then his tongue tracing my stomach at the rim of my long, loose skirt which lay at my hips. A hand reached down and teasingly pulled up the skirt, taking its time by gently ticking the inside of my thighs, his long fingers slowly finding their way under the edge of my panties to the now very moist opening of my vagina, tracing circles and increasing pressure on the old joy spot until his tongue followed in strong rhythmic motion, the heat in my body rising to meet the heat of the day as my groin pressed down and then arched upward, jolts of lusty satisfaction racing to my core. Before the sensations passed, he penetrated me, his long, thick firmness moving to the steady beat of my breathing until he, too, arched his back, groans gushing in tempo with the spurts of his satisfaction, his body then coming to rest on top of mine.

We lay there until the sun drifted below the horizon and the bugs found us, delighting themselves of our exposed flesh. We got the munchies and headed towards the kitchen to cook dinner together. Spaghetti tonight, like many nights. We were starved.

We'd been married in June, the ceremony held at the 17th century, Old Dutch Church of Sleepy Hollow in New York, made famous by Washington Irving in his tale of Ichabod Crane and the Headless Horseman. It was in this church that my father served his first congregation. For the wedding, I wore orange blossoms in my hair and a very short white satin dress that Dad thought was a slip, expecting a long wedding gown. It was a beautiful ceremony, after which we began the long drive to Florida to visit Cole's parents. Friends decorated our Chevy with the obligatory trailing cans and Dad had painted *Going to Florida for a little SON* in white along the light blue fenders.

Our stay with Cole's parents in the Florida panhandle had to wait until we'd made a trip further into the sunshine state that constituted our honeymoon. Cole and I drove from the gulf side where we'd quickly unloaded our stuff with his parents to the Atlantic side for the Apollo 11 lift-off to the moon. Before dawn, on a remote stretch of our drive to Cape Kennedy, we were sure we saw UFO's high above a conservation area: Five glowing, orange, blimp-shaped objects traveling evenly together at a slow speed towards the Cape. It certainly was an appropriate time to be watching what the earthlings were up to.

Arriving at the Cape, the impressively lit rocket was a startlingly bright visual against the still black night; a shining silver cone readied for its civilization-changing ascent. It looked like a poster for a science fiction movie, only it was very real.

The warm air was dense with moisture that carried the ocean scent. As the sun rose, you could see huge numbers of people standing in the great arc of the launch site perimeter, everyone hushed by a group reverence of the significance of what they were witnessing. I was excited by the prospect, but it was Cole who'd anticipated this since he first became conscious of the coming reality of space travel as a child reading Jules Verne. I watched him leaning against our car, an arm held across his chest propping the other uplifted arm, his fingers pressing against his teeth in a characteristic pose of barely contained exhilaration, his blue eyes dancing behind his thick, black-rimmed glasses.

"I can't believe we're actually here, babe," he whispered, not taking his eyes off the rocket. "I also can't believe I didn't bring the binoculars," he added, thumping his forehead.

"Here, borrow these," said a man standing near us, as tall as Cole.

"Why, thanks, man," Cole said.

"Not at all. I'm a space junkie. Wouldn't' keep a man from a good view," he added, handing over the binoculars. "Name's Leland."

"Great to meet you. Mine's Cole."

Public address speakers had been making announcements since we'd arrived. *This is Apollo-Saturn launch control; we've passed the five-minute mark in our countdown for Apollo 11; now four minutes, forty-six seconds and counting … on time for our planned liftoff of thirty-two minutes past the hour.*

The sun was well up now, and you could see the awkward steel girders reaching up to form the gantry tower, a stark contrast to the glistening rocket it held in its grasp.

"Amazing that it can rain inside that building," said the man, Leland, referring to the massive, windowless grey building where the rocket was assembled; the largest enclosed space ever constructed at the time. "It's like a successor to the Pyramids of Egypt, it's so damn big," he laughed.

"No shit," Cole reacted. He panned the binoculars over the building and then back over the crowd. "I wonder who's here besides us. Robert Heinlein, maybe? He's gotta be in his sixties, but he wouldn't miss this."

"Probably got a good seat," Leland said. "I'll bet Assimov might not be here, though." They both burst out laughing. Cole looked over at me and saw my perplexed expression. "He's afraid of flying," he explained.

The lift-off that soon came was no disappointment. The rocket emerged heavily out of the low, but intense rumbling sound and swelling fog coming from the boosters, the lengthening flames struggling to hoist the immense ship upwards, its slow gain in momentum encouraged by the delirious shouting of the crowd, almost pushing the rocket heavenward with its enthusiasm. The now more distant white streak labored to break free of earth's gravity, and then gracefully arced in spectacular triumph toward the waiting moon.

Cole and Leland had run up to the fence, ecstatically flinging themselves about like ten-year-olds. It was great to watch.

We'd planned our wedding around the moon landing at the end of July. Our other choice was to wait until August and go to the Woodstock Music and Art Fair before heading south. But we figured that a rock concert on some nearby farm probably couldn't compete with the Apollo mission. Of course we heard about the history-changing concert as it happened. And on our trip back north after visiting his parents, we saw the remnants of the concert on our way home.

After we got back, Cole took a job as a radio news man and deejay. He loved it. Being alone at the station suited him fine. Except for close friends, he really didn't like most other people anyway, though he could be a charmer and a great storyteller among those friends we did have.

His hourly news was a *rip and read,* he called it, from the Associated Press wire service, and he'd spin the records he loved to play. He knew music as well as he knew everything else. Cole read books by the pound and always had. His mental catalogue was crammed with information about so many things I didn't know where he found room in his head for it. His mother read Shakespeare to him when he was five years old and started an insatiable lifelong reading habit. He could speak on any topic with great enthusiasm and no arrogance. Cole just loved knowledge and greeted new information eagerly. He taught me things I doubt I'd have learned on my own. I was smart, but he helped me understand complex labyrinths of thought. I suppose the hallucinogens helped too.

I'd gotten a job at a commercial portrait studio as a "spotter." I'd examine all the black and white prints for imperfections created in the developing process where specks of dirt or bubbles in the liquid left marks. I'd correct the flawed areas with tiny paint brushes I'd dip into black ink and blend with water to make the perfect color tone to match the print, carefully filling in areas that needed to be darkened. Why they hired me I couldn't figure out as I had no experience, but I liked the work and became good at it. I'd even enhance the images a little.

Eventually I got inspired to have a darkroom of my own and Cole and I set one up in our bathroom, using the tub to hold the developer and fixer trays, a laundry line strung above it with clothespins to hold the prints. We'd spend hours making prints of photographs we'd taken around town and learn techniques or experiment with ways to create effects like increased contrast or odd juxtapositions. Our house was often completely dark except for the dim red light escaping from the black curtain we'd hang to keep out any light, although one night the darkness seemed to frighten Cole, who was sure that someone was walking around the house looking in the windows. We had to tour the house inspecting all the windows for a stranger's face and checking the locks on all the doors. It wasn't the first or last time Cole got paranoid like that. I just figured it was the pot, and let it go.

A dose of mescaline might inspire us to take up our acrylic paints and poster board. Years later I'd still have a painting of a huge multi-colored fish swimming among silvery weeds on a mottled blue background. It looked amazing while tripping, a little silly when not. I also got Styrofoam balls and string and we made a solar system strung across the living room ceiling like the one in my room as a child. We painted the planets with florescent colors that glowed in the blacklight we had, and when it was finished we'd sit in stoned wonderment, listening to the Moody Blues and having deep conversations about space and time that kept us talking into the night.

One of Cole's favorite subjects was "group mind," a concept he'd picked up from one of his favorite science fiction authors. He'd talk about Arthur C. Clarke and Issac Assimov like they were his buddies, like he'd just been hanging out with them at the corner tavern. In Cole's case, books' authors were his best friends.

"Group mind is where we're headed babe," he'd say, his blue eyes glistening beneath his thick black eyebrows. "A collective human consciousness existing beyond the physical world. Like a gathering of souls cosmically departed from this rudimentary plane, this evolutionary breeding ground we're on."

I'd nod and "grok," the hip word for understanding what he said, adding some corollary insight like "Maybe though united in harmony, we each bring with us some essence of our individuality, our uniquely evolved personal gift." And we'd nod together in an all-knowing way, *Days of Future Passed* echoing our thoughts in the background.

Much of this thinking was fodder for the science fiction stories Cole was working on. Having published in the school's student literary journal, Cole was intent on becoming a professional writer.

My ambition was to dance. I'd begun studying dance at Bard and wanted to continue, though I wasn't certain how. There weren't classes in the kind of dance I enjoyed. Modern dance was the main alternative to ballet, but it was still more restrained than what I envisioned as a really free dance form. And I wanted to combine dance movements with multi-media, using more experimental music, art, stage and lighting effects, all blended into intense visual rhythms where dance was only a part of the total effect. Nothing like that existed, and I had no clue how to develop it. So I spent hours in our living room choreographing dance steps to *Evil Ways*, a song Santana had played at Woodstock even before the album came out that fall. In the small space available, I created what at least felt like an explosive piece that expressed the energy and tone of the music. When I was confident enough, I looked for a place to perform it. I found an interested show manager at a resort in nearby Ellenville. He was pretty casual about it, not even auditioning me. I just described what I wanted to do and he said, *Sure, why not?* and we worked out the technical details. He'd pay me fifty dollars.

For some reason, I never felt nervous about the whole thing. I couldn't figure that out, but was glad. The day came; I chose an outfit to wear and headed for the resort. I asked Cole to come with me. I wanted him to see the dance, thinking I'd like to work on adding some visuals to it, building it up and maybe performing it again sometime. He might have good opinions to share.

I'd decided on a full bodysuit, ribbed black knit with long sleeves, and a turtle neck. Over it I wore a crushed deep red velvet skirt, short enough that I needed matching red underwear. The skirt was one of Cole's favorites, though he preferred no underwear. My hair was its longest then, hanging in thick, sun-lightened strawberry blond shafts almost to my waist. Sheer stockings and red leather dance shoes finished my evil ways outfit. I was a little afraid it was too much of a "Barbarella" look, but it was the best I could do.

We got to the resort and went into the main lounge. Cole took a table out front and I headed backstage. There were maybe thirty-five tables filled with diners enjoying their main course. Somehow, being a spectacle still didn't make me apprehensive. I was looking forward to trying my routine on a stage.

As the clatter of the dinner hour eventually began to subside, the show manager let me know that I'd be on in fifteen minutes. He took my music from me to set it up on the sound system. The lounge band certainly didn't know Santana. *Too bad*, I thought. *"Having twenty live musicians backing me up would be so much better. Having Santana backing me up, well there was a fantasy."*

The band stopped its dinner music set and I heard the manager announcing a new performer at the resort. He was gracious in his introduction, making me into the professional I was not. I walked boldly onstage and gave a slight wave of greeting to the diners, who were now politely shuffling their chairs to get a good straight-on view of the show.

Cole gave me an encouraging smile. The band members remained seated at their music stands, their leather-fringed, shiny shirts an odd backdrop to my performance. *Oh well*, I thought.

I took my starting position and waited for *Evil Ways* to begin. As the first pounding drumbeats slid into the guitar and organ riff with its tantalizing Latin tempo, I slid into a sultry dance, bending and twisting with the music. Quasi cha-cha moves alternated with extemporaneous free-style moves during the guitar and organ solos, my undulating exuberance escalating with the music right to the double-time rhythm of the song's end, my frenzied movement accelerating with Carlos wailing over the top, my long blond hair flipping wildly.

As I was dancing, a sudden realization came over me: *My audience was not at all familiar with this music and had no frame of reference for my dance.* As I spun around the stage I caught rotating images of placid-faced diners staring at me, some quizzically shocked, and then blandly smiling band members, faces beaded with sweat from the lights. *This music and my dancing made no sense at all to these people.* As I writhed my way to one side of the stage during a particularly orgasmic organ solo, I saw one young woman punch her husband's elbow off the table, protesting his intent gaze at my red satin underpants which flashed as my skirt swung side to side in motion with the music. As I grew more uncomfortable, the band members started looking like garishly costumed plastic dolls sitting against the gaudy stage set and the heavy velour drapes on the dining room walls made me feel like a cheesy bordello act.

What the hell was I doing? I had to ask myself. Now I was finally nervous. But the song wasn't finished and I had no choice but to dance it through. So I smiled at the band and the band smiled back. I flirted with the husband and motioned seductively at an old man. I threw Cole a shrug and he nodded supportively. I had to end this thing I'd begun and did so with gusto, knowing I'd never see any of these people again. *Thank god.* Finally, the song was ending. I did my last bold move, waved animatedly at the crowd and flounced backstage, hearing a weak, but polite applause as the manager shouted into the microphone, "Let's hear it for our energetic go-go dancer!"

Go-go dancer? I gathered my stuff and hurried out a backdoor into a hallway leading to the reservation lounge of the hotel, speeding my way through the front door and out into the parking lot. Cole eventually realized I'd left and found me leaning against our car, still shaking my head back and forth in disbelief at the gall I'd just shown.

"Way to go, babe! Or should I say way to go-go?" I threw my bag at his head and burst out laughing.

"Did you see the faces on those people?" I asked. "You'd think I just did a strip-show the way they reacted. I should've cruised the tables for tips!"

"Better get in the car before we get arrested," Cole joked. "I have a hard time imagining you behind bars in that little get-up you have on."

I poured myself into the front seat, holding my head low in jest. "You'd better bail me out," I said, still laughing.

"I don't know. I've got a good reputation in these towns. Everyone knows my voice. I can't be too risky," he teased. Reaching into the glove compartment, he pulled out a huge joint and handed it to me. "Better light this thing quick," he said, starting the car and heading out of the parking lot. "We gotta get stoned and outta here. This place is like something out of the 1950s, and I sure don't want to be stuck here." He zoomed onto the road heading north towards home. "Lily and Cole, out for a night on the town, headed down the highway, not knowing they were driving straight into … the *Twilight Zone*." We laughed hysterically, blowing pot smoke throughout the car.

I laid my head back against the seat and took in a long toke. The whole experience threw me into a giggle fit. I kept seeing the band leader's rosy, shiny, smiling face, only it grew larger and larger like a balloon being pumped up at a carnival, its cheeks bulging.

"You know, babe, you did have some really good moves tonight," Cole said sincerely. "I think you've got something there that can be worked on. I'd really like to see what you can do with it."

"Really?" I said, holding my breath and passing him the joint. "Well, I've got some ideas, like a big curved screen with a light show projected on it from behind. And two sets of dancers doing different movements, some more Salsa-like and some more modern jazz or pop. I'm not sure. It's not something I'm going to put together overnight, that's for sure. Just thinking."

"Go for it. I'd love to see it work for you." He smiled and nodded his head in a way I knew he meant it. Clearly stoned, he began talking about making videos and how with rapidly advancing technology we'd probably soon have computers generating images for us like nothing ever seen before and ways of making visuals out of musical rhythms. "It's all happening, babe," he said. "It's all coming our way." He smiled and even in the near darkness I could see his blue eyes sparkle. I returned his smile and, resting my head against the window, watched the stars glide by as our car proceeded slowly – very, very slowly – down the road, Cole's gaze focused some on the dotted lines in front of him, but some on the far distant horizon of his own imagination.

1970

I took the afternoon off from work for errands and a doctor's appointment before I met Cole to go to a new restaurant in town. Since we'd leave from the radio station where he worked and I wouldn't have time to change, I wore a dress for dinner while doing errands. It was one he really liked because he said the pastel flowers made me look like a Monet painting, innocent and pretty. I even curled my hair and used more makeup than usual. Later I'd throw on perfume. I was looking forward to a nice evening.

Work, banking, drug store and post office done, I headed for the doctor's office. He was a new gynecologist for me, but I figured it was a routine visit and shouldn't take long. I filled out paperwork and soon followed the nurse to the examining room, where she left me alone to wait for the doctor.

The room was ordinary, lacking patient information posters or any of the pink plastic body parts doctors use to explain things. The only patient amenity was a stack of news, sports and women's magazines. I flipped through *Cosmopolitan*, lingering on the article "I was an Overage Virgin," wondering what age was now considered appropriate and what kind of good or bad advice it had for young girls.

The doctor appeared, looking briefly at me while reviewing the medical questionnaire I'd answered. "Have a seat on the table," he said, motioning me to the sheet-covered examining table. I did so. "This shouldn't take long," he continued, and began asking me the usual questions about my medical history, glancing at me now and then, but expressionless. He was a short man and, from my slightly elevated level, the balding center of his head stared at me as he wrote things down.

Putting aside my medical chart and tucking his glasses in his lab coat pocket, he turned to me and matter-of-factly said, "Can you take down the top of your dress and remove your bra please?" I didn't remember ever being examined sitting up instead of being asked to lie down and was always given a sheet to cover myself. I felt uncomfortable, but he was staring at me, waiting. I unzipped my dress, pulled it down and unhooked my bra, which fell on my lap. His exam was done with his hands cupping and massaging my breasts. "Fine, just fine," he determined. "Now please remove your panties and lay back with your knees up." I didn't know how to say anything or even if I had the right to, so I did what he told me to do. The man was a professional, wasn't he? He pushed my knees further apart, and then a finger sketched the scar from my abortion. "Boy, they sure opened you up didn't they," he said loudly and with surprise. "Well, let's see how things are inside." He put his fingers just inside my vagina and moved them back and forth as his other hand settled across my pubic hair, his thumb pressing my clitoris and moving slightly. I froze. I focused on the dots in the ceiling tiles, trying to make sense out of them as if they were stars in a constellation. After a long minute he stopped, washed his hands quickly, turned and headed out of the room saying "Everything looks fine. You can get dressed now."

The door closed behind him, my knees snapped together and I sat bolt upright. Shaking, I clumsily stumbled off the low step of the exam table, gathered my underwear from off the floor and put it on, using paper towels to clean myself with warm water from the sink. I was mechanical and not thinking, my actions automatic. I opened the door and checked to see that no one was in the hallway. Quietly, but quickly, I walked out of the office, my head down, pulling my dress down against my thighs.

I had trouble with the ignition, but started the car and rolled silently out of the office parking lot, not wanting to draw attention to myself, accelerating in the street in the direction of Cole's radio station. My driving was careless and I couldn't stop shaking. I pulled off the main road and moved slowly down a side street leading to the edge of town. Meaning to stop the car next to a cornfield, I instead drove at an angle into a ditch. "Shit, piss, goddamn it, fuck!" I yelled. Tears came fast. I just sat there, my head dropping against the seat. The sun hit my shoulder through the window, and I faintly heard Paul McCartney singing on the radio. I realized I hadn't heard anything since leaving the doctor's office until now. Numbness was leaving my thighs and I could feel the hardness of the car seat. I shut off the engine.

The deep breath I took ignited heat in the center of my body and I felt the familiar burning in my gut, like an ulcer. It was in my solar plexus, the third chakra, my emotional core full of self-loathing and it flared hot. I imagined the doctor's hand running a finger under my rib bone and along the surface of my organs; a teasing touch, just to show how close he could get to me, just to scare me. My body recoiled into a ball in the curved bucket seat, my arms pulling over my head. I kept still and breathed slowly in and out until the burning stopped and my skin was cooler, the sunshine through the window soothing me.

What the hell was wrong with me? I thought. *Most women would've said something to that guy. Not me!"* I never said anything – not to friends, not my parents, not even a shrink. Everything unsaid became lines in my private pain-saga, the journal I kept in my head of the story only I knew. No one ever told me that sometimes bad things happen and I'd still be okay. I'd never be okay. I was damaged goods. I had this history I'd drag into who I'd become, making me different from who I wanted to be and maybe who I was intended to be.

And what am I doing in this fucking ditch? I'm such an ass. I can't do anything right. How can I tell anyone about any of this? It's way too embarrassing. I fucking roll over for this filthy doctor and then I drive off the road into a mud pit. Great. Yeah, you're doing real well, asshole.

The sound of a tractor that had been in the distance was coming closer. I turned to look and saw it was heading straight towards me. *Maybe it'll just drive over me and this shitty life will be done with.* I was almost amused.

The tractor turned and pulled up beside me, the overalls-clad farmer shading his eyes and looking into the car at me. "You alright, miss?"

"Yes, thank you," I called out. "Just a bad judge of distance I guess. Sorry about this."

"No problem," he said, jumping out of the tractor to survey my position in the ditch. "I'll have you outta there in no time. Not to worry. If you can open your door, just pull yourself out and step clear of the car, alright miss?" I happily did as he asked and then watched while he skillfully maneuvered his tractor into place, attached a chain to the car and very slowly hauled it up onto the road.

"I can't thank you enough, sir," I said, handing him some cash. "And I'm really so sorry."

"No need, miss. Not for me for cash or you for sorrow. You just go on and have yourself a better day."

When I finally got to the radio station, Cole was out the door before I parked. Expecting I'd be coming, he'd seen me out the news room window. He strode across the lot, waving and smiling and got in the car on the seat beside me.

"What's wrong, babe?" he said, seeing my face. He put his arm around my shoulder. I gave him a halting explanation, leaving out the ditch episode. He hugged me close. "What a shitty bastard! Listen, everything's gonna be okay. You just wait here and relax a minute. I'll be right back."

Cole sprinted into the radio station. I could see him on the phone through the window. I leaned my head against the seat and closed my eyes. After several minutes he came back and got in the car. His face was grimaced, his lips stiff as he talked. "I just called the president of the local medical society and identified myself as the station news man. I told him what happened to you and insisted on a meeting with him.

He told me to write the details in a letter to him, which he said he'd read aloud at the next medical society meeting, with our permission. He also invited us to meet with the members, after the letter was read." I couldn't remember Cole being so angry. He was a docile man.

"I don't know right now," I answered. "I just don't know if I could do that. Would that doctor be there?"

"No way. And with what I plan to say about this he won't even be in town for long. I'll make a news story out of this if they don't suspend that asshole's medical license." Cole stared out the windshield; his fingertips arched together, elbows on lap as was his habit when thinking intensely. "I want to take care of this, I'm so pissed. Let's not go out tonight, okay? It's kind of spoiled now. We'll go home and I'll write the letter. Yeah, I'll write a fucking letter they won't forget."

Cole drove us home and immediately loaded paper into the typewriter. He was madly clacking at the keys when I went to take a hot bath. He finished a one-draft letter and read it to me while I soaked. It was tight and bristling. Just hearing it read helped calm me down. "Thank you, Cole. This means a lot to me." This was one of the rare times I remember being so well validated for my feelings, and I was thankful to Cole for that. I was more used to my feelings being denied, ignored or glossed over, or made to think my feelings were wrong, that I'd been mistaken. Dad had particularly made me feel that way. Mom, too, at times. But now Cole was acknowledging my feelings as real.

Two weeks later we went to the medical society

meeting, Cole having convinced me it was best and assuring me he'd take the lead. I only had to say what I was comfortable saying.

We walked up the marble steps to an imposing building, a former mansion. Stone columns stood at the sides of ornately carved front doors, which we entered by pulling huge brass handles. Inside, a dark wood hallway accented with sizeable landscape paintings of the Hudson River and serenely lit wall sconces gave way to a large central room. Floor to ceiling bookcases of the same dark wood surrounded the room. A fireplace ablaze with crackling logs was featured in the center of the back wall. Elegant furniture graced a large Persian rug in the middle of the room, around which were seated at least thirty men in dark suits with somber expressions. I was nervous.

The society's president stepped forward and extended a hand to me, introducing himself and inviting us to sit down on chairs near the fire. Seating myself and feeling the warmth of the blaze, I relaxed a little. We were introduced to the group of physicians who nodded toward us and smiled welcomingly. The men knew the purpose of our visit, our host having just read them Cole's letter before our arrival, sparing me having to hear the details read in front of me. I could see they were taking this quite seriously. Cole and I answered clarifying questions from a few of them. With each answer I gave, I felt a little more confidence. That these men were listening made me feel heard, which I appreciated. I was wearing the same dress I'd worn to the doctor's and said so. I could hear feet shuffling uncomfortably when I did. I was then invited to speak. I still felt timid but now wasn't afraid of talking to them.

"I'm grateful for the kind attention you're paying to this matter," I said quietly. "It's important to me that other women don't have the same experience I did, and that I don't go through this again. I want to thank you for any helpful resolution you can find."

We were thanked for our visit with the group and graciously escorted to the front door, being told we'd hear from the society within the week.

The president's phone call came, and I was told the offending physician would indeed lose his license to practice. He also said the society members had discussed other measures to be taken to help ensure that my experience wouldn't be repeated. I later learned the doctor left the area. I've never been to a doctor's office since without a nurse in the room to assist the examination and without being instructed to remove my clothes in private and put on a hospital gown or cover myself with a large, crinkly, but effective paper drape. Validation. It was like a healing salve on a wound. Calming. Quieting the restlessness deep inside me. Soothing the burn. Reopening the lotus of the chakra.

ⓢⓢⓢⓢⓢ

Cole sold some short stories and his writing career seemed promising. We decided to move to Manhattan. He'd write and I'd study dance. We endlessly imagined creative things we'd do together. Somehow we'd make money. We'd have fun and life in Saugerties would quickly fade into just good memories of our early times together.

We sublet a furnished apartment on Bank Street,

having brought with us only a few treasures of our own. What furniture we did have either came from my family or we'd bought it at a flea market upstate. Having adult furniture was a luxury. It was a small one-bedroom apartment with the usual amenities of a townhouse in Greenwich Village: White walls, wood floors and an attractive, but non-working fireplace. Recessed lighting in the living room and kitchen lent sophistication. Our personal touches included favorite books and knick-knacks, a batik wall hanging I'd made, cheap but cherished art and two small woven rugs.

It was later in spring and the gaiety of street life was returning at the same daily pace of the melting snow. On the corner someone was playing a guitar and a harmonica, set into a wire construction that rested on his shoulders, Dylan-style.

Cole had been generally in an upbeat mood, his appetite for knowing about technological advancements well satisfied by reading in scientific journals and popular magazines about microchips and floppy disks and the inevitable coming of the computer age, which he thought would revolutionize the planet. He was psyched and talked about it in spiraling excitement; his fast track thinking propelling new interest in science fiction writing and ideas for stories that might or might not materialize on paper.

His enthusiastic talk opened new worlds for me I doubted I'd have found on my own. But I was also afraid of being too dependent on him for my own good. Life was becoming all about Cole and how he would conquer the instability of our lives through a magical attraction of abundant security. Our lack of money and station would be replaced by our soon-to-become world traveling selves, safely nestled in his reputation as an author and creative genius. His faith in his intellect was not arrogant though; his ego tempered by humility in the face of a universe he found endlessly complex and compelling. He was like a lanky, spectacled child who couldn't read, write, or think fast enough; ideas coming too swiftly to put into action, but soon, soon it would all come together. He promised me that, and I devotedly believed him although I was noticing that Cole's high-pitched excitement was becoming a predictable signal of a following mood slump. It was a subtle but noticeable pattern. For days he'd be ecstatic about something new he'd read or written, and then something triggered a switch and he'd feel insecure and tentative, wanting reassurance from me or just needing to be quiet and alone.

I got worried because when we'd stayed with his parents, I'd seen a similar pattern with his mother. She hardly left her room, her meals taken to her by Cole's Dad, who did all the cooking and housework with the help of a weekly maid. No one talked about it; it always seemed she was resting; only there was a secretiveness about it. Then she'd suddenly show up for breakfast, smiling and happy, wearing a red wig and a brightly colored bathrobe. She'd sit at the table smoking cigarettes one after another, regaling us with funny stories, one after another, about relatives and neighbors or things she'd read or seen on television in her room. She was amazing; very intelligent and as witty as a newspaper columnist. She had the most charming southern drawl with a low melodic voice she'd use indulgently in telling her tales. She'd laugh loudly at her own jokes, her hand slapping a knee, her clear eyes darting back and forth from one of us to the other to see if we'd gotten the humor. We'd laugh right along with her. And then this lovely woman would drift off and be gone again. For days. So I wondered about Cole, but then the tempo of our lives would change and it seemed both of our moods would too.

I was also distracted by taking quite a different route than Cole to what I hoped would be my own success. I still wanted to dance, though there was no easy course of study for what I intended. My generation was reeling from the dawning of the "Age of Aquarius," and I kept looking for a way into multi- media where dance would be only part of an intricate display of rhythm, music, light, sound and color. Shows like Rowan and Martin's *Laugh-In* spawned new horizons for visual media, both entertaining and serious. I wanted to be part of that creativity and my fledgling talent, from classical training as a child, dance classes at Bard and recently in contemporary movement would, I hoped, help me get there.

On this spring day, I was scheduled to audition for a show to open that fall called *Jesus Christ Superstar*. I had to both sing and dance and I was petrified. Musicals weren't what I was after, but I needed training and also to find some work, hoping not to just get a waitressing job, though I did realize that's what most other artistically aspiring women were sensibly doing.

After changing clothes several times, I finally decided on a beige fitted top and tights with pastel shorts. I wore sneakers and put dance shoes in my bag. My thick hair fell in lengths around my shoulders, and I left it loose. Throwing on a light coat, I went down the stairs, left the building and walked the few blocks to the subway, headed for midtown. Pressed against other daytime workers in the subway car, I felt my confidence rising as I identified myself with these very busy, productive and, I imagined, highly successful professionals. By the time I got to the rehearsal studio, I was ready.

Entering the hallway outside the studio, all confidence immediately drained away at the sight of a hundred or more women and men stretching their muscles and vocal chords in preparation for their chance at a musical role and future stardom. Movement and sound filled the room. Now I knew the meaning of a cattle call audition. This wasn't a funky upstate resort; this was Manhattan.

I made for an unoccupied corner and pulled out the sheet music I'd rehearsed for hours and began softly singing "Something in the way she moves," getting jostled off key by someone bumping me by reaching in their duffle bag. More nervously, I began again.

One of the first to be called, I left the noisy, busy room, entered the audition room and crossed the wide floor over to the piano, smiling and handing my music to the handsome accompanist. We agreed which key to use and he started to play. I sang as strongly and bravely as I could, still knowing I wouldn't land a role with my voice alone. When finished, I rejoined the others, looked at the faces of those near me and announced: "Well, if I can do that, all of you can do anything," which was greeted with amused and supportive laughter.

After everyone's singing audition, we trooped out to the dance floor in groups of twenty, creating a grid of dancers spaced a few feet apart. The choreographer, or an assistant, I didn't know which, very quickly illustrated the dance step sequences the piece required; those closest to classical or modern movements I knew, those more typical of a Broadway musical were newer to me, but I'd give it a try. Most of the dancers nodded their heads towards the choreographer, noting their understanding, many doing a few practice steps. I was clearly out of my league.

King Herod's Song began and instinctively, like a flock of starlings, everyone but me fell into step with the choreographer, fluidly sliding through the dance with easy grace. I gave it my all, but fairly stumbled through the whole thing, at one point smiling and shrugging my shoulders at the choreographer, who smiled in return. Afterwards, I didn't wait to find out if I'd made the cut. I gathered my dignity and left, feeling that at least I'd succeeded in trying out. *What the fuck*, I thought. *Waiting tables can't be all that bad.*

When I got back to the apartment, Cole was home. He'd left the apartment almost dark and I found him sitting next to the one lighted lamp in the front room. I could tell he was brooding, though I hadn't seen this mood in a while. Rather than launch into a frivolous description of my day, I asked him how he was, sounding upbeat.

"My last story didn't sell," he said, his voice raspy. "I got the rejection letter today. I was so sure of this one." He stared straight ahead, pressing his fingertips in an arch, his elbows dug into the armrests of the chair, a familiar gesture when he was upset.

During the following weeks, Cole drifted further into quiet solitude. He read a lot, watched late night television, went to movies, and sat by himself, thinking. It was difficult to rouse him or interest him in anything. It was usually best to let him be and let it pass. But this time it didn't pass; it deepened. For the first time since I'd met him, he seemed in real despair.

As he became unresponsive, our time together changed as he withdrew into himself. We spoke less, did less together, rarely ventured out and our intimacy vanished. I began to feel sullen myself and started taking everything too personally. I felt unwanted and alone and somewhat frightened.

And we were fast becoming financially broke. He wasn't writing so nothing was sold. The work I was finding was as a fashion runway model. It kept us in groceries, but his writing usually paid the rent. We still had some money saved, but it would run out soon.

One night I found him crying. I tried to soothe him, but it wouldn't work. I moved closer to him, hoping some intimacy would help, but he pushed me away. "I can't," he sobbed. "I'm not good enough. I never was. I'm not enough of a man."

"Yes, certainly you are," I countered, not for the first time trying to help him with this particular fear.

"No. I'm just the gawky, weird guy in the too-thick rimmed glasses with the oversized brain – the geek in the room. People always think I'm queer. I don't mean gay, just queer. Women like me because I'm smart, not for anything else. I'm just this odd, Frankenstein creature."

"Cole, that's just not true." I knew he didn't think much of his looks, even though I found him quite handsome. He was my tall, blue-eyed, black-haired Irishman. He once told me how surprised he was that I'd married him; that someone he thought was beautiful wanted to be with him. But this deeper self-loathing was new.

"Well you think that way, but I don't think other women do," he snarled, his tone bitter. "But how would I know," he continued. I haven't been with enough other women to really know how they feel. Not that I'm sorry we're married or anything, but I just wish I'd had more sex before. That might have given me some confidence. I really think that's it, that's my problem." He collapsed against the fireplace, tossing his eyeglasses on the mantel, grabbing his head, his white knuckles protruding through the black hair, his now even thinner body swaying sideways.

I had no idea what to say, feeling sorry for him and threatened at the same time. The next couple of weeks were extremely uncomfortable as we awkwardly maneuvered around each other. He gorged on reading, consuming books, magazines and newspapers or he slept long hours. I tried not to be home, keeping busy or finding useless activity to engage me. I walked a lot, sat on benches in Washington Park and watched the chess players or street entertainers, all without enjoyment or even much emotion. Summer was in full bloom and I was hardly noticing.

One afternoon I came home to find Cole pacing with a copy of the *Village Voice* in his hand. Seeing me, he rushed over to show me something in the paper. "I think I've found something that might help me – help us," he said, his eyes serious, his brows slanted down. He was pointing to an ad in the paper, which he handed to me.

"Couples Wanted for Adult Social Group," the headline ran. The ad went on to talk about "experiencing an exciting alternative lifestyle" and used other vague descriptors I took to mean sexual encounters. I looked at Cole somewhat blankly.

"I've read about swinging before," he said. "It's even talked about as a therapeutic intervention for marriages in trouble. It's not about the sex. It's what I need for my head."

It sure wasn't what I needed for my head. I really resented the fact that I wasn't enough for him. It wasn't a troubled marriage for me; he was all I wanted, even if I clung to him too much at times. I understood wanting sexual fantasy but "swinging" was not for me. Then again, maybe if we just got this fucking thing over with he'd relax and be satisfied with what we had. I didn't know what else to do. I only hoped things would change; that this would make things okay and he and I would be a team again; that we'd go ahead with our lives. I couldn't do it on my own. He had to lead me there, or so I thought.

"Okay," I said, hesitantly. "I'll try it," I added, my words stronger this time.

That weekend we found ourselves heading for a loft building in Tribeca. We'd quietly dressed for the evening, me totally unsure of what to wear to something like this. For Cole it was easy as he had a simple wardrobe of shirts and slacks he found comfortable and wore everywhere. I settled on a long sleeved black silk blouse, a long grey skirt with a tasteful slit up one side and leather boots.

A short cab ride and we were standing on a dark street, heavy mist turning to drizzle. Someone answered the buzzer to the building and we were let in to a nicely decorated hallway. The door at the far end opened and a medium tall man appeared; drink in one hand, cigarette in another, wearing a colorful towel around his waist, a long thick silver chain around his neck and otherwise nude.

"Hi there!" he called to us, waving his drink towards the inside of the loft. "Come on in. The water's fine!"

We exchanged greetings and stepped into a huge room filled with music, smoke, people, lights, pillow-covered couches, lava lamps, low tables with trays of hors d'oeuvres, a shiny row of booze bottles along a countertop and lots of talking and laughter.

Gill, our host, led us to the middle of the room and introduced us to several couples, seated or lounging on the floor. "Everyone, this is Cole and Lily!" he shouted over the din. Someone immediately handed us a joint.

We got as comfortable as we could and made an effort to join in. These were very uninhibited people. As we sat nibbling cheese and sipping flutes of mediocre champagne, others in mid-conversation with us would slide a hand down someone's shirt or up a skirt. Others would peel off from the group to head up some stairs to another floor.

I felt no desire to mingle any closer to anyone. Nice enough people, but I just couldn't get into it – the scene. Cole looked stiff as a seated oak tree, his smile strained. Thinking it would make him more comfortable, after a suitable period of time I drifted off to another part of the room to give him, or maybe myself, breathing space. I was vaguely pondering a Maxfield Parrish poster behind the bar when a man sidled up to me.

"There's a pool downstairs," he said, without introduction. "Want to check it out?" He was exactly my height, had short curly brown hair and a trimmed moustache. I felt absolutely no interest in this man, but didn't know what else to do. "Sure," I found myself saying. *Let's get this over with --* was my thought.

He moved towards a door leading to a short set of stairs and I followed, trying to look back at Cole, but not finding him in the crowd.

We emerged into a large room occupied entirely by a swimming pool curved in a lima bean shape. Rose and amber lights housed in the sides of the pool played in the water and reflected on the ceiling, giving a soft glow to the room. Tall, large-leafed plants sat in huge containers at points around the pool next to the many thickly padded lounge chairs. Towels, like the one our host had worn, were stacked on wicker shelves. Taped music played softly, an Al Green number at the moment.

I realized that my party friend was nearly naked, his clothes strewn over a chair while I'd been exploring the room. Without a word he came towards me and began unbuttoning my blouse. I'd never felt less turned on in my life, but went with it as I'd told Cole I'd do this thing.

In minutes we were easing into the shallow end of the pool, the water surprisingly warm. I've always loved to swim, enjoying the feeling of water encasing my body. It felt good until a hand slid around my waist and up over my breast. For about twenty minutes I tried earnestly to get in the mood, but just badly wanted to leave this party. I didn't know this guy from the rubber plant I could see above my head and had even less feeling for him than the plant, which I liked.

I endured his caresses a short while longer but then interrupted. "You know, this is my first time and I think another drink would help me relax," I offered. "I'll be back in a minute." I slid out of the pool and found a short terry robe hanging nearby, which I wrapped around myself as I headed back up the stairs, throwing a towel around my wet hair.

"Okay, I'll be right here," my new friend assured me.

Few people were now in the living room and I was happy to see they were occupied with each other. I made for the bar and poured myself a stiff Bacardi and tonic with little ice. Sinking into a couch, I buried myself in some pillows and sucked hard on my drink. Then for several minutes I just closed my eyes and listened to the Carpenters sing about rainy days and Mondays.

"Where the fuck did you go?" Cole harshly whispered in my ear. Jolted, I sat up straight. "To the pool," I said, nervously.

"You left me here! Did you just take off with some guy?"

"Yes. I thought it'd be easier for you if I didn't stay right near you. Someone invited me to go and I went. I haven't exactly been having a good time."

"Well I'm having a terrible time," he said, grabbing my robe firmly by the collar. "This isn't working out for me. We have to leave – now!"

"Okay, relax. I'll get my things." I hurried to the pool, excused myself from my swimming buddy, and quickly dressed.

Cole was standing by the bar, pouring a Jack Daniels and staring at me hard when I came back, jamming the bridge of his glasses to the top of his nose, a clear signal of anger.

We took a silent cab ride home, Cole slamming the front door when we got in. "How could you do that to me?" he shouted. "You purposely humiliated me, you bitch!" he said, grabbing my hair and pulling hard until he ripped a finger-full out of my scalp.

"It was your idea," I said in a low, angry voice, grabbing a kitchen towel and holding it to my bleeding head. "I just went along. The whole thing's a bit creepy to me, Cole."

"Just consider my feelings a little more the next time," he said, also low and angry and slumped off to the living room.

"*Your* feelings?" I shouted after him. "How about mine? If you had any feelings for me, we wouldn't even have been there tonight!"

I went to bed crying. He stayed up most of the night, falling asleep on the couch in front of the television – his favorite toy; his coping machine. The next morning I found my black silk blouse ripped to shreds on the bedroom floor.

᎒᎒᎒᎒᎒᎒

Trying to restore some dignity, I decided to do something about my fledgling dance career. I decided to take my *Evil Ways* choreography for an audition. I went from nightclub to nightclub in mid-town until I found a manager who said he'd watch my routine, only he called it "your *act.*" Act, routine, whatever. *Just watch, damn it,* was all I thought.

I gave him the Santana album and he walked into the sound-engineering booth at the end of the large dance floor, running a hand through his hair, a bit too long for a nearly middle-aged man. I asked if he could dim the lights which were on full for the janitor. He did so, and the room became vastly more suitable for the music, the backdrop a red velvet curtain. A broad spotlight came on, its oval shaft covering much of the black dance floor. I was wearing a short-sleeved, royal blue nylon wrap-around dress with a deep v-shaped neckline and a skirt of modest length over light brown sheer tights. I stepped onto the floor in my ankle-strapped dark brown dance shoes, finding myself a starting spot on the rim of the spotlight. The music began and I launched into my routine, my *act*, as it were. With no prim audience to restrain me and the music at loud volume, I made the most of every move, the dance segueing from sultry and expressive to sharp and powerful, giving the movements more contrast and drama than before. Along with a few balletic jumps and turns, I also threw in a bit of sensuality, running my hands through my hair, arching my back, swaying my hips and bending over, my skirt rising teasingly but tastefully. I ended strongly as did the music.

Silence. The guy said nothing at first. He came out of the darkness into the spotlight, smiling at me. "That's quite an act, young lady."

"Thank you," I said, breathing heavily from the exertion. "There're things I'd like to do with it, especially in this space. I know you usually only showcase local bands, but I think I could make an interesting visual out of this if I could use a screen to project some images and colors onto that'd work with the music." I was talking quickly, animating my ideas by walking towards the red curtain, using my hands to suggest whirling images on a screen.

"I bet you could," he said. "I've got some ideas, too. I've got some props you might be able to use. Want to see?"

"Sure," I said, glad to see he was getting into it, though not sure what props I needed.

"Come with me."

I followed him out of the room and down a hall to a small room that seemed to be part office, part storage room. The only light came from a green-shaded lamp on a table, the end of which was covered with long cigarette burns leading to stacks of papers and an open ledger. On the wall hung electrical cords and some handyman tools next to an open cabinet so loaded with odds and ends it'd probably been there for years. The manager hoisted a large hinged box onto a table behind the desk, which he opened with hands as pale as his face. I wondered if he ever went outside. "Come closer," he said. "Take a look."

I walked to the box and bent over to look, though there wasn't a lot of light to clearly see what was inside. I stuck a hand in and grabbed what turned out to be a whip. *Evil ways, perhaps usable, but pretty weird,* I thought.

"There's another club I belong to, where I'd love to see you perform," he was saying.

Next I felt metal and pulled out a studded leather strip with fasteners. *A collar? A little too S&M for me,* I thought.

"It's a private club," he said, his voice huskier this time. "I think the members would love your act."

The last thing I pulled out of the box was a leather face mask with buckles to attach behind your head. I became a tad concerned. Turning to the man,

I asked, "What exactly do you have in mind?"

He was bracing himself against the desk with one hand, masturbating with the other, his dick paler than his face and fully erect. Shocked, I just stared at it when it erupted, a white stream of jism spurting all over his hand onto the floor.

"What are you doing?" I blurted out, pushing him aside, stepping carefully by and stomping out of the room and down the hall. Back in the club, I grabbed my trenchcoat and started to leave.

"Wait!" he said, grabbing my arm from behind. "Let me explain."

I wrenched myself free and whirled to face him. "Explain what? That you're an asshole?" I yelled at him. "I came here legitimately because I want to dance." I paused. "Professionally," I continued, emphasizing each syllable. "And you took complete advantage of me, you fucking prick. How dare you be so disgusting!" I wanted to reach down his pants and rip his dick off. *How vile,* I thought, turning and heading for the door.

"But I've got work for you!" he said as I left.

I sped out of the building into the glaring brightness outside. Hustling down the seedy midtown street, I was afraid of him following me and dashed into a shell-and-shot joint, the only bar I could see on the block that didn't have a strip club attached to it. I grabbed a stool. Looking down the bar I saw I wasn't the only woman there. I was, however, the only woman without a massive head of hair and glittered cheeks. This was the theater district in the old days before they cleaned it up – an odd mixture of sex venues, dance clubs and legit theaters.

"What'll it be, miss?"

"Bacardi and tonic, please. Heavy on the rum," I asked the bartender in almost a whisper for some reason. Maybe I was pretending I wasn't really there. I certainly wished I wasn't. *What the fuck just happened?* I thought, but almost said aloud. Here I was trying to manipulate this sleazy club manager into hiring me as a dancer, and he manipulated me into being his private peep show. I was so pissed off I wanted to pound my fist on the bar. *But then again, what the fuck were you expecting, you asshole?* I kindly thought to myself. *An afternoon with Bob Fosse?* I slammed the drink and asked for another. By the third one, I'd decided my dance career would obviously have to find a starting point other than wriggling around in front of a sweaty, balding, middle-aged bondage freak. *How embarrassing,* I thought. *Some bio I'm developing.*

In the weeks that followed, when I opted instead to try and get modeling jobs, I was told by the major agencies that I had a 1950s look, meaning my full cheeks and round face were out of style and I'd have to wait until that look became popular again. Now it was all about being gaunt-faced and lithe with miles of legs for flared bell-bottoms, thin ankles for platform shoes and long necks for halter tops. I wasn't tall or thin. At five feet, seven inches tall, all I could count on for money was more runway and trade show work.

But that didn't stop me from trying for print work. There was always catalogue work – models pictured with kitchen appliances, living room furniture and such. You didn't have to be tall for that. *I'd probably look good in an apron holding an iron,* I derided myself. But I needed to build up my portfolio, what in the trade was called your "book." So I made the rounds of the photographers I knew and those who'd been recommended. Some were good guys willing to waste some time and rolls of film helping out a newcomer. They'd be very professional and quick, giving you what you needed along with valuable advice. I started getting some nice shots in my book and leads to small modeling jobs. One of them even complimented me on my low, resonant voice, suggesting I make a demo tape and try doing radio spots or TV voice-overs.

Other photographers I saw had different interests. At this point, at least I was beginning to see it coming and I'd heard all the sordid stories from other models I knew. But I needed to build up my stock of photos and I'd put up with them to get what I wanted. I learned to fend them off before it got too bad. I even found I had some power of my own and enjoyed using it. Saying things like "no" and "hands off" felt good and helped me learn some needed boundaries. I never sensed any danger, just sleaze.

Cole saw all the new photos in my book but didn't question me about them, often even complimenting how they turned out. He knew I needed to build it up for work and usually didn't have a problem with me seeing photographers. But shots taken of me in a black wig oddly triggered him.

"What's with the wig?" he asked. "I've never seen you wear a wig. Do you even have one?"

"No, I don't have one. The photographer had a few wigs and wanted me to try them on. We decided on the black one. Makes me look totally different, don't you think?"

"Yeah, the wig and that black lace dress. Pretty

sexy. And very flirty."

"Well, thanks," I said, surprised he found anything sexy about me these days.

"What did you do, fuck the guy?" he snarled. I was stunned. I was also going to lie to him. I did have sex with that one particular photographer. I had even lied to myself about it, telling myself that the photo shoot hadn't been very serious. The guy and I'd just been playing around. It wasn't like it was even modeling work. This one photographer was just incredibly handsome and, well, it just happened – in the black lace dress, in the wig, on the floor in front of the camera on its tripod under the still burning umbrella lights. It could've been a porno set it was so brightly lit. And the guy's tanned body and muscular arms as he held himself above me, pumping his champion cock into me, was more than suitable for a sexy flick.

It happened a few days after Cole had dragged me to yet another swinging party, and I was getting so tired of it and tired of feeling used by him for his own needs, while he ignored mine. I wasn't enjoying myself at all and it was making me feel shabby. So I fucked the guy. I wanted one fuck to be on my own terms. I wanted to get back at Cole. Not just for the swinging scene, but also because our sex life was so mechanical. Not that I'd tell him about the guy. It'd just be a personal satisfaction knowing that Cole wasn't calling all the shots. I hadn't even gotten off with the guy. And the really odd thing was that he'd gotten really pissed because I took off the wig while we were screwing. It was getting hot on my head and I felt weird having sex in it anyway. But this guy got angry and asked me to leave. Some kind of strange issue he had, for sure. I didn't care much. I was satisfied I'd been adulterous, which was against the rules of the swinging scene, which everyone understood to be no fucking around outside of the parties you went to only with your partner. I broke the rule and it was like saying "fuck you" to Cole.

"Cole, don't be ridiculous," I finally answered. I don't have sex with photographers. Even if I was attracted to someone, it just wouldn't be okay. I'm trying to be professional, not get a lousy reputation."

"Well I don't want you flirting with any of them, understand?" he said, more threateningly. "Look at your face in that picture. Your pretty blue eyes, your cute turned up nose and your sweet little mouth. Don't tell me you weren't asking for it." Cole was holding the photo in both hands, crumpling the edges. He was ranting.

"Cole, you're imagining things. Really, don't be so paranoid. I was posing for a picture, for Christ's sake, not coming on to the guy," I told him, meanwhile thinking he was probably describing exactly what the lens had captured.

"Well I don't trust you," he said, glaring at me, his eyes glassy and fixed. "Just be careful. And I don't want to see any more photos like this," he said, ripping it in pieces. "Have you got that?"

"You have nothing to worry about," I tried to say calmly. "This is work, not my social life. And if I did fuck someone, it'd sure be the first time I got laid in a long time outside of this obnoxious swinging shit," I shouted at him, already on the way to the bathroom, where I bolted to, slamming the door and locking it. I heard the front door slam and then it was quiet. *Fuck him*, I thought.

We didn't talk for a couple of days, Cole keeping to himself and getting immersed in his writing. I tried to not be in the apartment. Then he apologized, sorry for letting his feelings get out of hand. He thought he was smoking too much pot and said he'd cut back. I didn't say anything, but I didn't think it was the pot. I also didn't think it was just the photo of me he'd seen. He had these fears that intensified sometimes, even when he wasn't stoned. He'd been hearing unfamiliar voices outside the apartment and had added a bolt lock on the door just to feel safer. Sometimes when we were on the street he'd glance behind us, just to be sure no one was following.

He was also writing a lot and his themes were intriguing, dealing with people drifting out of present time, experiencing past or future lives and then returning again, bringing disconcerting information into their current lives that had to be kept secret even though it affected the lives of other people. Concentrating on this stuff would make anyone a bit strange. But there seemed to be some purpose to his writing, some effort at understanding himself and his relation to his world. His writing was good though, and I left him to it, trying not to disrupt him. Hopefully, he'd come around again.

A day came when he sold one of his stories that he liked the best. It delighted and excited him, restoring his self-confidence. He wanted to go out for the first time in ages. We hit the bars, the music venues, and the afterhours clubs. We had a great time and enjoyed each other a lot. We drank and danced and talked and danced and drank some more.

Sometimes Cole was like one of his characters, traveling to a dark dimension within himself where erratic things happened and then returning quickly to his likeable self as if stepping through a doorway into another room.

On those better nights we talked endlessly about fun stuff like recent discoveries in the galaxies or some tribe he'd read about in the middle of Brazil that'd had no human contact. For me this new mood was a holiday.

Cole told me about new plans he had, grand schemes about how he'd start making big money. He had no doubt he'd be successful and we'd become well known. He talked about celebrities like they were sure to become friends of ours. He'd read about a guy experimenting with combining computer generated graphics with mystery stories and making a computer game out of it. Cole was fascinated. He wanted to find this guy and talk to him about writing stories for him to use in the game. His happiness soared just thinking about it, his mind racing. I felt excited for him and for myself. I really wanted these dreams of his to happen and I wanted to be a part of it. I certainly had no idea how to create ideas like this and I hoped I could just be around when things began to happen for him.

His enthusiasm turned though. He became too energetic and restless and way over-wired. He couldn't sit still for long and started pacing when he talked. He kept making trips to the library doing research on computers and was building up a pile of notes he'd written, his handwriting frenetic, some of the notes looking more like symbols than anything sensible. He got more tense, his body stiffer. When he started cracking his knuckles I knew he was getting physically bent, the mind-body thing working in overdrive.

Eventually he said he wanted to try swinging again. It seemed to come from nowhere, but his tension must have brought it on. And the way he felt about himself vacillated. He'd waver between his ego ballooning and deflating. I guessed he needed some physical release and some reassurance about himself, which he always seemed to connect to his fuckability with women. His sudden suggestion surprised me but also irritated me no end since I was hoping for a return to real intimacy when his mood had lightened.

These days we were only occasionally having unemotional sex. Cole was very visual and liked it when I dressed and posed sexually for him, which became the main event of our intimacy. He liked pretending he was a photographer and I was his model. I'd done the lingerie thing for him, his favorite. He liked to take pictures of me with his instant camera and the bed would get covered with these badly lit, grainy photos of me taken at various angles, not always flattering. It was far from what inspired me sexually, though for him it was a major turn-on, these amateur photo-shoots always dissolving into me getting sexually ravaged by Cole, his face turning menacing, one time fantasizing aloud about biting my nipples off. Just lovely.

But when Cole was in a good mood he was a great cuddler and I tried to be satisfied with that. My sexual pleasure got put aside and we settled into a routine, though for me at some point I just gave up, which was stupid of me, but I wasn't confident asking for more from him. Sex became a performance. I guess I needed him to want to be with me more than I needed sexual pleasure. Or maybe I just needed to be his doll toy for a while and things would somehow get better.

Being with Cole was kind of like a jitterbug dance; as if holding my hand he'd twirl me away from him, do some steps on his own for a while and then pull me back in for a quick squeeze and a smile before twirling me away again. I just kept dancing to his lead, hoping a slow, romantic dance would come along. But it never did.

We went back into swinging, which got better for Cole and a disaster for me. I was trying to be more understanding. If having these odd sexual encounters with other women was what would level him out so we could stop this and get on with a marriage, then so be it. I wanted to have hope. I'd put up with the groping, bad booze, heavy floral incense and rug burns. Cole was getting more confident in his advances and was having some success. Any rejections would eat at his pride though. I'd have to rescue his fleeing ego, reassuring him he wasn't going to be every woman's type. He was fine. He was handsome. He was sexy. Yes, that shirt looks good on you. Your hair is fine. I like that new cologne. Whatever.

The only problem was that no amount of these let's-all-fuck in-a-pile episodes totally worked for him. He always needed something else. He made excuses like *She just did it to be nice,* or *I was the only guy available.* It was as if there was a greater achievement he was missing out on. We even went to a place he found called Lover's Lane, a free-love, nudist camp in upstate New York. For two weeks we joined a crowd of pink, burning bodies by the pool, watched movies and played card games in the social hall, and ambled about the wooded property of the camp getting stoned.

Given that it was a very hot August, the nudity was actually welcome, though I often found myself in some kind of loosely flapping wrap during evening social hours, never feeling entirely comfortable having casual conversations or playing poker in small groups while naked. Nude dancing, forget it. But sex outside of an established partnership wasn't happening in the camp as far as I could tell. A secret rendezvous between two people, maybe. But couples were not coupling with other couples. Cole tried to entice some of our new friends into getting together, but they excused themselves. Lucky for us as things turned out. We had the clap.

ᏬᏬᏬᏬᏬᏬ

The rent was due – again. Somehow we always managed to scrape enough cash together for one of our nights on the town, hitting posh bars and afterhours clubs. We didn't eat much, but drank plenty. Lump sums of money for rent were harder to come by. We were two months behind on our studio apartment on Seventy-Third Street on the Upper East Side, where we'd moved to save on rent. It was a nice address, a quaint apartment overlooking the pleasant, tree-lined street. Unfurnished this time, we slept on the floor on authentic bear skin rugs and huge suede pillows we'd bought with Cole's last check. The walls were the traditional creamy white with dainty floral plaster light fixtures on the ceiling, the prerequisite wood floors and non-working fireplace, though this time it was marble. The whole apartment had once been a rather decorous room in an elegant townhouse now broken up into six rental units.

Yes, the rent. Something had to be done. Not just about the rent, but our lives. Drinking and carousing kept us from thinking about it too much. Cole had again grown despondent and cynical. He was now prone to bouts of hypochondria and they were worsening. I'd recently had to talk him out of a trip to the emergency room for a rapid heartbeat he was convinced preceded an imminent heart attack. In getting him to describe all his symptoms as he might to the duty nurse, he listed so many ailments that even he finally began to laugh at the absurdity of his complaints. Calming down, his pulse quieted.

But he remained restless and anxious much of the time with an occasional flare-up of fear or anger. He'd taken to watching daytime television, claiming it was research for a novel he was considering writing. He had to study what was popular, what would provide the commercial juice for a book. So he swaddled himself in cushions on the bearskin rugs and watched soaps and game shows.

We weren't going out anywhere except a movie now and then and hadn't even been out to any swinging parties, though we never did when he got that withdrawn, mercifully.

I was, however, reacting rather badly to his reclusiveness and bouts of temper. He wasn't spending time with me and in my mind that meant I wasn't worthwhile. Worse, it meant I was unlovable, a feeling I couldn't handle well. It made me think I had nothing of my own to offer, and I felt scared I'd just slip away into the air, my leaving unnoticed, like dust particles drifting out a window.

I worked on my looks and my general attitude, trying to be as beautiful, energetic and desirable as a twenty-two-year-old could be. His depression deepened and my fears worsened. I told him I didn't think I had much personality. I certainly wasn't doing anything to create one. He advised me to choose one from the people I encountered, saying there were plenty out there to copy, his concurrence with my self-evaluation leaving me feeling even less substantial. I began to withdraw. He, in turn, watched more television and indulged even more in pornography, his now favorite pastime when I was out of the apartment or asleep. I'd found stacks of plastic folders, each a separate porno portrait of a different woman, carefully clipped from men's magazines. He'd been making these convenient little sex packets for a long time it seemed. I took them all and threw them out in the large rubbish bin behind the apartment building.

"I threw out your porn," I told him later.

"Why'd you do that?" he asked, as if I'd thrown out something precious like a stamp collection or valuable baseball memorabilia. "Well you can't throw out what's in here," he said, pointing to his head. "You can't take away my fantasies," he yelled.

To be accused of invading his human right to privacy was a little much for me. I'd been dragged to swinging parties, asked to perform like a sex doll and posed for his lurid picture taking sessions. In return I was feeling very neglected, unattractive and unloved. So I'd thrown out his virtual women because it felt like he was cheating on me. He always wanted someone else. Even when we had sex together it felt as if he was seeing another woman – someone he was fantasizing me to be. I wasn't expecting that the man I was with wouldn't have sexual fantasies or look at other women, but it'd be nice if occasionally he'd show up for a date just with me.

Feeling hurt and really pissed, I called up a guy we'd met at the nudist camp who'd given me his phone number toward the end of our eventful time there. He was married, but clearly interested in our getting together. I met him at his office on a Saturday and we had sex on a couch. He seemed to enjoy it. I felt like an empty paper bag. But we were nice to each other and that made me feel a little better. He paid me some attention and I laughed at his jokes. I never saw him after that. It was just as well. I felt guilty this time about cheating on Cole. I was just trying to level the playing field, but I felt crappy. I wanted things to get better between us, not worse. I also felt really scummy about the whole thing, aside from anything Cole would think. Screwing some guy on a couch at his office just wasn't what I wanted to be happening. It was a definite low point.

Some weeks later, on a bleak March day, I sat watching passersby out the window. I had to do something, anything, and especially something about money. I dug through the trade papers looking for modeling jobs. It was a slow time of year. One small notice caught my curiosity as it promised good money for easy work. Vague in describing the skills needed, it offered on-site auditions and I figured I might as well check it out since its location was only several blocks away.

I dressed casually but nicely in a long, shapely and soft brown sweater with pearl-like buttons over a darker brown skirt, its midi-length hem meeting the top of high-heeled leather boots that fitted my calves perfectly and made me a few inches taller. I ran a brush through my hair and put on some fresh makeup.

Leaving Cole to his late afternoon schedule of women's fantasy shows, I told him I was looking into a modeling job and would be back later. He waved his good-by, without taking his attention from the flickering screen.

The address in the ad was Sixty-eighth Street off Lexington. I strode the blocks, my heels striking the pavement as my confidence rose to meet whatever was ahead. The ad spoke of a private clientele and I wondered if, given the address, it might be some kind of private salon for showcasing high fashion to selective buyers, perhaps for the upcoming cruise season.

The recent thaw made the temperature bearable and the sidewalks clear but dirty from melting slush and car exhaust. My cashmere scarf, a holiday gift from a booking agent I used who was slightly too attracted to me, kept me warm tucked inside my double-breasted, ankle-length wool coat. There was little activity on the avenue. Yellow cabs swooshed by, headed downtown to livelier districts where fares could more easily be found.

I reached the street address from the ad and turned in to a wrought iron gated entry to a modest residential brownstone building. My curiosity rose higher. It was five o'clock and the ad had said new applicants were welcome for another hour. I pressed the bell for the first floor apartment, marked The Herald Agency. I noticed a small camera above the door and heard the buzzer sound. I let myself in and found the agency down a short, nicely carpeted hall. The door opened as I reached for the knob and a man ushered me inside.

I entered a pleasantly furnished room with low lighting. The man seated himself behind a desk at which a woman, probably in her thirties, also sat. He was wearing an open-necked black tailored shirt that matched his very thick hair. From what I could see of the woman, she was wearing a long, dark blue knitted sweater dress. No one else was in the room, which had only one other chair next to a small table and a tall brass coatrack.

"Can we help you?" the woman asked, smiling.

"Yes," I said, almost too quietly to hear. I cleared my throat and with more poise told them I was responding to an ad I had seen.

"I see," she said. "You'll need to talk to Richard. Please have a seat and I'll get him for you."

I took a seat in the only chair after hanging up my coat. While waiting I could hear muted conversation coming from the next room; women's voices rising and falling with the kind of light talk and laughter made from fond acquaintance.

A tall, handsome older man came into the room, an expensive looking ring on his outstretched hand. "Pleased to meet you," he greeted me. "I'm Richard. Kindly follow me."

He led me into and through the adjoining room, where several quite nicely dressed women were seated on couches around a table on which they were playing cards. "I'll see your two and raise you one," one of them said, glancing up at me as I passed.

I was invited into a smaller room that seemed to be the man's office. There were no personal touches to the room; it was outfitted for business only, though well furnished. He indicated my seat on a nicely upholstered chair in front of his glass-topped desk and I sat down, crossing my legs and looking as sophisticated as I could manage.

"So you read our ad," he began, seating himself while looking at me, appraising me it seemed, his fingertips running through salt-and-pepper hair.

"Yes, though I'm not entirely certain what kind of work you're offering," I said inquisitively.

He paused, his eyes fixed on mine. "Do you live in the city?" he asked.

"Yes," I answered, giving no details.

"What kind of work do you currently do?"

"I'm a model and do mostly print work. Should I have brought my portfolio?" I asked, my posture stiffening a little.

Again, he paused before answering. "No, that's not necessary," He unfolded his hands and reached for a cigarette. "We're an escort service for a discerning clientele and we need to be discreet; hence, the ad."

"I see. What would be the nature of my services if you were to hire me?" I asked.

"Nothing extreme," he said, his hand waving the air. "Our clients are well-to-do gentlemen, often from out of town, merely seeking the accompaniment of lovely, cultured women for anything from an afternoon business engagement to an evening on the town." Somehow, I knew exactly where I was as if I'd been there before.

"And I would come here to be assigned … a client?"

"Normally we would call you with your first

booking for the day," he explained, "After that it all depends on how busy we are. We might send you on to another assignment or you'd be called in to wait here until another booking came in. Anthony and Maria handle the bookings," he finished, folding his fingers together on the desk.

"How would I be paid?" I asked, relaxing into the back of the chair, this seemingly simple arrangement sparking my interest.

"Our fees are known to our clients beforehand. You just collect the cash up front and bring our cut in before the end of the night. Anthony will give you the details."

"When can I start?" I surprised myself in having no hesitation whatsoever in asking to be hired. It was as if something inside me was taking over. The whole scene intrigued me greatly and I still felt oddly comfortable.

"Tonight if you like," he smiled. "You're an attractive woman, you're dressed for a nice dinner and it's been busy this evening. You can find out if you're a good fit for this business. Would that suit you?"

"Yes, that'd be fine."

"I'll check with Anthony to see if an appropriate booking has come in." He rose from his chair and I followed him back out to the front desk. Only two of the women who'd been playing cards remained, and both smiled politely at me as I came through the room. One was standing at a bar I hadn't noticed before at one end of the room. She was making herself a drink and nibbling from a plate of fruit.

"Anthony, this young lady will be joining us for this evening. Please set her up." Richard turned to me, took my hand and shook it gently. "Welcome to

The Herald Agency. Anthony and Maria will take care of you. Let me know if you need anything. I'm here on the early end of most evenings." He backed away and then left the room. I rarely saw him again.

"Jerry called about twenty minutes ago," Maria said to Anthony. "He's got a reservation at seven o'clock. He's been hinting at wanting to see someone new."

"He'd be a good first client," said Anthony, turning in my direction. "He's an older man. Just likes a nice dinner companion and is very attracted to the innocent type. You'll be perfect for him," he said, smiling. The next fifteen minutes were a blur of instructions by Anthony, while Maria called this man, Jerry.

I suddenly realized I had to say something to Cole and asked for a phone, being told I could use the one in the living room. I hastily told Cole I was working with some other girls that evening on a modeling assignment that could become more work for good money. It was last minute as one of the girls had called in sick and they needed someone. I just happened to show up at the right time. I shouldn't be home too late. Cole said he'd take in a movie and see me later.

"Your cab's here," Anthony called from the front room. Everything was moving so fast I didn't have time to react. I felt a rush of anticipation, grabbed my coat and walked outside with Anthony to the waiting cab and got in.

"Plaza Hotel," Anthony instructed the driver. To me he said, "You're going to the Oak Bar to meet Jerry Feldman. That's not his real name, of course, but that's who you ask for. He'll be waiting for you.

Remember to call here an hour or less after you get there."

The ride to the Plaza wasn't far, but the drive down Fifth Avenue gave me a chance to collect myself. I watched the Central Park trees pass swiftly by and breathed deeply. The cab pulled up to the front of the hotel, and I stepped out onto the red carpeting, assisted by a uniformed bell hop. A slight feeling of apprehension coursed through me, but didn't linger. An older man, they'd said. I wondered what was in store for me.

Through the glass doors ablaze with reflections of warm spotlights, I walked down the beautifully appointed hallway and around the Palm Court, heading for the Oak Bar, where Cole and I'd been numerous times. I asked for Jerry Feldman and was led to a small table near the wall, just under the huge mural of Central Park in winter. There sat an impish, elderly man, well dressed in a dark pin-striped suit, a good complement to his graying hair. We introduced ourselves and I sat down.

What followed were two delightful hours with this amusing and well educated man who treated me with extreme respect and a courteousness more common to his generation than mine. Over drinks and then dinner in the Oak Room, I learned his entire history, his preferences in music and theater, and that he dabbled in sculpting clay figurines. He lived alone in a large condominium on Riverside Drive near Columbia University. He liked dining out and came frequently to the Oak Room because, he said, it took him back in time and place and helped him remember less lonely days. He said he was pleased to meet such a nice young woman as myself and hoped he might be able to have my company again sometime. He was going to get tickets to see *That Championship Season,* a new off-Broadway play opening at the Estelle Newman theater downtown in May, and he hoped I'd be able to join him. I said I'd have the agency get back to him. "*It'd all been too easy and natural,*" I thought.

Near the end of our dinner, and my second hour with Jerry, I excused myself and went to a phone booth. First I called Cole, but he wasn't home yet. Then I checked in again with Anthony to let him know I'd soon be leaving the Plaza.

"I've got another low maintenance regular if you're interested," said Anthony. "He's a talker, this one, but okay."

I wondered if Cole would get home and be worried or angry. But he knew me to always take longer than I said and it wasn't late yet. Anyway, I didn't feel too concerned about him. "Okay," I answered.

"Go to Café Carlyle on Seventy-sixth Street off Madison. Be there in a half hour and ask for Steve Jackson. Call in when you're there, same as last time."

"Okay," I said. "Way too easy," I mumbled aloud.

Another cab ride back up Fifth Avenue, this time with money in my pocket. Jerry had given me extra saying I was more conversational than most of the girls he'd seen. *I could get used to this,* I thought.

The Carlyle's art deco façade came into view as the cab pulled up to the Madison side entrance to the café. Once inside the smoky cabaret, I could feel the beat of the evening in the jazz filled room where guests were taking their places for tonight's performance. I asked for Steve Jackson and was taken to a table near the piano where a middle-aged man in a wide-lapelled leisure suit with an unbuttoned shirt sat sipping a frothy drink, longish brown hair framing his dark eyes.

"Hi sweetie," he said, standing up to invite me to the chair next to him.

"Hello Steve," I answered back, taking my seat, this time under another huge mural, one of a woman with her arms around the neck of a large beige horse. There wasn't much time for small talk as the band was assembling. But Steve was glad I could make it. He'd just gotten to town and called the agency on a lark, hoping someone was available. His business had him flying all over and he never knew where he'd land next. But he said the pace didn't keep him from partying. The band was ready to play. Steve lit a small fat cigar, smiled and winked at me, giving my knee a little squeeze.

"This is gonna be good," he said.

As the drummer began a slow rhythm, the bass player joined in and a voice over a microphone announced: "And now, ladies and gentleman, the Café Carlyle is proud to present the legendary Mr. Bobby Short!" An indeed smallish man with a wide grin walked briskly to the piano waving to the packed crowd, sat down and immediately launched into a Noel Coward tune, bringing loud whistles and hoots from the lively audience.

An hour and a long, but classy jazz set later, I was ready for the evening to end, calling in to Anthony to let him know so. Sometimes over the music and sometimes between songs, Steve had grilled me about my preferences ranging from food to fashion. Not deep talk, but Steve had fun, having several times put his arm around my shoulders and given me a tight hug and a fast kiss to show his enjoyment.

"This has been real nice. Now how about a disco?" he asked, still loaded with energy. I told him I was done for the night, but I'd have Anthony get him a new girl. "Nah," he said, adding that he was fine just throwing himself into the dance scene. "I always get lucky," he laughed.

We headed out of the club. "Say, you've been great," he said outside, eyeing the traffic and hailing me a cab. "Catch ya the next time." I slid onto the seat, thanking him and waving good bye. He'd taken my leaving so easily; he was low maintenance indeed. On the way to the agency, I let my head fall against the window to watch the buildings glide by, feeling exhausted but enthralled by my impromptu experience. I'd liked it. It made me feel more powerful that I'd felt in a long time. I wanted to do it again. I looked at the bills I'd stuffed in my wallet that evening. Subtracting the agency's take, I still had over half a month's rent, even after the cab fare. *Not bad,* I thought. *Not bad at all.*

The transaction at the agency went quickly. Anthony offered me another client, but I declined. "Short night first time out, huh?" he said. I nodded. "That's okay. Call us when you want to come in again and we'll have a booking for you."

"Thanks," I said. "I'll do that. What are your busy days?"

"They're all busy. It slows down a little the start of the week, but not too much 'cause of the travelers."

"I see. I'll give you a call soon," I assured him, though I had no idea how Cole would react to all this.

Getting ready to leave, I saw no women in the living room of the apartment. Then again, it was only eleven o'clock.

Walking the blocks towards home, I breathed the chilly air deep into my lungs. I began to slow down as I reached the apartment, wondering what I'd say to Cole.

"Well, here you are," Cole said as I let myself in. "What kind of job kept you this late?" He reached over and switched off the television, looking up at me without expression through his glasses, pushing the bridge to the top of his nose.

"It was a little different from the usual modeling job, but it paid really well," I said, handing him the money I'd made.

"What kind of work pays like this?" he asked, but not suspiciously. Cole was never bothered by my modeling assignments unless he imagined my getting personal with one of the agents or photographers. But once assured everything was cool, he was fine with it. It didn't seem to matter to him that men saw me half-dressed or even naked while changing outfits for a shoot. He was only threatened if he thought I liked someone too much or I was embarrassing him on purpose. Then he got crazy.

But this was business and I thought he'd see it that way. Not too tentatively, I explained how I'd spent the evening, saying I wanted to check it out before I said anything more to him. He just nodded his head and fingered the bills I'd given him.

"They'll give you more work like this?" he asked, unemotionally.

I hung my coat up in the closet and sat down at what passed for our dining room table. "Yeah, they will."

"Okay," he nodded, turning the television back on. I got up and headed for the closet-sized kitchen. Pouring myself a drink, I heard laughter from the set and then the familiar voice of Carnac the Magnificent.

⊙⊙⊙⊙⊙

I got to know the girls at the agency when I hung out in the apartment between calls. They got along really well for a bunch of women. No head games. No competition. In fact, they were a close group. I felt comfortable around other women for the first time in my life.

"Hey ladies," Anthony called out from the front desk. "Richard the Bald One" just called. Who wants him?"

"Not me," Juline said, the lithe, curly brown-haired girl stretched out on the couch in a low-cut, midnight blue cocktail dress playing dominoes with Eartha, dark-skinned and dressed in a colorful material that seemed to drape around her body with a scarf tied neatly around her short Afro. "I had him just a few days ago. It's someone else's turn."

"I need a call bad enough," Ruby said, the youngest among us. "I'll even take that guy." She hopped off her barstool and slid on the stacked shoes that added another few inches to her height, her short legs in black patterned tights that disappeared under a green velvet micro-skirt, the same color as the ribbon in the tiny curls of her platinum hair.

No one used their real name. Mine was Tess. It was a name I'd always liked and made me feel a little wild and unpredictable like a red-headed Scotswoman astride a roan horse, brandishing a shining sword as she raced across the moors yelling something aggressive in a thick brogue.

"Why do you call him 'Richard the Bald One'," I asked, comfortably seated in the large armchair watching the dominoes game. "What's his story?"

"He's 'Richard the Bald One' because he's not 'Richard the Hairy One'," Rosie said, just coming in from the apartment bedroom, used as a changing room. Rosie was the oldest, a beautifully curved Hispanic woman with long, straight auburn hair that she tossed to emphasize her words. "They look a lot alike, except one is as bald over his whole body as the other one is hairy," she said, very quietly this time, like she didn't want Anthony or Maria to hear. "If they stood naked next to each other you'd think one had stolen all the other's hair," she whispered. As she said this, she laughed and swayed her hips. She'd changed from jeans into a loose white blouse over a swishy knee-length skirt with a broad belt and lots of jewelry. "But they're both so boring you can't tell them apart otherwise."

The front door buzzed open and Audrey came bursting into the room, her long, wispy henna-red hair flying around her pale white shoulders like a Renaissance maiden in a Maypole dance. She flung her dripping umbrella into the corner and tossed her raincoat at the coatrack, though it fell to the floor. We were all like actors in costume coming and going from the same room every night as if in some odd play with unusual dialogue and no plot.

"What a creep! Don't take any more calls from that Fred guy, Anthony," she said, darting in sprints around the room with hands flailing like a mad woman on a psychiatric unit. "First he gives me a sweaty wad of small bills I'll bet he's been carrying around in his pocket for, like, ever. Then he takes me to this god-awful dark bar for watered-down drinks and I have to listen to him talk on and on about himself while some lounge lizard croons to a table full of tight-permed, middle-age women. I finally get him outside and flag a taxi to come back here, but he pushes his way in after me, the cab takes off and I've got this stubby-faced asshole forcing his tongue into my mouth while he's grabbing at my tits! He ripped a strap off my dress, the freak. Then when I get the cab driver to stop a couple blocks from here and let me out, I count the cash he gave me and he shorted me eighteen bucks! I'm not giving you the agency cut on this one, Anthony. And you owe me a good client for this one, pal." Her energy extinguished, she flung herself into the armchair opposite mine, almost knocking the dominoes to the floor with her huge red, half-open purse that hung off her body like an overstuffed mailbag.

"But he booked you for every week this month," Anthony kidded, sticking his head around the doorway from the front room, his glossy black hair grabbing a highlight from the wall sconce. "You can't let the poor guy down."

"Oh yes I can. Give him to Rhonda next time. She likes handling his type. She'll get every dime he has and a nice dinner, too. He'd be afraid to pull any shit with her. We should call her " The Intimidator" or something. Wish I was like that."

"Want to take my place at dominoes?" Eartha asked. "I got a call at eight o'clock. I'm outta here."

"No, I don't want to take your place at

dominoes," Audrey mocked, but affectionately.

"That's okay," Joline said. "I'm way ahead of this girl and I have to go out soon myself."

"Any decent booze in this joint?" Audrey asked.

"Just the same low rent vodka we always have," Rosie answered.

"Oh, great. Or maybe there's some of that delicious Chablis we never seem to finish. Whatever. I'll drink anything."

"And there's some leftover Chinese in the fridge," I said to her on my way to the bathroom.

"Fabulous. I'm starving. I ate two bowls of peanuts and some of those gross orange worm things," she said, holding up five orange tinged fingertips to make her point. "That guy really went out of his way to charm me."

I passed Rosie in the hallway and started to ask her what I'd been thinking about, but hesitated. She picked up on it right away. "What's on your mind, beauty queen?"

"Oh nothing really," I said. "I was just wondering."

"Well, spit it out, girl. It isn't like we haven't heard anything and everything around here."

"The two Richards," I said. "No one's been undressed on any of my calls. How do you know what they look like naked?"

"Well, we have to be very quiet with this kind of talk so they don't hear us out at the front," Rosie said, lowering her voice while drawing me into the bedroom. "I know you haven't been doing this that long, but sometimes with clients who've been around awhile who we think we can trust, some of us might be willing to, shall I say, extend the evening."

"But Anthony told me no sex is allowed."

"It isn't. If you ask any of the girls they'll say it's not done. If Anthony catches you, you'll never get a call again. You get me? So you have to be real careful. They are very uptight about cops."

"We got girl talk happening back here?" Eartha said, coming to get her raincoat from off the bed.

"Just filling Tess in on some of the rules," Rosie said. "It's different at different places," she continued, leaning against the dresser. "Here you got some protection. That's why they have us call in so often. So they know where we are. Anthony'd send someone to get you if they thought you were in trouble."

"Oh yeah," Eartha said. "He knows people in the hotels, clubs and places all over town. He checks on things. I know he checks on us, too," she said, laughing and heading out the door.

"What about other escort services?" I asked. "Some are different than this?" I sat on the bed and caught my reflection in the vanity mirror. I looked strange. I was Tess. My face changed with this new identity.

"Some don't care what you do," Rosie was saying. "You get lots of calls and you make a lot more money. A lot more. But if you're in trouble, you're on your own. Then they don't know you. And you might be in one of the smaller hotels or some guy's apartment. It's a lot riskier."

"You've used other services?"

"Hey, Rosie, Anthony says you've got a call," Audrey shouted from down the hall.

"Okay, be right there," she called back. "Sure. It's good money," Rosie said to me, glancing towards the living room. "I know I'm safer here, but sometimes I need the cash. I work it both ways. Hey, if you ever want to know more, just ask me. We all gotta help each other, you know? It ain't easy being us." Rosie laughed, pinching my chin, and then headed toward the front.

"How's that chow mein, Audrey?" I heard her say from the living room.

I had a call for eight-thirty, a repeat customer. We were meeting friends of his for dinner, some couple he knew from college just in town for a few days. He said he felt like a loser still being single, so I was the surrogate girlfriend. He was an okay guy; a little uptight, but amusing. He told stories about bizarre things happening to him in his travels that you wanted to believe were true. It passed the time.

I got my bag from beside the dresser and took out my makeup. *More money*, I thought. *Something to think about. Maybe kick this thing up a notch.* I had to smile at myself in the mirror. Feeling sassy, I chose the new lipstick I'd just bought. Barcelona Red.

♋♋♋♋♋♋

Still having a few modeling jobs by day, over the months my nights at The Harold Agency got longer and more frequent. I was going out for drinks, dinner, the theater, jazz bars or cocktail parties in elegant townhouses. I made regular hours out of it and to Cole it just became my job. He didn't seem to care that I was being escorted places by other men. He liked the money and it gave him his freedom. He didn't seem too interested in me anyway. He had his writing, his television and his pornography. The bills were paid and there was food in the refrigerator. My being out of the house meant more unspoiled time for him. I wasn't happy about it, but I didn't know what else to do. I didn't want to leave him because things might turn around and I wanted to be there when they did. I was only twenty-three and still had time to make a life of my own if I had to. Besides, I was intrigued with my new private life; there was something in it I wanted; only I wasn't sure what. But for some stupid reason, I sometimes felt guilty about leaving Cole alone, even if he didn't mind or even care. He'd made me jealous enough with other women, though. I should be able to do what I wanted. I felt guilty one minute and angry the next. I made up for my guilt and tried to feel less angry by asking Cole to come out with me sometimes. He liked going to the movies, so on a hot summer day I suggested we go see *American Graffiti*. He agreed and I drove a car to leased to me by Jerry to pick him up that afternoon from one of his occasional trips to see his agent. He jumped in, threw his briefcase in the backseat and we headed back uptown.

The movie was set in the 1950s when Cole was a teenager, and he seemed to really get into watching it. I was only a child in those years, but thought the movie was great. Afterward, we walked up and down the street looking for a bar.

"I really think George Lucas has a future," Cole said. Lucas made the movie loosely based on his life. "I think he could end up being a good friend of ours someday once we've gotten into films."

A movie review I'd read said Lucas had been a

geeky teenager who'd had as much trouble as Cole making friends. "Well, the two of you do have a lot in common."

"How about this place?" Cole said, pointing to a bar down the street from where we'd parked the car. It was where I'd sometimes go with the girls on a slow night between calls, but I chose not to mention that.

"Sure, that's an okay place," I answered. It was noisy with music, talk and laughter but we hustled our way through the bodies and found stools in the corner of the bar near the front window. Sawdust and peanut shells covered the floor, people tossing shells being a longstanding tradition.

"Hi there, Doll," the bartender said, tossing coasters in front of us. "What'll it be? The usual?"

"Sure."

He then turned to Cole, who ordered a Jack Daniels.

"The usual?" Cole asked. "Sounds like you come here often?"

"The girls and I come here once in a while when work's really slow. The agency's not far from here." Live music played in the back. A jazzy blues. After a long intro, a sultry looking black woman got up to sing and her breathy voice filled the room.

"Here you are," the bartender said, putting our drinks down. "So where're the girls tonight?" he said, leaning on the bar in front of me.

"Oh, I don't know. I took the night off. Gotta have a break now and then you know."

"I guess so. A pretty lady like you has to be real busy." Conscious that he was leaning in to me, I pulled back a little, noticing that Cole was watching.

Still, it felt nice to be paid attention to and flattered. "The next round's on me," he said, rapping his knuckles on the bar, winking at me and nodding at Cole.

"Well, thanks," I said, coyly smiling back.

Cole was quiet and gave me a hard look, before pointedly turning his back on me to watch the singer. *I've got those Monday blues, straight through Sunday blues.*

We listened without talking, me looking at my reflection in the mirror behind the various liquor bottles, their different colors softly gleaming in the subdued lighting. Tess looked back at me. Her face was thin and angular. It wasn't unattractive, just more sophisticated and older.

"Say, I found that Fats Waller record I was talking to you about." The bartender had returned. "Over on Broadway in that little place I told you I go for really rare records. I'll play it here sometime. I bet you'll like it."

"That's great. I'd love to hear it. I don't know his music much at all," I said.

"Oops, excuse me," he said, snapping his dish towel on the bar and hurrying away to serve someone further down the bar.

Cole snapped his head around. "Are you going to let me into this little conversation you're having or just ignore me?" he fumed.

"Sorry, I was just being friendly. I do know the guy," I said, knowing full well I'd been enjoying his attention. "Yes, well I can see that." When he pushed his glasses up to the nose bridge, I knew I'd maybe gone a little too far in making him jealous. He grabbed his drink, stood up and faced away again.

The bartender came and put the next round of

drinks in front of us. "I made them a little strong. Tell me if it's too much," he said, winking at me again and walking away.

Cole sat back down and glared at me. "Just how well do you know this guy, huh?"

"I told you. I come here with the girls sometimes. That's all."

"Have you fucked him yet?" Cole reached his arm under the bar, grabbed my nipple between his fingers and twisted it hard.

"Cole, please stop! There's nothing going on between me and this bartender," I whispered harshly. "He's friendly with all the women who come here. It's part of his goddam job." I pushed his hand off my breast, but he was squeezing it so hard it hurt to get it off me. He turned away and sat brooding with his drink.

"Nice boyfriend you got there," the man next to me said too quietly for Cole to hear. I thought he may have seen the pinching.

"He's not my boyfriend, he's my husband," I said, throwing him a sour look, but glad even for a stranger to validate what happened.

"Cole, I'm leaving now." I threw a tip on the bar, stood up and made for the door, pushing through the crowd. Cole just sat staring ahead at the singer. I could see the rage growing in his face. I left and headed for the car. As I walked around to the driver's side to get in I saw Cole coming toward me, walking fast across the street, his anger almost visibly preceding him. Afraid, I got in the car and locked the doors. He threw himself on the hood and grabbed the windshield wiper.

"Don't you dare leave me here," he shouted.

People were watching us from a restaurant's outside tables. I rolled the window down an inch.

"I won't leave if you'll calm down."

He slid off the hood and came around the side of the car. "Okay, I won't hurt you. Just open the fucking door," he said slowly. I looked at him and saw he was making an effort to relax. I opened the door and he got in. "Just drive home and please don't say anything," he said.

The drive down Second Avenue was so tense I could feel my stomach clenching and the rum I'd drunk pushing up into my throat, an unpleasant taste swilling over my tongue. "I'm sorry, Cole."

"Just don't talk. Drive." I got to our block and was relieved to find a parking space not far from our apartment. Cole got out, jerking his briefcase from the back seat. I came around the car and stepped on the sidewalk. "Don't ever embarrass me like that again," he said, raising his briefcase behind him, pulling it forward with speed and slamming it hard into my shin. Blood streamed from the gash made from the metal corner of the case. He turned and strode fiercely up the steps, the tip of his shoe bashing into the door before he managed to open it.

I couldn't even cry. I knew I'd brought this on myself, but his reaction was way over the top. I was hurt and pissed both at myself and at him. I found some paper towels on the floor of the back seat, staunched the cut and limped up to the apartment. I let myself in, cleaned and bandaged my leg in the bathroom and went to bed, pulling the covers around me to bury myself in something soft.

Cole was watching the replay of the day's Watergate hearings. I recognized John Dean's voice, the monotonous beat of his testimony helping me get drowsy enough to sleep.

I'd learned a new limit with Cole. I never made him jealous in public again. I still felt spite for hurt he'd caused me, but it wasn't worth arousing the anger of a six-foot, three-inch tall man with a briefcase for a weapon. When my own anger got intolerable, I learned to be snide instead. Over time, I honed my pissiness to a very subtle art, finding a talent within myself for being really cutting. Nothing to be proud of, but a handy skill when I got crazy enough to use it. I became more Tess and less Lily every day.

ᏀᏀᏀᏀᏀᏀ

Cole and I each kept our distance for a while through the fall, though eventually it was hard to keep it up. I wanted to be able to come home to a warm place where I could feel safe. It had to get better between me and Cole. I felt safer working as a prostitute than I did at home. I wanted that to change, and as I eventually learned, things have a way of changing on their own sometimes, tending to come back into balance. It was colder outside and I chose to spend more time at home when I wasn't working. In time and with proximity to each other, our anger softened. We both appreciated it, even if nothing was said.

On a Sunday, Cole and I sat on the bearskin rugs eating our favorite breakfast of scrambled eggs, bacon and sticky buns. Cole was immersed in reading the *New York Times* book reviews. I'd grabbed the magazine section and started the crossword puzzle, though at the moment I was gazing out the bay window, random thoughts passing by like the leaves whirling off the quickly emptying trees. The image of Audrey making one of her whirling entrances at the agency came to mind and I laughed to myself.

"What's funny?" Cole asked, still turning the newspaper pages, but glancing at me over his glasses.

"Oh nothing. Just one of the girls I work with. She loves drama and made one of her scenes last night."

"Yeah? Tell me about it. I haven't heard much about the girls. Which one is this?"

"Audrey," I answered, realizing I hadn't said much about them. I didn't think he'd want to know. "She's trying to break into acting, but so far's only been in a couple of TV spots. She goes to the Herbert Berghoff Studio downtown. It's turned out some good actors. If she keeps at it, she'll probably do okay. Audrey's just very dramatic all the time, making anything that happens into a story she'll act out. She does great with comedy. I think she dances, too. Like I could see her in a musical like *Grease* maybe.

"What about some of the other girls? What are they like?" Cole asked, putting down the paper and looking interested.

"Well, let's see. There's Ruby," I said, collecting our dishes on a tray. "I don't know why she chose that name for work, but it could easily be from Ruby Keeler. She's short, pert, blonde and blue-eyed, and I can just see her tap dancing in a Busby Berkeley musical. She's always playing music at work and shuffling around in little dance steps. But I heard her say she's putting herself through nursing school. She wants to work with kids in a pediatric practice."

I opened a window, but though it was sunny the November chill caused me to close it again.

"Then there's Rosie. She's a sweetheart. She's married and they live up in Spanish Harlem with their three kids. Her husband's been on disability from a bad accident at his construction job that messed up his back. Rosie's just trying to keep things going 'til he's working again. I don't think he likes her working, but he doesn't have much choice. Rosie never finished school and they got married young. She never worked; just raised the kids. She said the oldest plays the violin really well and she wants him to try out for Julliard. Rosie loves her kids. She works nights so she can be there for them during the day and after school. She's beautiful, too, and has real style. She's popular at the agency, I'll tell you. Men sure do love the Latinas.

"I guess I had a really different image of what the girls would be like," said Cole. "Not that you fit the stereotype, but I was expecting more like ...," he hesitated.

"Streetwalkers?" I answered for him, sitting down on the window ledge.

"Yeah, I guess so. Maybe not fishnet stockings and hot pants, but more low status. Pretty, but not much education or smarts and probably into drugs or something."

"No, there's a lot of class at the agency. Like Eartha. She's into fashion design, saving money to start her own business. She's black and beautiful and she knows it. She's got the body of a Nubian fertility goddess and she likes to play it up big time. Eartha: The name sure fits. She's always wearing one of her designs. She uses fabrics with all different textures and muted colors. She mixes them up in unusual ways, you know, like prints with stripes and she kind of fits the material to her body shape. There's no buttons or zippers you can see. The cloth looks like it's folded and tucked together." I mimicked how she might do that. "Really cool stuff. She uses lots of make-up, too. Bright eye shadow and lipsticks with gobs of lip gloss. And her jewelry! She's got huge earrings, necklaces and bracelets that dangle and bangle all shiny and clanging against each other. She's hot. Her smile fills the room. You just have to smile back. Yeah, she's class."

Cole was obviously fascinated, holding his hand to his chin in a gesture he used only when thinking hard. "Don't stop. More, tell me more."

"Okay," I said, curious about his sudden interest, but enjoying talking about these women who'd become my friends. "Well, there's Rhonda. She's a whole other story. I don't know where she comes from, but she's like a lion tamer from the circus or something. She's the most private of all the girls; doesn't say much at all, but when she does she talks tough, but with a good sense of humor, too. She's nice, just made of pretty hard stuff. I think she's done a lot of things and started young, really young – a vagabond with a criminal record maybe. It wouldn't surprise me if she keeps a gun in that big black leather bag of hers she won't let go of. If any of the women are into drugs it'd be Rhonda. She's only in her late twenties, but looks older. Not bad looking, just a little weathered. She's all black hair and intelligent dark eyes, fringed leather and high-heeled boots. She's a charmer all right. You don't want to fuck with Rhonda. But she also laughs at herself a lot. She has this deep voice and her laugh comes from her guts. She and Rosie are good friends. I wouldn't mind getting to know her better. I like her mystery." I paused and readjusted myself with a cushion on the window ledge.

"I don't think most people have a clue about who works at an escort agency," Cole said. He looked animated, pushing his fingers together in that "spider-on-a-mirror" way he had when he was conjuring. "You know babe, I think there's a really interesting book in all this." He got up off the rugs and paced around, his fingers back on his chin. "How many other women are there? How many stories like these?"

"Oh, lots," I said. "And I haven't even started on what they do and how they feel about it. You wouldn't believe some of the conversations that happen in that place." I thought about it seriously for a moment. "Yeah, it's pretty interesting stuff actually. It'd probably surprise people."

"You think any of these women would be willing to be interviewed?"

"I don't know. They're very self-protective and they stick together. It's not your typical bunch of chicks in a lot of ways. But some of them might talk."

"Can you ask a couple of them? See how it goes?"

"I'll think about it. I may want to get to know them a little more first. I'd want them to trust me. What kind of book were you thinking of? That'd be important to them, and to me, for that matter."

"I just think sexual mores are really changing with this generation, and I'll bet that interviewing these women would show that. It's not our parents' generation anymore. It's like in the Sixties the new freedoms made people think about their sexuality really differently. Just look at all the porno rags out there. And porno films! It's like a profitable alternative to film school; learn how to shoot live footage and make money at the same time. And they need actors. Not a bad way to earn money. Better than waiting tables." He sat back down on the rugs, stretching out his long legs and crossing his feet. "I think I could use this to make a real statement. I'm not just talking about cranking out a lot of sexy talk and images. This wouldn't be some kind of rank pulp fiction. No, I'm serious about there being some messages about changing morals – that an escort service isn't so strange a job for women anymore. I'd present it as a researched topic."

Cole was getting more and more intense and gesturing excitedly. I wasn't too crazy about his very definite knowledge about all the porn *out there,* but tried to put that unpleasantness aside to think fairly about what was looking to become a new project of his. He'd been stuck for a while. His "research" on afternoon soap operas wasn't yielding fresh insights about a new commercial venture. This book idea seemed like it might do that for him. I had to agree there was intriguing subject matter that'd probably interest a lot of women. Hell, I was fascinated myself. I knew I was into this escort thing for personal reasons that still weren't all that clear to me yet, but I could also see that other women and men, too, might be interested in what goes on inside "the life."

"Well, if you're really that serious about it, I can think of a couple of girls who might respect that. I can look into it," I said, not wanting to make a firm commitment, but willing to consider it.

"What did you mean when you said these weren't typical women in a lot of ways?"

"Well, let's see," I said, coming from the window and joining him on the rugs, stretching out and leaning against the big suede pillows. We hadn't talked this much in a long time and it felt good, even if I wasn't too sure about the subject. But it was nice to see Cole lighten up a bit. I laid my head back and as I talked I alternated my gaze between Cole and the tree branches dancing back and forth in the wind outside.

"They're much too streetwise to mess with each other's heads," I began. "They respect each other and everybody's got a way of striking back, so why bother, you know? And they don't need to compete. They can get all the business they want and they keep the details fairly private unless they want to share something with each other. Then it's usually about a really strange customer. Some of them've been around the block a few times and met a lot of guys. So what's strange to them is pretty weird. The girls newer to the business talk about the men as if they're feeling out the norms, you know? Like just what is normal and what should be avoided. I do that myself. How should I know? It keeps things in check. Otherwise, each woman is out there on her own. Sometimes it's good to bring it home, so to speak, and get some feedback. Being an escort isn't your standard occupation. There's no manual. You gotta write your own."

"I love this!" Cole said. "Even just hearing you talk about it is giving me ideas." He jumped up and grabbed a notebook from a pile of stuff on the dining room table. Settling back down on the rugs, he started jotting down his thoughts. I could see his mind working.

"What about these guys?" he asked. "I just figured they were all creeps."

"Normal. You know, the guy from Ohio just in town for a few days on business. He takes in a Broadway show, has dinner at some tourist trap, gets lonely and calls the service. He doesn't want to really cheat on his wife, but he wants the thrill of being with a pretty girl out for drinks in Manhattan. Something to tell the guys about when he gets home."

"So what happens when you get a call?"

For a moment I worried that Cole was setting me up by asking all this, but I could tell by how he was reacting that he was genuinely interested. I knew him pretty well and I was catching on to his triggers. If he felt jealous and betrayed he went insane, but otherwise was dispassionate about my experiences when I was up front about it. So I went on talking.

"Yeah. You meet the guy at some place he chooses or somewhere Anthony suggests to them."

"Wait, who's Anthony?" Cole asked, pen poised above his notebook.

"Anthony and a woman who works there make the bookings. They keep it clean and above board. No Times Square joints. Nothing like that. Classy places or trendy hot spots. Maybe some place in the Village or the lower East Side, but no dives.

I described Jerry, the elderly gentleman who'd leased me the car so I could drive up to visit him at his condo, though I hadn't mentioned that to Cole. I was afraid it would piss him off.

I left it at that, not wanting to describe too many

guys in case it began to upset him. "The guys are pretty interchangeable as far as the girls go. They're in it for the money, not the men. Going to a nice place is good; especially somewhere you wouldn't normally go. But money's the main thing. No one's thinking of doing this forever. They've all got plans. Some of them have been at it longer than they'd like, though. Expenses keep coming up for them and it's hard to turn down buying something nice when you've got a lot of cash on hand. Ruby keeps buying new stuff for her apartment. Ashley keeps taking more classes in acting, dance and voice. I have a feeling they'll all get where they want to go."

Cole was scribbling notes on his pad. "I've got to do this," he said, without looking up. "This book will write itself. You've got to keep using this escort place, babe. You're my research assistant."

I turned again to the window, looking at the now cloud crowded sky. Whatever I was looking for at the service, it wasn't researching a quasi- non-fiction book about female escorts. But, what the hell. If it made my working acceptable to Cole, I'd do it.

☙☙☙☙☙

I'd been out all evening on a call with one guy. Young, maybe thirty-three, he claimed to be a filmmaker in town from Los Angeles. I didn't care how true that was. He was younger, way more fit and way more interesting than most of the guys I usually saw – the insurance/computer/office supply salesmen in town for a motivational conference or the tourist/frequent flyer/traveling businessman with one long night to spend on the town. I liked this guy. He was cute, flamboyant, entertaining and totally crazy. He had greying temples that went nicely with his well-tailored, three-piece, dark grey pin-striped suit. He complemented the glittery, sequined, wrap-around blouse with its plunging neckline that I wore over flared black pants slit up the side to my thigh, the hem draped over ankle-strapped platform shoes. I'd worn bright red lipstick that jazzed up my long, thick and swishy blond hair. We were a striking pair.

He'd called the service because he wanted a good looking woman on his arm who he could have fun with and not worry about pleasing. An easy pick up and drop off kind of girl. That was me. That was my job.

His having money didn't hurt. We had dinner at La Grenouille, a fabulous and very expensive French restaurant on the upper Eastside, a townhouse beautifully lit with huge vases of fresh cut flowers and carefully selected art nicely framed and positioned on the walls. We had a delicious meal, mine the quenelles of pike Lyonnaise with a nice bottle of Pinot Blanc. Then, after dinner liqueurs at a classy neighborhood bar before a cab ride to catch Ziggy Stardust at Max's Kansas City, a music and art venue downtown. He was meeting artist friends of his there, and while we were all hanging out his friends would greet other artists I'd never heard of while he'd casually gossip about famous people who were there. Some I knew, most I didn't. I caught glimpses of Andy Warhol, Abbie Hoffman and Faye Dunaway. But the crush of glam freaks, high fashion models, and wanna-be celebrities made the experience into something like taking acid on a carousel ride with faces and garb of all descriptions sliding by you, mixed with odd bits of dialogue, various perfume scents, the pleasant aroma of marijuana and the occasional whiff of an Eros-inducing inhalant. Of course with the 151 proof rum, several Sambucas and his unending supply of cocaine, I was getting drunk and high enough to enjoy anything.

At the tail end of the evening, he paid a cab driver to take us on a long drive around the Manhattan waterfront. Up the Eastside Drive we went, lights blazing across the river. It was pleasantly warm out and we had the windows rolled down, taking in the night air and soft city sounds after hours in smokey bars with music blaring, shouting at each other to be heard over the din of drugged and drunken carousers.

We were each leaning back on our own side of the back seat and he was grinning sweetly, handing me yet another line of coke on a very small silver tray he carried with him in an inner jacket pocket. I declined. One more snort and I'd need an emergency room. Time to slow down and suck in some oxygen. But I was relaxed and enjoying myself. It didn't even faze me when he reached over and began fondling my breasts under the thin material of my loose fitting top. A hand slid under the cloth and pulled it away, exposing my skin to the breeze coming through the window. A mouth found my hardening nipple, a tongue making small circles around it. I was just getting into it when he leaned back, unzipped his pants and pulled out a very erect penis, stroking it with a happy grin on his handsome face. My groggy mind settled on the realization that I was still on the job. This was my first sexual encounter and I had a decision to make. I glanced at the cab driver, barely visible through the yellowing and cracked plastic partition. I doubted this was his first long fare. I doubted he cared anyway.

"There's an extra fee for that," I said, smiling and nodding at the dick in his now busy hand.

"Don't worry, lovey," he said. "I'm an old pro at this. I'll take care of you. You just take care of me."

And so I did. Without much thought. It just seemed the thing to do at the moment and he wasn't being obnoxious about it. When he was done, we lay cradled in the back seat, the lights of New Jersey coming into view as we headed down the Westside Highway.

It was late, and I asked him to drop me off at the all-night mid-town diner that for the escort girls was the usual last stop after work for eggs benedict and a snifter of cognac. I knew I'd find at least some of them there. He obliged and as the cab pulled up he handed me the hundred dollar bill we'd been using to snort lines of coke all night. He'd given me the usual agency fee at the start of the evening.

"You'll have to work at flattening it out a bit," he laughed, "but I want you to know I've enjoyed your company. You've been great fun."

I tucked the rolled bill into the pocket of my evening bag. "Thanks." I smiled and touched his cheek. "Hope I see you again." I ducked out of the cab and headed into the diner. Towards the back, seated at our traditional table, were Rosie, Eartha and Rhonda.

"Hey beauty queen," Rosie called out. I made my way back, nodding at the waiter who always took our orders, and slid in beside them on the horseshoe-shaped, padded booth bench.

"Why do you always call her that?" asked Rhonda.

"Because that's what she is: A beauty queen. Can't you just see her up on a parade float dressed in a lovely pink gown with a *New York* sash across her boobs?" All blond hair and blue eyes and red lips, waving to the crowd like a princess?" She laughed and patted my arm.

"That's a nauseating idea. Doesn't that piss you off, Tess?" Rhonda asked. "She's making you out to be some Barbie doll for Christ's sake."

"Well I guess that's what I do look like sometimes," I shrugged. "I don't mind. Rosie can say anything she likes. She's my good friend," I said, lacing my arm through hers.

"Yeah, Rhonda. Everybody's got their own style. Like that hippie-bandit thing you got going for yourself," Eartha chided. Rhonda was wearing her black fringed jacket over a short blue denim skirt.

"Okay, okay," Rhonda said. "Let's order already. You got here at just the right time, Tess. The special tonight is smoked salmon benedict." She waved the waiter over.

The restaurant was a renovated railway car diner made in the 1940s with lots of glass and mirrors, black plastic and shiny aluminum. Art deco sconce lights illuminated the bar and soda fountain area that was lined with fixed swivel stools with black leather seats and aluminum pedestals. Our booth was at the end of a row of booths by the diner windows, hanging lamps over each table. Silver-framed black and white photos of old movie scenes covered what wall space there was.

"I'll just have some tomato juice," I said. "I'm not hungry tonight. I kind of overdid it on some really fine coke so I'm a little wired on top of a lot of booze."

"Yeah, you've got a little remnant of white powder ringing your left nostril," said Rosie. "You get some for the road? Any to help out a couple of tired working girls?"

"Sorry, I didn't ask. He sure had enough. But I was a little flipped out when he dropped me off."

"By what?" asked Rhonda, smiling slyly. "The coke? Or do I smell a story coming. Do not leave out any details!"

"Well, I guess I just got initiated," I said, shyly. All three women leaned forward, listening intently when the waiter showed up.

"Oh great timing, Phil" Rhonda said. "But that's okay. We're starved." Everyone ordered and then leaned towards me again. "So, spill it girl."

"I, uh, blew a guy tonight," I said, almost whispering.

"You blew a guy. That's it? That's the whole news flash?" Eartha said, sitting back and lighting a long, thin cigar, her eyes rolling under the rim of a broad headband holding her thick black curls away from her face.

"Now ladies," Rosie said. "This is a first for Tess, I think. I'm assuming you negotiated a price increase?"

"Well she's not the guy's wife," Rhonda said, snorting a little. "Of course she did. Right, Tess?"

"Yes, Rhonda," I said, pulling the twirled-up bill from my bag. "Is this about right?" I flattened it out on the table. Specks of cocaine bounced off of Ben

Franklin's face. Eartha licked her finger and dabbed at the specks, running her finger over her gums."

"Eartha, that's disgusting. All the germs on that bill?" Rhonda said, throwing back a shot of Jack Daniels, her favorite brand, and chasing it with beer.

"Guess I'm not as proud as you," Eartha said, laughing. "We don't get enough germs in the work we do? At this stage of the game, I think I've become immune to anything life-threatening."

"Seriously true," Rosie said. "And that's a fair price, Tess. Congratulations." She lifted her glass. I met hers with mine and smiled.

"Well it wasn't all that bad and I sure like the money," I said, putting the bill away.

"There's more where that came from if you want it," Rhonda said, glancing at the other women.

"Yeah, we told Tess about our alternative call service," Rosie said.

"You can make a lot, but you just have to be careful, that's all," Rhonda said. More drinks arrived at the table and everyone fell silent until the waiter left. "You can turn down a call if you don't want it. Most of them are fine. But stick to the good hotels or first class addresses."

"Yeah, sometimes they get calls from hotels west of Seventh Avenue or the cheaper mid-town hotels. Stay away from those," Eartha added. "Safety's one thing, but you also get real creeps sometimes. You'll learn how to handle them, but don't set yourself up for them in the beginning."

"What kind of creeps are we talking about?" I asked, taking a swig of my tomato juice.

"Oh, not psychos, but just creeps," Rhonda said. "Guys into fetishes or weird tastes, that's all. Some aren't so bad. Like the shoe enthusiast I have. I spend an hour trying on different open-toed stilettos and walking around him lying naked on the floor while he licks my toes. He loves it. And he pays for it. What do I care what he likes? But you don't want to start out with that."

"You'll freak her out with this talk. She'll be fine. I think Tess has the smarts for it," Rosie said. "You tell me what night, Tess, and I'll introduce you to Charlie. He'll understand you're new and he'll give you good calls."

"He better or I'll fix him," Rhonda said, stabbing out her cigarette in the ashtray.

"Oh you're always threatening to do something to Charlie," Eartha said. "What would you ever really do?"

"Just wait 'til he fucks with one of us and you'll find out," Rhonda said. "This business gotta be a two-way street. I just don't mind having Charlie a little bit afraid of me, that's all. He talks tough, so I talk tough. Being around my step-father taught me that," she said, an angry tone rising in her voice. "No need for Charlie to think we're pussies."

Food arrived and plates of eggs were served around the table with toast, cream cheese and jam.

"God, I'm hungry," Rosie said, sliding a garnish of sliced orange into her mouth. "I had no dinner tonight."

"I got to eat at La Grenouille," I said. "Quenelles of pike Lyonnaise," I said, drawing out the vowels.

"See?" Rosie said. "Beauty queen food."

Everyone forked into their meals, bantering between bites, an easy camaraderie among trusting friends.

"Lord it's late and I got to get the kids up in the morning 'cause Frank's got a doctor's appointment," Rosie said.

"You're a good mom, Rosie," Eartha said.

"Gotta be. They're good kids. I finally got me a good family to be grateful for. But don't you worry. As soon as I get the kids at summer camp for the day, I'm off to get my legs waxed. I know how to take good care of myself, too, when I can. I'm no fool."

"Where do you go? I got to get mine done. And I need a pedicure bad," Eartha said. "My nails, too. You gotta keep yourself up in this business, that's for sure. It's damn rough on the body" she said, and we all laughed.

I let the conversation drift by, words and laughter a comfortable pillow for my thoughts. I was finally feeling a little sleepy and decided to head home.

"I'm getting woozy, ladies," I said, yawning. "I think I'll take off. See you tonight."

"Okay, precious girl," Rosie said. "And don't forget to let me know when you're ready to meet Charlie."

"Yeah, we'll break you in," said Rhonda. "Not to worry."

"We can even do a double-date if you want," said Eartha. "If that's easier for you, doll."

"I'll think about it and let you know," I said, paying my share of the tab and getting up to leave. "Night, ladies." Once outside the diner, I hailed a cab quickly. It was a slow time of night. I relaxed against the seat as the car started for uptown.

I'd never been around women who made me feel so comfortable. They all seemed to understand me and each other without having to say too much. It was like having sisters who came from the same background but were all different personalities. There were unspoken agreements about how to talk to each other. You knew what buttons not to push, and you knew the buttons were there without even asking or being told. And we knew what ways to comfort each other and when to do so. There was a shared past and we all knew it was there. We'd been to the same painful places and could feel the terrain of each other's emotions without knowing any specifics. With them I didn't feel I had to hold back, but I also didn't need to explain myself. They already knew. And it was okay. I was okay. And I wasn't alone. We were all different together.

♋♋♋♋♋

It was a gorgeous summer evening and I decided to walk to my first call of the night at the Plaza Hotel on Central Park South. I was snaking through the Eastside blocks to get to Fifth Avenue by the park. As I got closer I could hear the chanting of collective women's voices. Heading west across Fifty-ninth Street I could see them marching north on Fifth Avenue, carrying banners and waving signs. Approaching the avenue, I could more clearly hear them shouting: "We will fight, we will fight, we will fight for women's rights," the refrain repeated by women marching in rows for several blocks. Their protest signs supported the Equal Rights Amendment, which had passed in Congress the year before, though it still had to be ratified by the states. I reached for one of the flyers being handed out by women on the edge of the march. It explained that though many states had quickly backed the E.R.A. last year, the pace had slowed and these women were advocating for a speed-up of ratification across the country.

I stopped at the corner to watch women of mixed ages passing by, some with children in strollers or carried on a hip or shoulders. Banners signified different women's groups and most wore large E.R.A. buttons on their shirts or hats. A few men were sprinkled among the rows of marchers, including a number of supportive gays, the fems among them proudly flashing their colorful garb. Drumbeats kept the march moving and an occasional cow bell or whistle punctuated the chanting and shouting.

It was a peaceful march, even festive. Mounted police took unthreatening positions at the intersection, just to keep the crowd flowing. Traffic was temporarily stopped for the distance of the march, safety controlled by police cars. A couple of television crews followed alongside, grabbing close-up shots of the marchers. People lined the sidewalks and watched. Those obviously opposed to E.R.A shouted back at the women and waved hands in dismissal; progress bringing fear out in some people, fear of change they aren't sure of and can't control. That women could be equal to men suggested they could also be heads of industry or presidents or maybe even soldiers. Unthinkable to some.

I took advantage of a slight break in the crowd to cross the avenue to the Grand Army Plaza at the mouth of the park. The marchers were curving around it and into the park along the East Drive. As I crossed the rows of women I flashed back to my marching band days, remembering planned maneuvers of rows of us marching through each other at angles. I dropped into the cadence of the women and managed to cross without running into anyone or getting bashed with a sign.

I emerged onto the sidewalk which was lined with information tables covered with literature of the women's movement: Leaflets on issues, brochures from women's groups, flyers of upcoming events, pins and buttons littered the tables. I had time before my appointment and glanced through a reprint of Gloria Steinem's article "What Would It Be Like if Women Win," printed a while ago in *Time Magazine*. "Want to buy a button?" asked the smiling woman behind the table, her floppy hat a display of all the buttons and pins she had for sale. She held out one of the ubiquitous E.R.A. buttons.

"No thanks, I'm just browsing," I answered.

I was pretty out of touch with the details of the women's movement. I knew the Supreme Court had decided *Roe v. Wade* earlier that year because the abortion issue was meaningful to me. I knew Congresswoman Shirley Chisholm had been the first black candidate to run for president because my mother had avidly supported her campaign. The issues were as important to me as any woman, but I was on a different trajectory. I wasn't exactly sure what my issues were, but the path I'd taken seemed the one to get me where I needed to go. Rights? Sure. Just let me figure out a few other things first – like who the hell I was and why I didn't like myself very much. I was living outside the world of women with normal adult pursuits like getting a job, running for office, starting a women's magazine – these were things other women did – other, mostly white, middle-class, college educated women like those on the march. I wasn't capable of anything as sane as that. Years later the women's movement would work to *take back the night*, as the slogan went, so women could defend themselves against male intimidation, sexual aggressiveness, assault and rape. Not yet though. The movement, in this country at least, wasn't ready. But I was. Not just looking for equality, I wanted payback big time. I wanted triumph. I just didn't know how to do it, though I seemed on my way to finding out. At the time, I didn't even know how angry I was. That realization was still to present itself. Now in hiding, that deep motive drove me on, me putting one foot in front of another down a shadowy street looking for power and control on my own terms, looking to take back the night – today.

"I'll take this one," I said to the floppy-hatted woman, picking up a small button that said " Woman Power " on it, black letters over white with a grey clenched fist in the background.

"That's two dollars," she said. I handed her a ten, smiled and walked away. "You've got change coming," she called out.

"That's okay," I called back. "It's a donation." The woman smiled and raised a power fist. I raised one in return, smiling and continuing on.

Crossing Central Park South by the Plaza, I hopped onto the curb and circled around the fountain to the hotel entrance on the back side of the building. I'd been to the Plaza enough times that I used different entrances so as not to appear as a regular visitor. But this time would be different. Days ago I had been introduced to Charlie by Rosie. This was my first call.

I spent the elevator ride brushing out my hair, reapplying lipstick and tugging up stockings that had crept down my legs during the walk. I strolled down the elegant hallway, found the room and knocked, my hand sliding back into the pocket of my suede gaucho pants where I found and fingered the *Woman Power* button.

A man I could name "Mr. Ordinary" opened the door. He was wearing one of the hotel's terrycloth robes and was pink and gleaming. Steam was still coming from the bathroom. "Am I too early?"

"Not at all. Just in time. Please come in," he said, waving his hand into the room. "I took the liberty of ordering some champagne. I hope that's all right."

"That's lovely, Mr. Williams. Thank you," I said, seating myself on the floral setee in front of the polished wood table on which stood the champagne cooler. He sat down beside me, pulling out the bottle and drying it with a serviette. It was a good sized room, a huge bed visible through open French doors.

"Please call me Fred. And your name is?"

"Tess."

"That sounds like a delightfully wild name," he mused, his robe falling off his leg as he reached for the champagne opener, revealing a very pale, hairless, freckled, fleshy thigh. I gave him my practiced coy smile while passing my attention out the window behind the settee. I could see down to the thinning end of the women's march in the street, bits of paper trash trailing the last stragglers as they headed into the park. The sun was setting over the Westside buildings, a rosy glow reflected in their windows. The evening had just begun. It'd be a long time until midnight.

Woman power. I could feel it coming on as I accepted the offered flute of champagne.

ᥫᥫᥫᥫᥫ

For the next several months I alternated between the two escort agencies, eventually spending more time on the higher paying sex services as I gradually got used to it. I'd read about sex workers in European countries, especially Scandinavia, who were accepted as part of the general economy. Services were wanted and services were provided. No one thought too much about it. The women I worked with operated with the same sophisticated efficiency. Like any business, production and profit were key. As I got better at it, I learned to avoid unnecessary time and unpleasantness with the men. I could size up a guy and deliver the goods with a minimum of physical contact and a maximum of material gain. I had regular customers who'd give me lump sum rent payments. I had a car leased to me by someone living far enough away that driving to his condo was cheaper than using cabs. I cashed in gifts of jewelry that might just get stolen off me, but wore the expensive perfumes and clothing. I infrequently went to dinners, bars or Broadway shows at this point. I was in and out of top hotels and penthouse suites like a high-priced plumber stocked with gold pipes and platinum fittings. Always on the move, I had no time to waste. I had power for the first time in my life and used it to manipulate the men I serviced. Nothing happened without my consent. I was making up for the all the boundaries crossed by men in my life by my holding firm to my own preferences and decisions. I never worried about getting hurt. And if someone had tried, I'd have taken them on. Crazy perhaps, but I might have enjoyed it. I kept myself smart, careful and in charge. And either it worked, or I had one hell of a guardian angel. I learned a lot about the trade from girls in the business, but mostly the ambition came from within me, from that old smoldering place in my gut that I transformed into an engine of power and control. I was tougher than ever. I took the advantage and grasped it firmly, like fingers curled around the handle of a gun, safety off. My choice to fire or not. It was the one time in my life I was always calm, strutting casually on New York streets in high-heeled boots, my wolf soul prancing happily alongside me, tongue out and drooling.

I gave Cole the stories I wanted to tell him for his book and he wrote them down. I found a couple of girls for him to interview; he listened and wrote their stories down. Gradually he built these stories one onto another and created a picture of the modern call girl, or at least his understanding and fantasy of what that was. It wasn't entirely accurate, but I didn't care. He was busy, he wasn't hurting me, we were getting along okay and the book was getting good enough that it just might sell. By this time he knew about the sex I was providing and didn't even care. He pretended, and wrote, that I liked it – or at least that my character in his book liked it. He liked having sex with his hooker-wife, and I serviced him too. He complained a few times that he wasn't getting any outside sex, still needing to embolden his frail ego. So without him knowing, I paid a couple of girls who worked out of their apartments to have sex with him, asking them to pretend like they wanted it from him.

And they gave him good interviews for his book, too.

Winter came. I took a work break over Christmas. I wanted to enjoy the holiday. I'd never had money for frivolous Christmas shopping. I bought myself a camel hair coat with a huge fake fur collar and a rabbit fur hat. I bought good leather boots and a baby blue cashmere mini-dress. Cole and I visited my parents in New Jersey and brought them gifts. I gave them nice things for the house and expensive clothes. I gave Mom an autoharp. She didn't play it for years. After seeing me in camel and rabbit apparel and after opening her presents, she knew something was up. Cole's writing couldn't be selling that well. I was as animated on that visit home as a wooden character in a cuckoo clock at midnight, gesturing and moving and talking with a confidence she'd never seen. Of course the cocaine helped. Something had happened to her daughter that she couldn't ask about. She sat in her blue padded rocker with the autoharp silent on her lap, looking at me and suspecting, her lips stretched over her teeth in a failed attempt to smile. She wouldn't ask and I wouldn't tell. Merry Christmas, Mom. I'm a grown up now.

᠁᠁᠁᠁᠁

After the holidays, work resumed: Hooking for me, writing for Cole. His mood completely swung around again. He was animated and happy. He had purpose and he worked hard at the book. He started getting outside more, walking and browsing in bookstores. He found a comics shop and brought home some old issues with superheroes. He made popcorn and sat cross-legged on the bear rugs reading them like a kid and laughing. "Hey babe, you gotta see this!" he'd call out. He was engaged again and I was glad to see that.

Over the next few months my confidence grew to fit how bold I'd become. I began to feel proud of myself, even liking myself. When I was with men who had some class I felt taller and physically stronger. I was poised and managed a womanly charm.

I was now seeing Jerry frequently, one of my calls who I didn't mind. He was certainly old, seventy-five years to my twenty-five, but very sweet and he wanted to give me a nice time. He always had something for me to eat, some odd Jewish thing, the name of which I loved hearing him pronounce. "I made you some nice Gefilte fish," he said on one visit with him. "Whitefish, not too much matzo," he added as he shuffled around his kitchen in his comfy slippers. I took my usual seat at his small table and he served me the perfectly formed patties with a side of horseradish. He sat down opposite me and watched me eat while he opened and poured us both some wine. "Pinot Blanc. I know you like a dry wine. A little fruity, but it goes with the fish," he said, the pale skin on his lean face wrinkling into a smile as his light blue eyes looked into mine. "Eat, eat, and then I'll show you my new sculpture. It isn't fired or glazed yet. I haven't been to the senior center to use their kiln." He prattled on while I ate, words rolling along endlessly like a Yiddish Proust: "… a   guy I play bridge with, oy, what a headache, not like Harry, he's a mensch, but Saul, Saul's an unmensch …"

When I finished the very delicate fish, well-seasoned with just the right amount of onion, he took me by the hand and guided me into his living room.

There on his baby grand piano sat a little clay bird perched on a clay branch. "Jerry, that's beautiful," I said, meaning it.

"It's a bluebird," he said, the long fingers on his frail hand gently running down the bird's sloping back. "It's singing, can you tell?" He tilted his face at me, at the same angle as the bird's head was tilted, and opened his mouth.

"Why, yes! His beak is open. How sweet."

"Her beak." He chuckled as he said this. "Females, always females. I have no use for males. Females are the delicate ones."

Jerry did love women. At his age he was still smitten with them. He'd told me all about his wild days as a young man, courting several women at once. He'd been married twice, though both had died. His second wife was a prostitute before they married, something he was proud of. He'd loved her for her earthiness and her honesty, telling me he'd never known anyone so wisely in touch with herself. He still grieved her passing.

"I want to make a sculpture of you someday," he said, bringing in more wine from the kitchen and handing me my glass. "I want to pose you naked. Would you mind?" He turned to glance at me, pausing in closing the curtains to speak, also closing the tremendous view of the Hudson River, tiny lights twinkling on the other side, a freighter silently heading north, its lights casting long beams on the water.

"I wouldn't mind at all, Jerry. That'd be nice." I sat down on his elegant, silk threaded couch, my toes curling into the soft white carpet and leaned back against the cushions, the wine and his easy conversation making me nicely woozy. I always felt safe at Jerry's.

He sat down beside me, tugging up the knees of his grey trousers. "I'll have to photograph you first so I have an image of you to work with when you're not here. Nothing dirty," he winked. "Just a nice innocent pose. Like a mermaid. That's how I see you. Like a beautiful mermaid sunning herself on the shore." Smiling, he put a hand on my knee and snuggled closer.

Jerry was the most benign and easygoing man I saw. Others could be very demanding. I'd traveled more than a half hour recently through thick traffic on a very snowy night to reach the apartment of a man I'd never seen before who, on greeting me at his door, complained bitterly of his disappointment.

"I said I wanted someone with a dancer's body," he griped. "I don't mean to insult you. You're very pretty and all, but that's no dancer's body," he said, gesturing at my full breasts.

"I'm so sorry you're upset. I'll take care of it." I called Charlie and explained the problem as discreetly as I could as the man could hear me.

"Dancer's body, my ass," Charlie replied. "None of my girls are flat chested for Christ's sake. Who the hell wants no tits?"

"Perhaps Laura is available?" I hoped. She was also not flat chested, but she was very tall and willowy so her curves weren't as obvious as mine and she moved like a ghost.

"She's still got thirty minutes," Charlie answered. "Just tell the asshole she'll be there in half an hour. She's not far away. You take the call over on Park and Seventy-fourth. Hampton Towers. It's on the corner.

Name's Fred Sevino. The doorman will send you up. Call me when you get there."

I thanked Charlie, hung up the art deco phone and turned to the man, now standing over by his wet bar, an ornate mirror reflecting his torso in an unbuttoned gabardine shirt that revealed a smooth, hairless chest I hadn't noticed before. He was smoking a long, thin cigar and whirling cognac in a huge snifter, looking aggrieved. I wondered if he was gay and in heavy denial. A flat chested woman with no hips would be a bearable alternative to that still hidden desire.

"Not to worry, sir. I've requested Laura for you. I think you'll find her much to your liking."

"I'm sorry to make such a fuss," he said, taking a quick sip. "It's just ... it's what I want," he flustered.

"There's no need to explain. I completely understand. We're a service, after all. We aim to please," I smiled, putting on my camel coat and rabbit hat. "Laura will be here in half an hour."

"Thank you," he said, stubbing out his cigar and sailing across the room to see me to the door. "Here's something for your trouble. At least for your cab fare." He managed a smile while opening the door, looking much relieved.

"Well, that's very kind of you." I gracefully took the folded bill and slid out into the hall, grateful to be leaving. Once in the elevator I unfolded the fifty-dollar bill and tucked it in my purse next to that evening's thickening take.

Still other men I saw had emotional problems they were working out or some other need for which a sex worker was the best choice. There was the wealthy middle-aged Chinese man I'd seen who, after an evening of cocktails and quick, almost ritualized sex in the sumptuous bedroom of his elegant apartment, told me he wanted to introduce his three sons to sex. These virgins were ages seventeen, nineteen and twenty. I was to start with the oldest. From him telling me this, I realized that his own sex with me had been something of an interview for the job. I agreed and saw the eldest son the following week in the same apartment, apparently the man's city apartment for business, the house he actually lived in situated elsewhere, probably with a wife in it out in a wealthy suburb. I'd yet to meet the two younger sons, but if they were as polite and well-mannered as their big brother, I was fortunate to have the work.

Some men clearly had more serious emotional issues. I counseled a number of them about troubled marriages, worked out sexual dysfunctions and had my share of beastly-looking, sexually frustrated men. If I'd had a psychotherapist's license I wouldn't be making as much money. With some of these men, I genuinely felt good about helping them.

But on the whole, most nights were pretty forgettable. After a while the men looked the same, sounded the same, and wanted the same. I began to drink too much and was hitting the cocaine a little hard, but I still felt strong. Gradually I got to a plateau of confidence and it seemed I could comfortably stay there. It was like I'd passed the crest of a hill and I just wanted to coast down, which I did for a long time. I'd work maybe four calls a night, stopping for a drink, a cup of coffee or an ice cream in between. I'd meet some of the girls for an after-work dinner or I'd stop by my favorite pizza parlor and get a slice with everything on it but anchovies. I hate anchovies.

Sometimes the guy would see me coming down the street and have the slice ready for me when I got to his little corner shop.

After a few seasons passed, hooking got routine and I was numbing out. Being strong felt satisfying and familiar. I knew how to handle myself better, and I was getting better at creating boundaries. I'd been able to play things out more the way I wanted them to happen. As I understood it much later on, I was recreating the past with new endings – my endings. Prostitution was an odd but effective role-playing therapy to stumble upon. Each scene was a small play and I was the playwright and lead actress, the men responding to my lines. And if they didn't follow the script, I'd ignore them and change the scene to my liking.

But after a time I realized I wanted to stop hooking. I didn't need it anymore. I'd achieved what I wanted. And there's only so much sex you can perform. It was wearing on me. One more blow job and my head might explode. I wanted out.

"Cole, I'm done with the service. I've had enough," I announced.

"You can't stop now babe. I'm well into the book but I need time to finish it. Trust me. This thing will sell. I've got a good feeling about it. But I have to finish it before I can show it to anyone. Give me just a little more time."

"How much time?" I asked. "I've made enough to hold us a while, but it won't last forever."

"Well, how about you just slow down some then?" he asked hopefully. "I promise. I'm working hard on it, but I've got lots of character development still to do and tons of notes for a couple of new characters. A couple of month maybe."

I kept going, though I did tell Anthony and Charlie I wanted to slow down. I took nights off. I insisted to Cole that we get out together more often, have dinner and go to the movies. I also suggested I help him more on the book. I read some of the chapters and gave input. I gave him more information and invented some new stories. I did anything I could to make the thing write itself faster. I also found I had a lot to say.

"You know, Cole, I think you've focused way too much on sex in the book," I said one day while he was writing at the dining table and I was cleaning the apartment.

"How so?"

"Well, the sex is really much more irrelevant than you've portrayed it. Especially for the women. This isn't something they enjoy. Maybe a couple of the women you've interviewed have expressed some degree of satisfaction with it, but mostly what's gratifying for these women is the feeling of being in charge – in charge of the sex and in charge of their lives. They have money power and sexual power where before they'd felt very un-empowered," I said, waving a roll of paper towels in the air. "A lot of them come from poor homes or middle class families where their fathers ruled with a heavy hand especially against the mothers and daughters. I don't think you've emphasized that kind of aspect enough."

"Tell me, then," Cole said. "Describe some of their circumstances to me and how what you're saying fits in."

"Well, take Sadie, for instance." Sadie was a woman I'm met a few months back who I'd introduced Cole to over drinks one night but he hadn't interviewed. "She's from what most people call a white trash background. She grew up in a trailer park somewhere in south Jersey with two sisters and three older brothers." I was spraying antibacterial cleaner around the table where Cole was working, wiping it energetically with towels as I talked. "It was the classic scene: Her dad was a drunk, he beat her mother, he threatened the girls, and the boys took after him by humiliating their sisters and even their mother. Sadie was the youngest." It occurred to me while I was telling him this how unusual it was for one of the girls to be so open about her history. I paused to wonder why, but went on, moving my cleaning frenzy to the bookshelves. "She ended up on drugs, stealing money from her father's wallet. Then as a teenager she started trading sex for drugs. Eventually she got into the city but was so strung out she got counseling for the drugs and got clean. But she didn't give up hooking," I said, turning to look at Cole who was fixed against his chair in fascination. "Now she's earning top dollar and her specialty is foot freaks. They always pay a lot. Especially the politicians. It's shut-up money."

"Sadie? That little blond I met?" Cole said, surprised.

"Yeah." Sadie was not quite five- feet tall, had wispy platinum hair and an angelic face. She looked like a stiff wind would send her flying. She always wore four-inch spike heels or big platform shoes. She had a closet full of shoes of every color and type that looked great on her small feet at the end of her thin, shapely legs. Her shortness was in her torso, not her legs. Wearing mini-dresses in bright royal colors, her legs were strikingly attractive and it was little wonder the foot freaks favored her. They probably didn't even notice her rather large breasts.

"Sadie's got'em by the balls. She's worked very hard at it. She spent a fortune on clothes, on her hair and makeup and on her nails. She has her legs waxed regularly and her toenails buffed, polished and glossed like jewels. She had a nose job, too. Sadie's made herself perfect." I was now concentrated on cleaning my collection of rabbit figurines on the middle shelf. "She hasn't seen her family in years and acts like they're dead, though she misses her sisters and wants to look them up sometime. She's made big bucks and lives in a penthouse overlooking Central Park that she had a designer decorate to look like a Japanese house with paper partitions, low tables, bamboo light fixtures and woven grass mats." I stopped cleaning the rabbits and just looked at them, thinking about the one time I'd gone to Sadie's apartment. She'd looked so young and fragile then, dressed daintily in a beautiful silk Japanese dressing gown, standing against the soft light of a paper lantern. You'd never guess her strength. "When she's not working," I started up again, not talking so fast this time, "Sadie studies flower arranging and watercolor painting and she knows how to perform a traditional tea ceremony. She's done it for me. She's amazing. Totally self-created, Sadie is a perfect example of the kind of self-empowerment I'm talking about. She's also learning some martial arts thing and if I was a man I wouldn't mess with her. She's a petite powerhouse from platinum head to polished toe. She's come a long way from the trailer park and she's making sure she never goes back. She even talks about buying the fucking place someday and tearing it down to make a park she'd donate to the community."

"Really," Cole said, without a questioning inflection. "From looking at her, I had no idea she could kick ass like that," he laughed. "She was so soft spoken that night."

"Yeah, well a lot of girls are like that. Once you start feeling that kind of confidence you don't need to create attention for yourself." Cole was writing notes again. As I watched him, I realized I'd been talking about myself more than any one of the girls I knew. Not that Cole saw that. He'd never commented on any change in me. I don't think he'd seen any. At least he hadn't said anything. What I also realized in talking about Sadie was how fully empowered she really was. Maybe living on her own had something to do with it. She didn't answer to or have to please anyone. I envied her freedom to be herself.

Cole did start including me even more in the writing of his book, asking me to read over chapters and make more suggestions about the text. I also had him talk to a couple of the girls he'd interviewed again, telling him some specific questions to ask that I knew would come with interesting answers the girls wouldn't mind sharing. The book started to have a more serious, real feel to me. The characters were becoming fleshy and whole. People had no idea what really went on in this secret little world. The women's movement wasn't just happening in street protests or in elite circles of advocates who put their ideas in print. It was happening in the minds of all women who felt betrayed and put down. Between birth control pills and the coming reality of sperm banks, women were becoming aware of their ability to control reproduction and, ultimately, sex, as well as the waning power of men over their lives. They had choices. They could get educations, have jobs and finance their own lives at their own pace. In time, I at least thought, a matriarchy of strong, cooperative, peaceful, nurturing females would replace the long-standing survivalist, rugged individual, greedy, sex-addled, artery-hardened, pugilistic patriarchy. Thanks for the memories, boys. Thanks for the animal skins, the winter shelters and the machines you built. But you've gone way overboard and look at the mess you've made. Step aside. Our time has come.

I began to resent having to keep hooking. It'd served its purpose. I was losing control. It wasn't my choice anymore. It was Cole's. He was essentially pimping me. Being with men got more distasteful. The confidence I'd built up was being deadened by the repetitiousness of the work. I drank more. I did more cocaine. I started using downers to get through some nights. I sat alone in bars or just walked the streets sometimes; finding a park bench to sit on and watch night fall. *This is crazy*, I thought. *Why the fuck am I still doing this? Just two more months, Cole had said. It had been three so far.*

"Good news!" Cole brightly greeted me one evening. "I showed the first hundred pages of the book to a literary agent and she likes it! I just have to finish editing the next hundred pages and I might get an advance on publishing it. Isn't that great?" he chirped.

It was, in fact, great, but I felt unaffected by his enthusiasm. Obviously I still had to work to keep us afloat a while longer. The money was too good and there was no other way I could make as much to cover our expenses, especially since Cole had long before ceased writing and selling any short stories. I'd been irregularly working, taking long breaks but not motivated to do anything with myself. The most I'd done to keep from slowly going mad was pick up a five thousand piece jigsaw puzzle of a Brueghel painting called *Netherlandish Proverbs*. I distracted myself with the complicated scenes of peasants doing all the things that comprised well known proverbs. I spent hours on the floor of our apartment putting the pieces together and guessing at the proverbs, which were listed on the inside cover of the box. Men gutted pigs while women gossiped. A man beat his head against a brick wall while a woman strangled the devil. And on and on it went. My dreams during sleep became broken up into jigsaw patterns and brilliant colors of currant red, burnished gold and royal blue. And the moon shined over it all. I was possessed by the puzzle, thrilled by each discovery of a piece long sought after by combing my fingers through the box of still unsorted pieces or staring at the colored groupings of pieces laid out on the dining room table – green leaves, brown buildings, yellow straw. Slowly the pieces fit together. I finally saw the blue hat over the face of a man standing in the middle of all the chaos looking bewildered. Perhaps it was the artist's comical self-portrait.

One morning I looked up from my puzzle and sat watching Cole biting his fingernails as he worked on the book. Nail biting meant heavy concentration.

"Cole, I'm done. I won't do any more hooking. I've made enough money to last us another month. You've got that one month to finish editing the pages."

"Yeah, yeah, okay babe. It'll be done," he said,

glancing at me and forcing a tight smile. I could use help retyping some of the edited pages though."

"Yeah, okay. I'll do it." I returned to the puzzle. The woman in red placed the blue cloak over the man with the walking stick. *Ah yes, I see, over there ... 'a bird in the hand' ... but there, why is that man's ass sticking out a window?*

"You know, babe," Cole suddenly said. "This will all be worth it. I'm telling you. This book will sell and you'll never have to make money again. I'll take over. I know I can. And I'll not only provide for you, I'll make it great. This is just the beginning, babe. There's lots to come," he said, lifting himself out of his chair and swinging his arms wide. "I've got other books in my head. I've been thinking about it a lot. I've got a terrific idea for a science-fantasy book," he said, spinning around to face me. "Just you wait. I promise. I really do. We'll be able to travel like we've always wanted to. I'll take you to Europe," he said, swooping down onto the rug beside me and the puzzle, his hand grabbing at a shank of his hair. "We'll do it all: London, Paris, Berlin, Zurich, Venice and Rome. It'll be ours! We'll go to the opera, we'll dance in the clubs, we'll swim in the Mediterranean. Just help me finish this. You'll see."

I just stared at him. He had a jigsaw puzzle look. His face was pieced together and his royal blue shirt gave off a golden shine as the afternoon light tilted in through the window. It was impossible not to believe him; he was so sure and enthusiastic. His eyes were dancing in their familiar way when he was excited. He meant everything he said and I felt he could do it. He really could. His passion for life would make it happen because he avidly wanted to succeed and enjoy the world he loved living in. In that moment, I loved him again. I understood him. He was working through his own problems and fears just like I was. We were both growing up and learning and we were still so young. We were a team and we'd make it. I believed in his dream and it could be mine, too. I had to give him a chance.

"Yes, I'll help. I think you mean it and I know you've been working hard. I'll help you – and us."

"I love you, babe," he said, leaning over and kissing me for the first time in a long while.

"I love you, too," I found myself saying. And I meant it.

He gently pushed me to the floor and we descended onto the puzzle. As he unbuttoned my blouse and pulled it away, its leaf green sleeve swept the mound of red pieces into the air, rubies twinkling in the streaming light as we laughed.

ᑫᑫᑫᑫᑫ

By late summer, Cole had finished and submitted the required editing on the book and received a contract for publication. He was flying high. Now we just had to wait for the advance payment of twenty thousand dollars. It was a small fortune to us. I'd also saved a few thousand, which I'd squirreled away.

"This is so fabulous, babe! We're set! It'll take me no time to finish the book and there'll be more money coming. I'm already really psyched for the next project, too!"

We were sitting at the bar at Sign of the Dove, our favorite piano bar, where we'd gone to celebrate his success. It was such an elegant place, all mirrors and huge sprays of flowers in vases. I'd dressed in my cashmere sweater and tweed riding skirt, its voluminous folds always making me feel classy. The piano music was lovely and I just felt good sitting there. I'd only been here with Cole and thought of it as our place. He took off his glasses, laying them on the bar. Blue eyes dancing, he leaned in to me and gave me a light kiss, followed by one of his sweet smiles, the one where he tilted his head to the side and his mouth slanted upward a little.

"I promised you this would happen. I know I've owed it to you, and now it's real. It's all about our future now. We can do anything, go anywhere." He signaled the bartender for two more drinks. Wiping his glasses clean and putting them back on, he suddenly looked straight at me. "What do you say we get out of New York, babe. I'm done with this place for now. How about you?"

"I've been done with it for a long time," I laughed. I'd be real happy to blow this pop stand. What do you have in mind?"

His tilted smile reappeared. "How about we leave the country for a while? What would you say to that?"

"Mexico," I said without hesitation. "I'd love to go there." Images swirled through my head of hot red hibiscus, diamond sparkled sand, waving green palm fronds and clear turquois water. A postcard paradise.

"On the coast somewhere?" Cole said, getting as excited as I was.

"Yes, the coast. I have no idea what's on one or the other of them." I laughed at the thought of exploring our options. It would be so freeing for both of us.

"Well, then let's just check it out!" he said, giving

my shoulder a gentle squeeze. I started to tear at the feel of his tenderness. He traced his finger along my cheek to catch a falling droplet. "Wow, babe." I felt the smooth suede of his shirt sleeve against my neck as he ran his arm under my hair and around my shoulder.

"It's just been such a strain for so long," I said, blowing my nose on the cocktail napkin. "It's hard to imagine being able to leave all of it. I mean there've been some good times, too, but I was really beginning to wonder if we'd just be in these lives forever."

"I know. It's over now. It'll be like it used to be. Like it was in Saugerties, only way better. It'll be Mexico for god's sake, babe! Sun and surf and Sangria all the time!"

"Sounds really good," I said, now smiling again. *Amazingly good*, I thought. I felt more tears coming at the idea of Cole and I being able to find each other again. He can be a real shit sometimes, but so can I. *It'll be different now.*

"Hey, let's get over to the bookstore before it closes and find a travel guide. We've got to decide which coast we'll live on!" We paid up, slid off our stools and headed out. Cole surreptitiously plucked a lily out of the immense flower arrangement near the door and handed it to me as we left.

The decision to leave having been made, the next couple of months went quickly. We planned to arrive in Mexico with little more than our bags and Cole's typewriter. To accomplish this, we had to sell or store the things we had, which wasn't much, but it all had to go somewhere. I gave things away to the girls I'd worked with, Cole sold all but his most treasured books to the used book store, we donated lots of stuff, and what we wanted to keep we'd store at my parents' house. Before the next month's rent was due, we loaded the leased car and a small trailer and left for New Jersey.

Over the following month we stayed with Mom and Dad while we made definite travel plans, studied some Spanish, got passports and vaccinations and reduced our belongings to summer clothes and the few things we'd need for travelling.

Cole also had to keep working on the book. He owed his agent and the publisher the remainder of the edited pages after we got the check for the book advance. He worked intensely on it, using the desk in the upstairs den. We'd told Mom and Dad very little about the book, saying it was just a story based on popular culture that had been written as a commercial seller. Cole focused on telling them about his next project, the science fantasy novel, which he said would be a true literary effort. Nevertheless, Mom and Dad were excited that he'd sold a book at all. On an afternoon when Cole and I were downtown buying some new clothes for the trip, parental curiosity peaked and they went into the den to see if any of the book was there to read. Cole had unfortunately not made a great effort to hide it and the chapter he was editing was in easy view.

When we returned from shopping, grim-faced parents greeted us from the living room. "Lily, we have to talk," Mom said through lips taut over teeth, her hands frozen on the arms of her rocking chair. Dad was similarly unmoving in his chair.

"Sure, Mom, what's up?"

"Don't think it rude of us, but our curiosity about your book got the best of us and we read the chapter that was laying in a folder on the desk upstairs."

"Oh, I see," I said, sinking down onto the couch. Cole stood immobile in the hallway, still gripping our packages.

"Lily, does any of this book have to do with you?" Mom asked. I considered lying, but couldn't bring myself to do so. This was too heavy to avoid honesty. I hoped, in the end, that I could make sense of it all for them. I hesitated a long time before answering her and when I did I couldn't look at her.

"Yes," I said, my head bent down, my hands shifting awkwardly in my lap. "But it's not as bad as it sounds," I said, finally looking at her. Her eyes were closed, obviously working hard to keep her composure. I glanced quickly over at Dad who was staring down, his hands curled into fists on his lap. "It's mostly made up," I said, struggling to continue. "Some of it's loosely based on real experiences I had just to research a project we thought would sell. But mostly Cole either interviewed some women we reached through an ad in the newspaper or we made it up completely." *A few lies just to make things easier would be okay*, I thought.

Mom was now staring at Cole. "I'm sorry you read the chapters," he offered. "What Lily's saying is true. Please believe her. I think it's best if I stay out of this. I'll be upstairs if you need me, Lily," he said, heading for the stairs.

Dad watched him go, got up from his chair and left the house. Mom and I were left alone.

"What do you mean by 'some experiences' were yours, Lily?"

I thought hard before answering. I wanted to be

honest, but I didn't want to hurt either Mom or Dad in any way. "I worked briefly for an escort service," I said, leaving out the rest of it. It'd be enough for them to accept that. "I just acted as a date for dinner or a theater show. There was nothing to it, really, Mom."

"What about the sex described in the book? Did you have sex with these men?"

"No, I didn't," I lied. "All that information came from the women Cole interviewed. Plus he did some research on how morals are changing for women," I lied again.

"Why would you even think about doing something like this though, Lily? There are other books for Cole to write, I'm sure. Why this? Did Cole talk you into it? That's what Dad thinks. He's too angry right now to even be here. You're lucky he hasn't thrown Cole out of the house. I told him we should talk to you first and find out what had gone on."

"Cole didn't talk me into it. It was my idea. I thought it might make a good book. I was looking at it like I was being an investigative journalist," I said, almost believing myself.

"But you did go on dates with these men, didn't you? How could you possibly do that?" She had at least sat back in her chair and her expression was less strained. She seemed more concerned now.

"It wasn't difficult, Mom," I found myself saying, my own feelings intensifying. I wanted to tell her how I really felt. I wanted to talk about a lot of things having to do with why I might want to prostitute myself, the hell with just being a female escort. *Fuck that,* I thought. But I kept calm, if defensive.

"I needed to do it. You don't know all the things

that have happened to me. I've never told you," I said, my voice rising. "But there are reasons why it felt right to do it. I needed to feel some control over these men and that's what this did for me. I may have been paid, but I felt I was in charge. It was the first time I'd ever felt like that."

"What things have you never told me, Lily?" She'd gotten out of her chair and was now sitting down on the couch beside me. I let it all out in a stream of disconnected words, but it was all there: The father at the birthday party, my flute teacher, the doctor, all the men over the years who'd felt me up in subways and elevators, the men who'd hooted and howled at me on the street, the constant looks and comments, the seemingly unending harassment and manipulation and how it had made me feel trashy, ashamed and afraid. I'd needed to get back at them, I told her. "I needed to have control over them, not have them trying to control me," I said, finally. She reached out a hand and put it on my knee.

"Lily, I'm so sorry. I had no idea. I always wondered about some things though. It makes sense now." She leaned back and took a long breath. "I didn't do right by you."

She looked so small pressed against the back of the couch. She was wearing one of her ancient sweaters, the one with the big brocade flower sewn on the front, the stitching coming loose in places. She'd gotten older. I looked down at her hands, full of dark veins and wrinkles now, though her fingers were still long and graceful and her nails nicely shaped. I smoothed the lines on her hand with my finger. "Well, I haven't exactly made things easy for you, Mom. I never came to you with any of these things. I kept it all to myself. How could you have known?"

"Mothers should know." We sat silently for a few moments. I felt her nearness and the sorrow between us. "I should at least have known to ask. I'm afraid I wasn't much help to you. I didn't explain things, not that my mother explained anything to me. I had to figure it out by myself. But I'm sorry I wasn't there for you when you needed me."

I was stunned by her insight and admission after all this time. It validated me and so much of the bad feeling I'd had toward her wafted away like white-feathered dandelion seeds. She was a very intuitive woman, a strength and a voice within her that I thought hadn't been sufficiently expressed in her life, kept silenced by her low self-esteem and dependency.

"Well, it's all behind us now," I said softly, not unmindful of the words I'd chosen. I leaned back and we looked across the couch at each other. "The book's finished. It's written under a false name. We've got the advance money for it and we're ready to move on. Things'll be fine." I looked away for a moment and then back at her again. "I learned a lot from what I did. I learned that I can be strong and take care of myself. I learned that I like myself, Mom. I've never really felt that before."

"Oh, my beautiful little girl. How could someone like you not like herself? But I do understand. It took me a long time to like myself. But I don't think life's meant to be easy. It's the hard things that give us grace." She paused. "We almost named you Grace, have I ever told you that?

"No. That's a nice name."

"Dad thought of it. But Lily is the old family

name and so we chose that. But you have grace and always have. After all these years, I'm beginning to understand why. You've always taken the road less traveled – the more spiritual journey."

Over the next few weeks, the emotional maelstrom that the book created slowly got resolved. Mom talked Dad out of banishing Cole. Cole had been perturbed by what he'd seen as an invasion of privacy in their reading his book, but was talked by me out of staying angry. Dad and Cole walked circles around each other for a while like angry dogs, but gradually became better tempered through conversations about politics and literature. Mom and I spent time going through old photos of family vacations and Christmases years ago. Dad eventually made Cole pay by sending him a bill, once we were in Mexico, for six hundred dollars' worth of his food and laundry services while he'd stayed at the house. I thought it was such a typically Scottish thing to do. So trifling, but it was what worked for Dad. Cole actually felt better by paying it, feeling he'd at least symbolically made up for any harm Dad still worried he may have caused me.

Cole and I studied maps and guide books about Mexico and decided to go first to Mexico City and then check out Puerto Vallarta on the Pacific coast. We practiced more Spanish. We finished readying ourselves for the trip with plane tickets for just after Christmas. The holiday came and went; so much more enjoyable than the one the year before. No fancy gifts this time. Mom made me a pretty sundress and gave Cole a small blank notebook, having made a cloth cover for it out of his family's Irish plaid. Dad gave me a little handpainted covered dish he'd found with rose buds all over it, telling me it was for me to keep my dreams in. His gift for Cole was a leather case he'd had, but never used, for Cole's passport and travel documents. We gave Mom a bonsai tree to take care of and for Dad a laughing Buddha to keep on his reading table, both gifts from a Japanese store in town.

The day came to leave and Cole and I finished the last of our packing. As I came up from the laundry room with the final clothes we were taking, I passed through the kitchen where Mom was fixing lunch. Dad came over to me, it seemed, to help me with the laundry, but instead he said "We're going to miss our little girl so much. I've just got to have one last taste of piggy meat," and planted his mouth once again on my neck.

"Don't do that!" Mom cautioned him. "She's a grown woman and that just isn't right. That's an erogenous zone, for heaven's sake. You must know that, don't you?"

I don't know who was more shocked, me or Dad. We both just froze and looked at her. "Well, I'm … I'm sorry," Dad said. He shuffled over to sit down at the lunch table, his head bending over and seeming to fold into his large body as his weight sagged onto the chair. "Mom's right, Lily. I shouldn't treat you like a child or bother you." He was gazing at a point vaguely in front of him. He could've been a big clown sitting at his dressing table after the circus show, the heavy makeup not hiding his fatigue or maybe sadness that the show was over and he had to face himself again.

"That's okay, Dad. I won't make you go down to the garden to eat worms." I kissed him on the top of his now balding head.

"Well, thank you for that. But just so you know, I'd be willing to dig through the snow and frozen ground to find them and eat them for you if you want me to. That's how much I love you." He looked up, but not right at me. I could see that his eyes were glassy with tears. I kissed his cheek and gave him a hug with my free arm.

"No need, Dad. I love you just the way you are, faults and all." I knew I meant it. In recent years I'd finally given up on being angry at him, had surrendered to the fact that he wasn't likely to change at his age or ever. Why not just let an old man go. He'd had his own challenges and done the best he could and I loved him for all the comfort he'd given me and for what he'd made of himself: A brilliant, educated, cultivated world citizen, even though he shared a body with a narcissistic, forever needy old grump.

Turning to Mom, I gave her one of the biggest smiles my mouth could manage. After all these years, she'd finally spoken up and challenged Dad for me. I was so grateful and so proud of her. She smiled back and playfully held her chin up, recognizing her own courage. She looked at least half a foot taller. She may not have prepared me much for adult life, or even taught me much basic self-care, but I loved her then. She was teaching me that we all do what we can, that we all have to help ourselves grow up at some points and that it may take a lifetime.

♋♋♋♋♋♋

We'd flown almost thirteen hours to Mexico

City. As it was early January, the ground we'd left on was deep snow-covered. But we'd crossed the gulf and were now flying over central Mexico. We could see hills and valleys covered with trees, even pine trees. I hadn't expected it to be so green and lush. I'd pictured more of an extension of Texas or Arizona with patchy verdant areas. I did expect it to be warmer though, and both Cole and I had changed into summer clothes mid-flight, with jackets for any January chill.

On landing, as we stepped down the gangway onto the tarmac, the feel of fresh warm air tinged with humidity was a thrilling relief from the dry, cold winter air of the Northeast.

"This is so far out, Cole. I can't believe how good this feels."

"Oh, yeah," was all he said. I couldn't see his eyes behind his new prescription sunglasses but his smile was beaming as he nodded at me and rolled up his shirt sleeves.

Grabbing our few bags, we sped through customs and got a cab. On the ride to the hotel we went from the barren airport grounds down dusty roads that gradually broadened into city streets crisscrossing through blocks of buildings that got taller as we neared the city center. We'd be there for two nights before heading to Puerto Vallarta on the coast. We'd arrived on January sixth, Dia de Reyes – Kings Day. That night, during dinner on the hotel's top floor, blinding streaks of celebratory fireworks shot off the roof and plummeted down outside the windows surrounding the restaurant. From our table, this sparkling shower seemed to come right out of the sky.

"We've arrived, babe. We really have." He lifted his glass towards me. "Here's to the most beautiful American woman in this city tonight."

"And to the best American writer in this city tonight," I added, raising my glass to his, lovely Spanish guitar music playing in the background nicely elevating the effect.

That meal was the best I ever had in Mexico, just from my own excitement and happiness to be on a new adventure and, hopefully, a new journey for Cole and me. My introduction to chicken molé, a spicy chocolate sauce, wasn't bad either. I was going to like this country very much.

A few tequilas after dinner, we decided to go dancing in a disco down the street from the hotel. I'd put on my bright red dress with the fitted bodice and flowing knee-length skirt. Cole spent the night alternating his stare between my tits and my face before we finally headed back to the hotel to make love under a slow-moving ceiling fan, a mariachi band making its way down the street outside our window.

"I learned in the guidebook that mariachi is a musical form created in the colonial period," I said.

"Please, babe, I'm in the middle of something here," Cole joked as his penetration of me deepened.

"And it began in Jalisco, the section of Mexico where Puerto Vallarta is," I added, now laughing.

"Why that's just fascinating," Cole kidded as he flipped us over so I was on top. "Now get to work, babe. I'm enjoying the hell out of this." As was I. We hadn't had this sexy a time together in ages. Cole was even looking into my face. I made it as good for him as he was making it for me.

The next day we slept late, had a continental breakfast in bed and then took a bus for a dusty ride out to the ancient Aztec city of Teotihuacàn and the site of the Pyramid of the Sun. We climbed the steep steps of this immense structure, over two hundred feet to the top. Halfway up, I looked straight out and the perspective made all viewpoints seem equidistant, as if I was as close to the ground as I was to the sky. It was like being in the center of a globe where you could reach out and touch its inner surface. Little wonder the Aztecs were so mystical.

"The steepness of the pyramid was planned for the quick disposal of sacrificed victims. The height of the steps was intentional as only the taller Aztec priests could step up that high," our guide informed our group, which was somewhat dissembled over the steps. "This kept men of lesser status from climbing the pyramid, even though they would have built it, using scaffolding. The priests achieved the climb wearing sizeable headdresses, the weight of which they'd have to balance to keep from toppling over."

"They probably also took hallucinogens," Cole whispered discreetly. "Can you imagine the view they got?"

"Yeah, and when these tripping dudes of high holiness got to the top they killed lots of virgin women," I said, struggling to climb the steps myself. People had generally gotten taller since those days. I'd have hated to miss the view. Then I noticed all the shorter, squatter people waving from below or taking pictures.

"Well, you know, things were a bit different then." At his height, Cole was having no problem with the steps. He reached out a hand to help me up, playfully grabbing my ass as I moved by him. "But you have nothing to fear. I know you're no virgin."

The view from the top was worth all the sweating and dehydration. The feeling of being at the center of the universe was even more powerful. This was certainly the place to worship anything, quite aside from the bloody, still-beating hearts wrenched from their hosts and held high to appease the deities. We sat contemplating in silence for a while. I felt a hint of kinship with the gods, or god, or group mind, or maybe just my higher self from the view of the closeness and unity of all things.

We made the trip back down, me partly on my ass with some hopping carefully between steps, my nails gripping the edges. By the time we got to the ground I was filthy and exhausted, but enthralled.

"Pyramid of the Moon next?" Cole said. I threw handfuls of sand at him and headed for the bus. "Hey, it's smaller!" he yelled.

"I've had my enlightenment for the day, thanks." And I had. It'd been great.

The next day we left Mexico City early for the long bus ride to Guadalajara, our last overnight before the drive to Puerto Vallarta, where the airport had been completed, but we'd decided to take a slower route, allowing our anticipation of reaching the coast to grow. We hired a car and driver for the next day's trip. The man had family near Puerto Vallarta and said he'd easily find passengers for the return trip. The three of us took off in the morning and spent the entire day getting there including stops along the way. The roads were passable, but getting close to the mountains they wound around bends and then natural passages through the hills. There were often trucks loaded with people to pass by and herds of animals in the road. It was slow going but it was great and our driver had the best suggestions for places to eat, drink and browse through small family-run shops that dotted the roads.

I had my first plantains on this drive, the sweet fried bananas I washed down with fresh mango juice. Children peeked out from behind doors to stare at us. We were still among the first American tourists taking this route.

"Hello," I said to one older girl who came over to our table and pointed to my blond hair, reaching out to feel it.

"Cómo te llamas?" I asked, hoping my effort at asking her name in Spanish was right.

"Maria," she giggled and then ran off to join what must have been her little brother and their scrawny goat, its bell clanking as they sped away smiling and laughing.

Once over the mountains we caught our first glimpses of the Pacific Ocean, and on our descent the driver pointed out Banderas Bay and the town of Puerto Vallarta, tiny in the distance. In 1975, it was still mostly a fishing village with nothing taller than the Cathedral of Guadalupe to mark our destination.

Nearing the town, the ocean's salty air got stronger and we could faintly hear the low roaring of the waves crashing on the shore. It'd been a long drive. I was tired, but happy to be finally arriving at this place I'd read so much about.

There was only one road into the village, which led to the center of town on the north side of the Cuale River. The driver worked his way through the quiet streets towards our hotel. The waves were louder; the air heavy with moisture. Late afternoon sun cast a rosy light on the town. I imagined the yellow adobe buildings pulling the heat of the light into their stone, making it warm to the touch. Nearing the beach, the palms crowning the trees swayed in the gentle ocean breeze.

We parked outside our hotel, which was just off the beach, one of the few hotels in the town. The driver helped us bring our bags into the lobby, a simple but very nice room accented with brick and decorative tile.

While Cole checked us in, I walked through the lobby out onto the patio leading to the beach, removing my sandals as I got to the sand, digging in my toes and feeling the remaining heat of the day on the soles of my feet. The warm, moist breeze brushed my cheeks and curled into my hair. I walked to the waves, my skin responding to the salt spray. I closed my eyes and walked until the sand became hard and wet under my feet. The edge of the wave licked my toes and I waded in until the water swished around my ankles. Taking a deep breath, the spray felt as if it was opening my whole body, any tension in my neck and arms falling away. A smile spread over my face as I lifted it skyward.

"Not a bad place to hang out for a while, eh?" Cole slid his arm around my waist. I opened my eyes and looked up at him, the sunset colors reflecting on his face, the sea breeze tossing his hair.

"This was such a good idea."

"Yep. I think so, too." He took my hand. "Let's check out our room. We can have some drinks there before dinner. How does that sound?"

"Fabulous."

We were on an upper floor with a balcony overlooking the ocean. The hotel was old and the room was worn. The walls had cracks behind faded pictures of old Mexico. Wood furniture, beams and window slats were weathered from wind and salt. Both the living room and the bedroom opened onto the balcony. A double bed left little room for an armoire and a dresser, on which rested a flecked mirror, colorful images of Mexico painted on its yellow frame. The white tiles in the bathroom were chipped here and there; an ancient claw foot tub had a rusty drain. A small, but adequate kitchen was set off from the living room by a short wall. I loved it there.

A restaurant waiter brought our margaritas and we took them out onto the balcony where two wrought iron chairs waited for us. We had indeed arrived.

We spent the next couple of weeks on vacation, even taking a weekend trip to Acapulco. The hotel began to feel like home, especially with the kitchen we used when not exploring the restaurants. There was a manageable range of places to eat, drink and dance; tourism still largely in the minds of local municipal officials and land developers. It'd be years before the big hotels were built along with the required attractions and amenities. All we needed was a nice bar, a good restaurant and a dance club.

During the day we'd stroll down the Malecòn, a broad paved walkway along the beach that bordered the town for a mile from our hotel to an old amphitheater at the southern end. Or we'd spend time at the beach or walking through town. Lunch might be corn on a stick bathed in a white sauce, coated in cheese and roasted in foil, which a bright-faced, middle-aged Mexican woman sold from a cart on the bridge over the river. She always seemed to be there.

We gradually relaxed into our surroundings like plants drawing in moisture after a long rain. Cole and I were learning to be friends and even lovers again. I was glad to be alone with him and return the attention he gave me. It'd been awhile since I'd felt like that.

It was also great there wasn't a television in the room or that I'd seen in town. And mercifully, in this very Catholic town, I hadn't seen any pornography for sale. What a relief not to compete with that on a regular basis. It was probably available somewhere, but hopefully there'd be time before Cole sniffed it out. I needed the break. I had my husband back and I was content to be his wife.

Within a few weeks, Cole got started on his next book, a novel. I was satisfied for the time being to lie comfortably on the beach sunbathing, reading, going for long swims in the incredibly warm salt water and ordering pineapple juice from the beach bar. I'd brought books and more were sold at the newsstand and other hotels. The best pastime was just watching the dolphins arcing their way across the waves. I was settling in just fine. I could feel myself slowing down, especially at night as I lay in our big, comfy bed by the window overlooking the beach, the breaking waves pulsing a gentle rhythm into me, sleep coming easily, enticing my soul out for a midnight dance on the sea.

Cole worked in the morning and joined me for lunch. We'd swim and play in the surf before diving onto our towels where he'd tell me the latest development in his story.

"I'm really into this novel, babe. All that research I did at the library in New York? It's paying off. I know exactly where this plot has to go and how to get it there," he said, sitting up cross-legged and cleaning sand off his glasses with his towel. His now tanned chest had just the right amount of hair that gradually lessened and disappeared under his low slung bathing trunks. He was a sexy man.

"This woman? My main character? She's headed for one hell of a ride. With the scientific experiment she's part of she'll start travelling back and forth in time, visiting the life of a woman in the past – seeing what she sees, meeting people in her life. It's fascinating stuff. You gotta read what I've got so far."

"I'd love to. From what you told me about this woman before, I'd like to see how she's coming along. What about her husband? How's he doing?"

"Oh fine, just fine. I feel sorry for what the poor bastard is in for though," he chuckled, laughing, I knew, at the creative power he had over these fictitious lives.

In the afternoon I'd throw a sundress on over my bathing suit and head into town to get food for dinner. Street venders sold fresh vegetables and fruit and the small grocery store had most everything else I ever needed, including locally raised meat, which came with all its parts. Chicken came packaged with the feet sticking out. Once as I was throwing them away, the hotel maid asked if she could have them. I stood there, feet in hand, feeling awkward as hell; the rash American tourist caught disposing the goods. I wrapped them in clean paper and handed them to her, along with an offering of gizzards, which she gratefully took. She'd make soup, she said.

I loved it that things happened slowly in the town and that everyone was always so calm and patient. I wasn't used to that. It took a long time for a sidewalk to get built. Once finished, I still walked in the road until the day I discovered the sidewalk was there. But I missed the workers who'd tipped their floppy hats and called me "Bonita Senorita." They meant it. They were nice guys. I wondered where they'd gone, where they lived.

There were few tourists yet, but they expected more to come. While we were there, the first grand hotel appeared at the edge of town. On the Malecòn I'd often see the same woman selling shell and bead necklaces hanging in a display on her outstretched arm, their colors like those in the beautiful dresses she wore. Her tiny assistant was often with her, huge brown eyes peering from behind long strands of thick black hair. I had nearly a dozen of their necklaces hanging on the dressing table mirror at the hotel, doing my part to help alleviate the poverty I imagined she shared with so many other Mexicans. Perhaps I was wrong, but I doubted it. I wondered how many necklaces she and her daughter could make in a day and how far they'd maybe walked to get here. She was persistent. When the tourists all came, she'd be ready.

I loved the town with its dust, heat and big-faced flowers, its music drifting by along with village sounds and a language slowly becoming familiar to me. I'd been accepted by the people I met in the town, which was important to me. I'd worked at it. I felt a lightness, strength, safety and freedom that I hadn't known for a long time. I wore loose blouses and long skirts and had sand in my hair. And I was more womanly, leaner, browner, blonder and happier than I remembered being in a very long time.

Within several more weeks, though, an ignored fear began to manifest itself. Cole's writing became more intense and so did he. He got more aroused with each new chapter. His characters took hold and began to develop on their own, as he'd explained to me they were apt to do. It was a sign of good writing, he'd said, for them to suggest actions subconsciously to the writer and to begin having lives independent of his intentions. His main character had come alive and Cole was excited by what he called her *enigmatic charms.*

"She's thinking about acting on her own, now. I can feel it happening. Within another chapter or two she'll be the one, not me, deciding when to time-travel. It's becoming more her choice than mine!" he almost squealed.

The more excited Cole got, the more animated and energetic he became. He wanted to stay up late going to clubs and we danced ourselves into exhaustion. He slept shorter hours. I'd wake up and find him on the balcony well into his work for the day. And inevitably, as his anxiety returned so did other impulsive feelings.

Of the regular diners in the hotel restaurant, he'd noticed a young couple about our ages. I noticed him one evening striking up a conversation with the man at the bar and shortly afterwards he'd invited the couple to our table. We'd met plenty of people in town, spending whole evenings over drinks having great conversations about traveling, learning people's histories, and sharing crazy aspirations. But this was different. Or rather, very familiar. I knew what was coming and dreaded it.

"Lily, these are the Bradshaws from Edmonton, Alberta," he enthused as he pulled out a chair for the woman to sit down. "This is Clara," he gestured, "and this is Bill. They're here at the hotel until the end of the month. Isn't that great?"

"How nice," I offered. "What brought you to Mexico all the way from Canada," I asked Clara. "Of course I'm sure it's freezing up there right now."

"We left a new three foot snowfall that was on top of the four feet of packed snow already on the ground," she said. "I love snow, but I couldn't wait to get out of there! With our long winters, you just need to get a break."

"When you start thinking you ought to abandon your car and just lash some huskies to a sled to get to work you know it's time for a weather change," Bill laughed.

"Say, let's get another round of drinks," Cole said, flagging a waiter and placing an order. "Now Bill, tell Lily your ice fishing story." Turning to me he said, "You won't believe this one. I might have to find a place for it in one of my books. It's priceless!"

Cole was rarely quite this gracious with anyone, especially men. As I listened to Bill regale us with the details of hacking and torching his way through the ice, after a long drive to the lake having left his ice drill at home, I stole glances at Clara. What was striking about her was that she looked amazingly like Cole. Her shortish black hair was pinned back and she wore somewhat thick glasses with a black frame. She'd used little makeup on her pale skin and her features were very angular like Cole's Cherokee cheeks. A thin white sweater covered her shoulders, bare in a sleeveless navy dress that was modestly buttoned. During the conversation, it was evident she was very bright and well read. She'd been a literature major in college before now embarking on a graduate degree in library science. She was a female version of Cole, the nerd. Seemingly more intelligent than Bill, she was obviously enthralled with Cole, especially fascinated that he was working on a novel. Though very shy, she flung questions at him about the library research he'd done as a background to his writing. The subject of parapsychology sparked her interest, and she was quick to mention the experiments of J.B. Rhine, whose work meant nothing to me but was very familiar to Cole. He became immediately absorbed in deep dialogue with her about this, while I was left as Bill's audience for a monologue about Edmonton's reputation as the "Gateway to the North" and the future home of what was anticipated to be the world's largest shopping mall.

"Well," Cole said later after we'd detached ourselves from the Canadians and were back in our room. "Nice people, huh?"

"Nice enough. I think you got the better end of the deal though," I said, smiling.

"What do you mean?"

"Well Bill's an amiable fellow, but not the most fascinating. I imagine Clara had more to say."

"Probably, but who cares?" he said.

"The one who gets stuck talking to Bill, that's who."

"Oh, you weren't that stuck were you?"

"Not as stuck as you were on Clara, I guess."

"It wasn't that bad!"

"You got close enough to fog each other's glasses," I said, heading for the bathroom to brush my teeth.

"Oh, now babe. It wasn't like that," Cole insisted. "She had a soft voice. I had to lean close to hear her."

"Funny, I didn't have that problem the few times she spoke to me," I called out.

"Besides, Bill's nice enough looking. Don't you think?" I didn't answer. "You know, we haven't made any real friends here yet. We should invite them to Carlos O'Brien's for dinner."

"What do you mean by 'friends'? They'll be gone by the end of the month," I said, coming from the bathroom. Cole was hanging up his pants in the ornately painted armoire I'd admired since we'd moved into the room. I tried to focus on its intricate designs rather than listen to what I knew he'd probably say next.

"Well, it's enough time for us all to have some fun together. You think they might be into swinging?"

I loved the way the deep red hibiscus turned to gold leaves along the grain of the wood, the dark blue bird to black feathers. "Cole, I'm done with that." I opened the balcony door, felt the fresh breeze waft in and heard a wave break and crash on the shore. The sound of the pounding waves was the most consistent pleasure I'd felt over the weeks. I knew I'd always remember it.

"Hey, babe. It's been awhile. Like you said, they're leaving anyway." His voice was like that of a still tall, but miniature man in the other room. I imagined him standing there in his underwear, putting his tiny shoes under the enormous bed. Another wave crashed.

"What harm can it do?" he said, now large and

hovering at my side, his voice loud again.

Another wave crashed. "A lot of harm, for me." The lights strung in the palm trees gave off enough light for him to see the tears now sliding down my face. "I just thought we'd gotten back to being together, just you and me."

"We are together, babe. And we do things together like we always have." I said nothing and minutes passed. "That's okay. We'll talk about it another time," he said, heading back into the room.

Another wave crashed.

๛๛๛๛๛

For a few days, Cole and I were civil, but didn't talk much. Bill and Clara weren't mentioned. Cole also didn't come down to the beach for a writing break. I kept to myself, but after a while I was lonely. One midday, I gathered my beach stuff and started back to the hotel, hoping we could work things out. Nearing the front of the hotel, I saw Cole and Clara sitting close together under a palm tree by the Malecòn. She was gesturing and Cole was laughing.

I went up to the room for a shower, my mind struggling to rationalize the scene. Cole came back as I was toweling off.

"Hi, babe. Done with the beach for the day?" I didn't answer, but walked in from the bathroom and just stood looking at him. "You okay? What's wrong?"

"I saw you and Clara."

"Well, that's alright isn't it?" He came into the room, removing his sandals and shaking sand into the wastebasket. "I like her and she seems to really like me," Now he was aimlessly pacing around the room. "It's good for my head, babe. I haven't felt this with other women. Clara has kind of a crush on me. It's sweet and it makes me feel good about myself. I need that. Otherwise, it's no big thing. I'm not in love with her or anything like that." He sat down at his writing desk, took off his glasses and rubbed his hand over his face. "It's just that she and I are so alike. For someone who's like me to like me so much, well, it shows me I'm worthwhile, I guess. It makes me feel desirable." He was talking to the floor, but looked up at me, waiting for me to understand.

I stood still and expressionless. He had to know how this affected me. *How could he not realize that?* I thought. I needed him to see how I felt. I glared at him, still holding the towel, strands of wet hair hanging over my eyes.

"Cole, I don't mind you having friends or feeling good about yourself. But you know where this is going." My anger rose a pitch. "I sure know where this is going and I'm not buying a ticket this time." I'd gotten stern and loud.

"Listen, we'll talk about this, but right now, how about you get dressed. I've got to get to the newsstand before it closes. The first ad for the book is due out today and I ... we've ... got to see it." He jumped up and slid his sandals back on. "Then I'll get us some drinks from downstairs. Would that be nice?" he said, going for the door. "Then we can talk about this some more. I don't want you to be hurt, babe."

He sounded far away and I seemed to be fading, almost invisible. I looked in his eyes, but they didn't find mine.

"I'll be right back," he said, leaving the room, his voice sounding like an echo.

The warm sea breeze through the balcony door brushed the drying hair off my shoulder. I had no idea what to do, but felt so lost it didn't matter. Any direction I took would make more sense than standing still. My feet took action before my mind did. I walked to the armoire and pulled my suitcase out from underneath it. I grabbed clothes off hangers, putting on the sundress Mom made for me that I had not yet worn. I slipped on my sturdiest sandals and took a week's worth clothes out of drawers. I grabbed toiletries from the bathroom and from my bedside table I pulled out any important papers I didn't keep in my bag or money belt and threw them in the suitcase. I ran a brush through my hair and threw it in my bag. Slamming the suitcase, picking it up and throwing my bag around my shoulder, I walked to the middle of the living room. I didn't want to leave a place I'd come to love, a place we'd filled with happiness. On the center table was a large, beautifully handcrafted ceramic bowl I'd bought for us, covered with rose, rusty-red and purple bougainvillea, the ubiquitous regional flower. I walked to it, picked it up and hurled it against the far wall as I broke into tears.

I looked out the balcony door; taking in the sound of the crashing waves as it'd be the last I'd hear it from this room. I welcomed its gentle pulse, took in a deep breath and calmed down slightly.

Turning and leaving the room, I walked to the back stairway and headed down to the rear entrance. As I stepped onto the beach and walked in the darkening sunset around the well-lit bar, I saw Cole through the window, coming into the lobby and going to get our drinks. I stepped from the sand onto the Malecòn and began walking.

The waves were close. I listened, the ocean's rhythm guiding my breathing. My pace slowed to match it, four steps inbreath, four steps outbreath. After a while I stopped walking, dropped my bags onto the sand over the lower, deeper wall of the Malecòn and stepped into the darkness on the beach away from the streetlights. The town looked peaceful and distant, though I could hear its music softly playing. No one was nearby. Spontaneously, I took off running in a huge circle around the beach, running into and out of the water's edge, the music playing first in my right ear and then the left, right then left, the sunset over the water alternating with the rosy color of the town's lights. I slowed my running into long strides around my circle, the effect wonderful and trancelike. I closed my eyes, going slower still and was reminded of a meditation spiral I'd once walked as I closed in on the center of the circle and dropped like a sack onto the sand. I felt free and safe, spreading myself out and opening my eyes to see stars twinkling high above against a deep blue sky where a sliver of moon was rising. Friendly stars, rolling waves, warm colors and a pleasant, salty breeze brought comfort. My breathing slowed even more and I relaxed, watching the sun set and the moon rise.

I lay there for a long time, it seemed. The tide was coming in stronger and the waves crashed more insistently. The breeze was getting cold and the sky was dark. I became aware of my aloneness on the beach and felt vulnerable in the dark. Calmness left me and panic set in.

It scared me to leave Cole. I was terrified of being by myself. *How could I run out like that?* I thought. But I knew I had to. I couldn't tolerate what was coming. He didn't give me a choice.

The darkness was scaring me. I gathered myself and my bags and went into town, heading for the center square and its lights. As I got nearer I heard voices and laughter. People were scattered around the square and on neighboring streets going in and out of bars and restaurants. The breeze died as it hit the town's trees and somewhere a guitar was being played. I eased myself down onto a long bench. An elderly woman sat alone at the other end, a large sun hat on her lap, protection for her weathered, paper-like skin.

"Just getting into town?" she asked, seeing my suitcase. It took a moment to realize she was speaking to me and I struggled to find my voice.

"Why yes, I am," I said, the lie feeling uncomplicated. I was grateful for her company.

"It's a wonderful place. You'll love it."

"I'm sure I will." I sat quietly, afraid to talk, but wanting to. "How long have you been here?" I managed to say, assuming she was a tourist.

"Eight years."

"Really? What brought you here?"

"John Kennedy," she answered, turning to face me more directly. "After he died, I just didn't like America anymore. Johnson was alright I suppose, but the war ... I couldn't abide the war. And then that horrible Nixon man. It's all such a shame really."

Listening to her was calming and I began to feel safer. "Well yes, I have to agree with you there. I can understand why you came here, although it must have been quite different then."

"Oh my, yes. In some ways better, some ways worse. We have more utilities now; that's nice. But the town's set for a tourist boom. Not that you're part of it, dear," she said, smiling at me. "It's still to come, but it'll come faster than I'd like, I'm afraid. Our little town will get swallowed up."

"I hope not. It's just perfect now. From what I've seen so far, that is," I hastily added, remembering I'd supposedly just arrived. "Are you here with family?"

"No, I came by myself" she said. "I was alone anyway. Might as well be somewhere you like to be. I'd come to Mexico before with my husband on vacation and I knew I wanted to return."

"You husband died then?"

"Oh yes. He was a bit older than me. Bad heart."

"I'm sorry."

"Don't be. We weren't getting along anyway. It was all for the best. He didn't even like Mexico. Too hot. Too many bugs. Funny how things turn out." We sat quietly, the cicada song emanating from the trees nearby offering a nice backdrop.

"I just left my husband," I said, somewhat feebly, surprising myself with this disclosure to the woman. She just seemed easy to talk to. I needed someone to care.

"Oh my dear. I am sorry to hear that." She paused. "Unless of course it's for the best. You'll know in time. Vallarta is a good place to test your feelings. You know, they tell you to follow your bliss. Well I haven't found bliss yet, but I have found a lot of comfort here." She looked over at me and smiled again. "Don't worry, dear. You'll be fine. I'm seventy-two and the scorpions haven't gotten me yet. It's amazing how well we girls can do on our own."

I glanced over at her. Her being on the bench when I came was magically strange. People say things happen for a reason. It felt right that I'd met this little wise woman.

"I hope you're right about that. I actually haven't been on my own before. I'm frightened about it. I've just been putting one foot in front of another." *And haven't even gone that far,* I thought.

"Well then, perhaps it's time for you to try it. You needn't be frightened. The world's a welcoming place if you look closely enough. A little dusty in spots, but it becomes familiar in a short while. You'll get used to it." She laughed. "And then things will change again. That never fails to amuse me. Just when you find a bit of comfort – poof – it's gone again." She waved her hand as if following the path of the disappearing comfort. "But it comes back."

"You seem to have managed pretty well," I said. "Thank you for your encouragement. I needed to hear that. I'll give it a try." The woman was quiet again and I felt awkward. "In fact, I should probably be getting settled into my hotel."

"Yes, it's getting chilly. I'd better be off myself. I'm like a vampire, mostly out after midday. I can't take the sun and today I got too much," She rocked forward to put her small weight onto her feet as she stood up. "It's been very nice meeting you. I hope I'll see you again. I live up near the top of Corona Street, in what has unfortunately become known as Gringo Gulch. I got here not long after the Burton-Taylors made the area famous with his movie and her Cleopatra-like lifestyle. My house is one of the oldest and has the most bougainvillea. Do come by if you like. I'd love to know how you're doing."

"Yes, thank you. That would be nice. It's been lovely to meet you." I stood and held out my hand, which she took and gave a small squeeze.

I watched her leave the square, a quite upright and strong walker for her age. I picked up my bags and walked on, looking for a hotel. I'd often gone by the Chulavista and decided to go in. I got a small room and was led to it by a young, very smiley Mexican boy who carried my suitcase for me. We passed by the mandatory hotel courtyard, the short palms and sprays of flowers showing some wear and lack of attention. All the rooms were on one floor and mine was toward the back.

I left my door open after the boy left, happy with my generous tip. "Me llamo Pedro," he'd said, introducing himself.

"Me llama Lily," I'd said in return.

I wanted to be able to see the courtyard, feeling afraid of closing the door, as if with its closing I'd be locked out from the world. Standing in the doorframe I felt safe again, secure in knowing I'd made it this far. I could quell my panic by moving forward, doing the next logical thing.

My hands slipped into the pockets of my sundress where I found an envelope. I pulled it out and slowly opened it, unfolding the note it contained. It was from Mom.

Hi honey. I hope Mexico is all you hoped it would be. But for those inevitable moments when it, and life, may disappoint you, I want to give you this poem to keep with you. It's always been one of my favorites. Handwritten in her almost illegible scrawl was Robert Frost's *The Road Not*

Taken. She'd underlined the last three lines of the poem:

> *Two roads diverged in a wood, and I –*
> *I took the one less traveled by,*
> *And that has made all the difference.*

Next to these lines she'd written:

Like I said, you've always taken the road less traveled, and I trust it may make all the difference for you as well. Take care on your journey. I love you so and will always. Mom.

The ocean salt on my cheeks mixing with the salty tears tasted good sliding into the corners of my mouth. I felt Mom was there with me. There in a moment I really needed her, with words to comfort me and tell me I'd be okay. I'd been feeling more alone than I could ever remember being, but I was where I needed to be and it felt as if she was nearby.

Now able to close the door, I could better appreciate the room and knew that I could, as my new friend had said, be comfortable there. I filled the small drawers of the dresser with the few things I'd brought and put my toiletries on the bathroom shelf. I draped a shawl over the corner of the mirror to add a contrasting blue color to the otherwise very yellow room. After pulling open the blanket and sheet on the bed and placing my pajamas on the pillow, the room looked more like I belonged there.

Though exhausted, I was starving. Near the hotel was a tiny café and I had a small meal of rice and beans with red wine. I was the only American and it seemed by the banter that the Mexican diners were members of the family that owned the place or at least were friends of theirs. After I ate I had to immediately leave, thinking that if I sat there alone I'd start to cry.

Coming back to the room, I undressed and left the bathroom light on when I crawled into the single bed. It was a bit hard, but the large pillow was soft, the cover smelling clean and fresh. I cuddled under the summer blanket, trying to be cozy, but felt totally out of place and miserable. *What was I doing here?*

I read Mom's note again and cried. Looking through the slanted louvers of the window, I could see the edge of the moon and watched it until finally I fell asleep. It wasn't a restful night. Several times I woke up, confused by where I was. Then remembering, it took a while to doze off again. More towards dawn I was harshly awoken by my old dream of being chased along the beach, the men's' faces visible in their torch light. I hadn't had the dream in a long time.

The new morning brought panic. It seemed as if I'd awoken on the deck of a sinking ship to discover I was the only passenger left, everyone having fled in lifeboats I could see as bobbing dots in the distance.

The glaring daylight and the harsh bustle of street and pedestrian traffic outside my window woke me further and I sat up. "I can't believe all the shit that's happening," I said aloud, becoming conscious again.

I hurriedly got dressed and rushed to my favorite outdoor restaurant for breakfast. I knew the waiter and seeing him helped me find some bearings.

"Buenos dias, Seniorita," Felipe greeted me. I took a table and sat with my back to the sun, Felipe politely holding the chair for me.

"Buenos dias, Felipe" I replied. "Huevos rancheros, por favor," I ordered, hoping eggs would settle my stomach.

"Hugo di pina?"

"Si, gracias." He always remembered my favorite juice.

I let the sun warm the tense muscles of my neck and back and gazed at the street scene around the café. It was still early and shop owners were sweeping out their stores and setting up stands outside to display their goods. Children ran by in the direction of the school passing by a woman swatting her donkey with a handful of straw, urging it probably to the square with its burden of vegetables she'd sell there in the baskets strung over the forlorn looking animal.

The waiter brought my eggs and I gratefully ate the spicy meal. Over breakfast I wrote Cole a note, which I'd leave for him at the hotel. He was undoubtedly worried and even though I felt awful, it wouldn't be fair to not contact him.

I know it's crazy, the note began, *and you probably think I'm being silly, and perhaps I am, but I got a room at the Chulavista. Maybe this doesn't make sense but I need to be quiet for a little while and get my strength pushing me in the right direction.*

Breakfast in a familiar place made me feel much better. Afterwards, I stopped quickly by the hotel, leaving the note at the front desk for Cole. Being in the hotel made the panic return, as I was afraid I'd see him. So I left immediately and took off down the street having no idea where I was going. I found myself heading for the center square, hoping I'd perhaps run into my new old lady friend, but she wasn't there.

I sat on a different bench, partly hidden by a large hibiscus bush, its branches reaching around the end of the bench, my head competing with its huge pink flowers for a spot in the sun. Neighboring it was a frangipani plant, its smaller yellow and white flowers giving off a faint scent, only a hint of the fragrant strength it had at night to attract moths. I wanted to be hidden in daylight, comforted by the sounds of people around me, but safe from the view of anyone who might bother me. I needed to think, wanted to figure out my next move. My panic was easing in the camouflage gained by the hibiscus, but my thoughts were unraveling fast.

Okay, I've left Cole, but where the fuck am I going? I could get money from him, plus what I have, which could get me somewhere, but where? I can't be alone and there's no one to go to. We have no friends. I don't want to go home. If I go back to New York, what can I do? I'd run out of cash and there's no way I'm going back to hooking. I have no college degree and no skills. I can type. Great. That'll get me some low-level secretarial job – not the world-traveling writer's wife I was counting on. Damn Cole, I thought.

Maybe I'm not good enough. He needs a Clara I suppose, someone smarter than me. He's gotten successful. What does he need me for? Maybe I don't fit in now and he wants me to go. But I don't want to. I don't want to give up having Cole support us for a change. He owes it to me. Why should I leave? Fuck him. But why should I stay if I'm not wanted? I can't do that. I just want a fucking happy marriage. Is that really asking a lot? What do I do to get that? What part of this is my fault? I've tried giving him everything. Even other women, for god's sake. Maybe I haven't done the right thing. I should try writing. He might think more of me. Or he might just find that too cute, like I'm his groupie. What did I have that he might really want? Nothing. I've never done anything. I can't create shit. No wonder he's bored."

"Collar, seniorita?" Startled, I realized I'd been found by the necklace-seller from the Malecòn. She was holding a long string of pink and yellow beads for me to consider. "Rosa y amarillo. Precioso por la seniorita, si?" She held the necklace to my hair and smiled, her wide and even white teeth shiny as sea shells. Then she held it up to the *rosa y amarillo* petals of the flowers around me, my memory of Spanish words for colors racing to my frontal lobe. Pink and yellow, yes. Yes, they nicely complemented my blond hair.

Si, esta maravilloso," I told her, stumbling through the words but indeed finding the beads beautiful. "Pero no gracias," I said, declining her offer. She walked on and I watched her offer a necklace to a woman slowly walking by, arm in arm with a tall man. "Rojo y blanco," she said: red and white beads to match the woman's black hair and white cotton Mexican peasant blouse, the bodice embroidered with red hibiscus flowers, a traditional pattern found in most of the shops. She held the beads up to the woman and then offered them to the man, who dutifully bought the necklace, placing it around the neck of the very receptive woman.

The necklace seller's interruption of my circular thinking was welcome. I was nowhere near being able to decide what to do. I didn't even know how I felt. Feelings, ideas, feelings, ideas – swirling around in my head like freakish animals on a merry-go-round.

Maybe I'll go swimming, I thought. Or go to that soap and perfume shop. Buy myself something nice. No. I shouldn't spend money I might need. It's too early for drinking and I'm not hungry yet. I was hot. It's midday. That's why the old woman isn't here, it occurred to me. My shirt is too hot. I should change. Yes, I'll change. That's the next thing to do. Put on a bathing suit under some shorts, or maybe under a skirt if I go get a drink after. Bring a shawl or maybe a sweater for later. Later when? What the fuck am I doing? Go change, girl. Do one thing first. Okay.

I'd made myself so nervous I almost sprang off the bench. Sprinting out of the square, my gait slowed as I succumbed to the local pace. Apparently others weren't as crazed as I and were enjoying their lethargy in the heat. I was sweating just from my ruminations.

Getting back to my new hotel home, the half-asleep manager handed me a note he pulled from my message box. I went into the courtyard and sat down on the plaster pedestal next to a fraying palm shrub. A salamander squiggled up the pillar supporting the passageway roof. The miniature bell hop I met the night before was swabbing the area around what stood for a fountain, its singular waterspout rising pathetically before plunging into the cracked and yellowing basin.

"Buenos tardes, seniorita," the boy said. I smiled and gave him a wink. Or it maybe it was the onset of the facial tic I got when overwrought. I wasn't sure. I opened and read the note.

I'm out on the beach drying my head out. Will be in the usual area. Come on out. If I'm rapping to anybody it won't be because I particularly want to. I'd rather just sit and think and talk to you. Honestly. So don't bash my head in in the unlikely event that I seem to have company.

My indecision roared into overdrive and I decided I just needed to not think for a while.

The heat blasted out of my room when I opened the door. I left it ajar, turned the slats in the window to their full open position and started the ceiling fan. I stood in the small breeze that now crossed the room, letting the air ride over me. I had to go swimming or I might pass out. I closed the door, opening the slatted window that overlooked the courtyard, giving the breeze a continued destination. Undressing, I slid into a cool shower. Then, freshened a bit, I dressed in my bathing suit under a long, loose fitting cotton tunic that was clean and dry and good feeling. I put underwear for later in my bag along with all my beach stuff, slapped my big hat on my head, slipped into my sandals and was off to the ocean. I'd made no decision about Cole, just focusing on going swimming. I'd see how things went.

The sand was packed with bodies. I chose an open spot next to the water's edge where the sand was hard and wet from the waves. It seemed cooler there. Laying out my towel on the dry sand nearby, I dropped my stuff and sat. When I was very young I'd told my father on a trip to the Atlantic Ocean that it looked like America's bathtub. It looked the same here. The ocean was full of white-bodied tourists all bobbing in waves in their bathing suits like brightly colored children's toys. A few locals were sprinkled among them.

I decided to swim and waded through the waves until I got to bigger surf. As soon as the next large wave began to swell, I dove straight into the middle of the rising water, allowing the crest to ride over me, while I surfaced beyond in the deeper, calmer water. Only a couple of other swimmers were out that far. I loved this part of the ocean where I could swim parallel to the beach, back and forth, back and forth, meditation-style. All the noisy sound subsided and I was alone in the salty water. This far out it was deep, colder and nicely bracing. I swam for a while and then floated onto my back to rest, gently rocked by the current, gazing at the endless blue sky, hoping a shark didn't bite my legs off. Just in case, I turned my face into the water and approximated a few high pitched dolphin sounds. Probably not very effective, but I felt safer. I looked around in the water, prepared to punch my assailant in the nose if he appeared, as I'd read you should do, though panic and screaming seemed a more natural reaction. You might be lucky in your flailing to get a punch in. Assured there were no sharks for the moment, I went back to resting for a while and then body-surfed back to the beach and clamored out, trying to look graceful as I slipped and stomped over the stones at the edge.

Returning to my towel, I saw that a little girl had settled herself nearby and was busily packing the sides of her sand castle. Not more than seven years old, she hardly noticed me as I sat down to dry off. I watched her intently working on her creation, tongue fixed between teeth, blond hair coated with wet sand.

"Nice castle," I said.

"It's not a castle," she said.

"Oh?"

"It's an enchanted island," she said, briefly glancing at me, the person too demented to not realize this obvious fact. "It's called Avalon."

"Ah, I see," I said, leaning over for a closer look. "Yes, now I clearly see those are cliffs, not castle turrets." She snuck another furtive glance at me, as if wondering if I could be trusted. "What's that mound there on the island?" I asked, pointing to a sculpted structure atop the flattish island mass.

"That's where Morgan lives," she answered.

"Morgan Le Fay."

"Well, that's quite a name."

"She's an enchantress."

"Oh, of course, it being an enchanted island and all. So she has magical powers?" The little girl sighed and sat back on her ankles, looking straight at me.

"She's a sorcerous," she said adamantly, as if I clearly needed an explanation. "She can cast spells and she's also a healer."

"So she practices witchcraft," I said, trying to show some knowledge. Looking beyond her I noticed what must be her mother a few yards away, a bemused look on her face as she watched us. I smiled and she nodded.

"Well, kind of, but she's not a bad witch." She was placing tiny shells on a small piece of driftwood she'd placed near the mound on top of the island. "She's powerful like Merlin," she threw in as an afterthought.

"Oh, she's friends with Merlin, then?"

"No. They're rivals," she said, enunciating the last word as though perhaps she'd just learned it. "She's King Arthur's sister."

I admired her confidence and ability to engage with a stranger without fear. I never could have done that at her age.

"Oh, my. Well, she's quite an important lady isn't she?"

"Yes, she is." She paused, rocked back onto her feet and popped up off the sand as only small children can do, then quickly ran off to her mother's side, jabbering away, the frilled skirt of her sky blue bathing suit flouncing as she ran.

Her mother and I exchanged smiles. I leaned back

to rest on my elbows, turning my gaze to the ocean.

Watching the waves roll in and out, an old memory came to mind, one of those odd, very sudden flashes from out of nowhere. Actually it was a memory of something I'd been told by my mother of a time she and I were at some beach together when I was very young. It seems I'd toddled off out of her sight. When she realized I wasn't there she panicked, frantically looking up and down the beach to find me. I was nowhere to be seen. She went to the lifeguard in total distress. It'd apparently been awhile since I'd disappeared and he arranged a long line of men who clasped hands and began walking together into the water, slowly advancing in case one of them turned up my drowned body. By then the whole beach had been alerted. The men were waist deep when someone from the beach yelled out that I'd been found playing alone by a sand castle not far from where my mother had been sitting.

I was tired. I turned to lie face down, lowering myself on the towel, the hot sand underneath now feeling good, like a heated, muscle soothing pad, my face pressing into the nubby cloth, my eyes closing.

"Hi babe."

Cole plopped himself onto the sand next to me.

"I saw you out swimming. You're the only one who ever goes out that far. I could see you from down the beach."

Wide awake now, an amazing amount of tension returned, my slack body stiffening. I half rolled onto my side to look at him. He was wearing his long white pants, a shirt slung over a shoulder. I could see him looking at me through his sunglasses.

"I'm sorry if you're hurt. I didn't mean that to happen." He was picking through shells in the sand. I let the moment be quiet. Then brushing the caked sand off my arms, I propped myself up to half-sitting.

"Cole, I can't imagine anyone thinking for a moment that I wouldn't be hurt. What were you expecting?" He leaned back, bracing himself with his arms and looked at the sky.

"I don't know. I really don't. I guess I wasn't thinking at all. I was just … I'm not sure,"

"Responding to attention?"

"Yeah, I guess." He took off his sunglasses and pressed the bridge of his nose. "But I think she wants attention even more. She has no intention of sleeping with me, just so you know. It seems she – "

"I really don't want to hear your analysis," I said, cutting him off. "I'll say only this: I'll be at the Chulavista until you decide you're ready to be with me and me alone. I want a husband, not some other tourist's boy toy. Not a swinging buddy. Not a pimp." I sat up. "So if you want to woo her, fuck her or forget her, the choice is yours. When you're ready to be with me you can come find me." I lay back down on the towel, pressing my face into its welcoming heat. Nothing was said for several minutes. I'd no idea where this rush of strength had come from within me. It just gushed out like blood spurting from a knife wound I'd been staunching to no effect.

"Okay, babe. I got it." The sand crunched beneath him as he stood to leave.

I lay there for some time, trying to relax and feel comfortable, but shifted around like a troubled sleeper. This was killing me. I was hurt and angry, but I wanted Cole. I couldn't stand being away from him. I didn't make sense to myself without him.

Why is it so hard for him to just love me? What do I have to do? I love him and he's good enough for me. Why isn't that enough for him? Why does he always need someone else? Normal fantasy, fine. But other women? Reams of pornography? I don't fit in his voyeuristic fantasy land of sex thrill rides and hoochie-coochie girls. I might have to just let him go, but I don't know how I can do that without completely losing myself. I can't even tolerate these racing thoughts, for Christ's sake."

I stood up too fast and got dizzy. I threw my long tunic over my now dry bathing suit and headed for one of the ubiquitous grass shacks set up on the beach.

Dropping onto a barstool in the shade I felt a little better. "Hugo di pina, por favor." The icy liquid appeared quickly and I chugged it down, asking for a refill. I'd dehydrated myself badly. And I was hungry, realizing I hadn't had any lunch. I pulled myself together and left the shack, planning to get an early dinner. I stopped outside before leaving the beach, ran a brush through my hair and put on some lipstick. I wouldn't change out of my bathing suit, going somewhere just as I was.

I walked up the main road and found myself automatically going to Carlos O'Brien's, the one touristy place in town that catered to Americans. I wanted a steak. I wanted American music. This was where Cole and I often went, but I didn't care. He wouldn't come this early anyway. And if he did and brought Clara with him, I'd just leave.

It was much cooler in the restaurant. I sat down at the usual table and was served by the usual waiter, our now almost friend, Alomar.

"No husband tonight?" he asked.

"No, just me. He wasn't hungry yet and I'm starving. I'd like a steak. And some fries."

"Sure. Medium rare, like always?"

"Great. Thanks, Alomar."

"Coming right up," he said, with a friendly wink.

I got up to play the jukebox, starting off with Linda Ronstadt's *You're No Good*, which fit my mood fine. I stayed by the psychedelic machine, a rainbow of colors swooping back and forth across its top. I half-danced to the song and quietly sang along, trying to take my mind off everything. After my next selection, Alomar slid close to me.

"Your salad's on the table," he whispered, giving me another wink. I winked back.

The salad, steak and fries were more delicious than I remembered that meal could be. Satisfied, I paid the check and left the table, taking a seat at the bar and ordering another Bacardi and tonic. Someone else had followed up my jukebox choices and David Bowie's *Fame* came blasting out.

Alomar came dancing by and playfully bumped his hip on mine repeatedly, teasingly trying to knock me off my stool. I got up and bumped him back, our moves becoming slightly more suggestive.

"You are one sweet lady," he breathed into my ear, laughed and danced off. A few Bacardi and tonics later, he was regularly stopping by to flirt with me between serving tables. I'd never been there alone and I was thoroughly enjoying his attention and his pressing himself into my hip and the muscular brown arm he kept sliding around my waist. I knew

It'd be so easy to stay until he was done with his shift and just go home with him.

Perhaps I'll slink into the hills above town where I know he lives. I can move in with him. Have a couple of pretty brown babies with blue eyes. Learn to cook spicy things. But no. I have to be whacked out crazy in a love generation marriage with a sex-addicted geek whose mind travels in science-fantasy adventures. Yeah, that makes sense.

I was getting drunk and it was a lousy thought anyway. Maybe not Alomar, but some of the waiters and bartenders were finding extra money entertaining lonely women tourists and I didn't want to seem like one of them, even if I was lonely and a tourist. Before I fell off my stool, I gathered my stuff, blew Alomar a kiss across the room and left. I felt flattered and pretty and that was enough.

Getting to sleep that night was easier and I slept almost all the way through only waking a couple of times and lulled to drowsiness again by the incessant song of the cicadas outside my window.

I had all the next day to focus on relieving my hangover, which helped take my mind off Cole, though I did feel even more hurt than before and afraid my ultimatum might back fire and make me a permanently lonely tourist destined to wither and die in a yellow cinderblock hotel room.

I decided to take my hangover for a walk down the Malecòn and back, stopping for plain eggs and toast on the way and lots of coffee. A couple of blocks south of the Chulavista I found the soap and perfume shop in another hotel lobby and treated myself to a lavender sachet. Then a bloody Mary in the hotel bar took the edge off the shaky feeling that wouldn't leave me. On my way back to the Chulavista

I bought a large bottle of water thinking that more hydration and a short nap would be good. I had no ideas for after that. I didn't want to think about anything else beyond the day I was in. Feeling in crisis brought on panic. I had time and if that was supposed to heal all wounds, well then taking a nap was okay.

Pedro, the miniature maintenance man, was in the entrance to the Chulavista. "Senorita, senorita" he called to me using something of a stage whisper, his hand beckoning me to join him. He was adorable. I couldn't imagine what he was excited about. "Un hombre te está esperando," he said, pointing to the courtyard. I knew "hombre" meant "man" and I had a good idea what the rest of the translation was.

"Gracias, Pedro," I said, patting his thick mat of black hair. Heading into the courtyard I saw Cole from behind, resting against one of the roof supports. I walked toward where he was sitting and looked over at him. He was gazing pensively at the fountain; his jaw set in a way I knew meant he was deep in thought.

"Buenos tardes," I said in Spanish for some reason, injecting a note of pissiness.

"Hi," he said, seemingly surprised to find me there. "I need to talk to you." Turning to fully face him I saw Pedro's head peering around the laundry room door, eyes wide with anticipation. I smiled slightly and he shot back into the room.

"Okay. Why don't we get a drink?" I asked, clearly abandoning the water and the nap. It was still only mid-afternoon, but having another drink would quell the anxiety I was now feeling from the mix of fear and hope squirreling around in my chest on top of the hangover. "I just discovered a bar we actually haven't been to together yet. It's just down the street." Somehow the bar seemed like it was in my territory since I'd discovered it on my own. "Let me put my things in my room and I'll be right with you." I let myself in and put the bottle in some cold water in the sink. Taking a long whiff of the lavender sachet for courage, I stuck it in my underwear drawer and relocked the room.

"I've been thinking a lot," Cole said, as we slowly walked to the hotel bar. "I don't want you to leave. I need you." He paused. "I want you with me." I continued strolling along, my head almost compressing from me trying to squeeze out all unpleasant sensations and thoughts.

"That's nice, Cole. But I just can't be worried all the time that you're going to leave me for someone else, or that you're going into your emotionally absent mode even when I'm with you. It makes me feel like a roommate or a piece of furniture in your life, not your wife. I'm afraid I'm not good enough for you and if that's true, then I wish you'd just go. I can't stand it otherwise."

"You're more than good enough for me. You're perfect. Too perfect. I've told you that. It's me that feels I don't deserve you."

"Well you have an odd way of showing it, Cole."

We reached the hotel and walked through into the bar. It was a newer hotel and obviously designed to attract a higher class tourist. We took stools at the more private end of the bar even though few people were there yet.

"Jack Daniel's en hielo para mi, y un Bacardi y tonic," Cole said to the bartender.

"You want the rum on ice, too?" the Mexican bartender asked me in very clear English.

"Yes, thank you," I said, returning his amused smile. He left to make our drinks.

"I know I've been an asshole, Lily, and I'm sorry. That's what I've been thinking about. I really don't want to lose you. I'll figure out my problems, but I don't want to hurt you. I need you too much." He'd put his hand on my knee and was looking at me intensely. He wasn't even blinking so I knew he was serious. Then he leaned over and kissed me gently, started to pull back and then kissed me again, more firmly this time. I started to cry, I was so confused. He smiled and touched my cheek. "Really, babe. I mean it."

"Yes, I think you do, Cole. I just need you to know that I can't take being hurt again. I love you and want to be with you too, but I need to know that you really want me, that you love me, and yes, that you desire me."

"Yes, babe. I do. I love you and I want you."

Our drinks came and Cole threw some money on the bar. "Listen, babe. I've been looking into something today. I want us to find an apartment here. I need to focus on my writing and I need us to be together and I want us to live here awhile. We've been here two months and we can afford to be here for another six months if we want to. By then I'll have another advance on the book I've started. The last book is doing well. The ad came out and they're running it everywhere. The fucking book is selling, Lily. It's no bestseller, but I didn't expect that. But it's selling well enough for us to get some royalties out of it. What do you think? Do you like it here? I mean, would you like it here if I wasn't being such an asshole?"

"Well that'd be nice," I said, half smiling. "Yes, I love it here. I'd like to stay." I sipped my drink, my hangover subdued by more alcohol. "And I'd like us to try to stay together. Look, I don't want to leave you. I need you, too. I really have no idea what I'd do on my own. I can't even think about it, it scares me too much."

"We'll be alright, babe," Cole said, smiling for the first time, his head pointed down in his humbling way. I could tell he felt some guilt. "Listen. I found one apartment that you might like. I stopped by a realtor earlier and they knew of this woman who has a big house up on the hill with a smaller gatehouse that she rents. I took a look at it and I think it's just what we'd both like. Want to go see it? I told her I'd bring you by."

"Really?" A rush of hopeful excitement shot through me. It felt like he wanted to show me how things could really be for us. Maybe this was what we needed. Maybe it would make things different, or new, between us. I had to believe it was possible. To feel otherwise was too painful. This was a huge relief and I had to go with it. I couldn't get anywhere on my own. I had to have Cole. "Okay. Let's go see it."

We left the bar and went back down the street a few blocks until we came to Corona Street where Cole turned and headed up the hill. I thought right away of the nice older woman I'd met who lived at the end of the street and thought it was a good sign. Halfway up the block Cole stopped and gestured with his hand towards a huge white wooden gate. I caught up to him, panting, and he rang the buzzer.

"Yes?" a woman's voice answered.

"Hello, Mrs. Whalen. It's Cole. I stopped by earlier to look at your rental?"

"Oh, yes, certainly. Come right in and I'll meet you there." The gate unlocked automatically and fell open. We walked up the stone driveway and I could see a large house set into the hill above us with a long veranda covered with a huge awning, its pink and white stripes matching bushes of flowers amid the lush greenery around the base of the porch. A woman was waving to us. "Go on in. It's unlocked," she called to us. I'll be right down."

The gate house was just to our right, also set in thick greenery with the same flower theme. It was white wood like the gate. I saw the woman emerging from her home, walking down a stone pathway towards the driveway. She had bleached blond hair, a tanned face and wore a bright red dress. I waved and she waved back.

Cole had gone in the front door and I followed. It opened into the kitchen, which was a level above a huge living area you could see below, the apartment built on a hill. The ceiling was vaulted to about twenty feet, a sleek light fixture hanging from the highest point. A curved couch that could fit a crowd of people filled the corner of the living room with a few upholstered and very tasteful chairs set in front of it, a long teardrop-shaped dark wood table in between on which were several sizeable art books. Large pillows decorated with brightly colored sprays of tropical flowers were placed here and there on the beige furniture. Large ceramic pots were spaced around the room containing a tall rubber plant, a broad ficus, a small palm tree and some other spiky thing I couldn't identify. Cole had already found a low bookshelf and was thumbing through paperbacks. White walls held a few abstract and colorful paintings and over the kitchen counter hung pots and pans with shiny brass bottoms. On one side of the living room were windowed French doors that looked onto a courtyard.

"Well, you must be Lily!" The woman had come in behind us and was now almost sailing down the wide stone stairs into the living room. "What do you think? Hhmn?" She swung her way towards me. "I'm Patricia, Lily. How do you do?"

"I'm very glad to meet you, Patricia. And this apartment is wonderful."

"Yes, isn't it?" she laughed. "I have a terrific decorator. I love it myself. You absolutely must see the rest of it." She almost pirouetted towards a door leading to what had to be the bedroom. "Please come along!" She led us on a tour of the large and nicely decorated bedroom, similar in taste to the living room but more subdued and intimate. A door led into a long bathroom with two sinks and a large glass shower stall. "And of course you must have a look at the courtyard," the woman said, already back in the living room.

It was a large flagstone courtyard with stone walls topped with more greenery and flowers. Trees outside the walls gave it some privacy though through branches you could see the wide lawn leading up to the woman's house. A large glass table supported by wrought iron legs was surrounded by padded patio furniture including a couple of lounge chairs. There was a grill built into the wall and a dry bar. Wall sconces held lights casting a pleasant glow over the courtyard. "It's just perfect for a writer," Patricia was saying. "A good place for a creative mood. And if you want even more privacy for writing there's a stairway over here that leads to a smaller, one-person apartment built into the hillside. It's a maid's room, but there's no one living there. You can use it yourselves or for guests or even sublet it to someone else if you like. It has its own entrance. I won't mind. My maid will be down once a week to change your linens, do your dishes and any laundry you have. Her service is included in the rent."

"Well, babe, what do you think?" Cole had stretched himself out on one of the lounge chairs, looking quite at home.

"How could I say no to this? It's beautiful."

"Then we'll take it," Cole said to Patricia.

"Excellent. You'll love it. Everyone always does. Let me just get the paperwork I left in the kitchen."

"Can we really afford this?" I asked Cole after she'd gone back into the apartment.

"We're paying the same rent here that we had in New York for a studio apartment. Not to worry. We'll be fine."

After the lease signing, we went back to our respective hotels for our bags, and returned to the apartment. Cole came by taxi having stopped on the way to get a couple bottles of white wine and fresh red snapper to cook on the grill for dinner.

In our absence, the maid had stopped in to put fresh sheets on the bed, turning down the cover and thick clean towels were stacked in the bathroom. Two white terrycloth robes now hung by the shower.

"This is too inviting," I said. "I've got to take a shower."

"You do that, babe, and I'll get the fish going."

There were tall candles in the bathroom that I lit and a delightful jasmine scent filled the air. A lovely purple and orange bird of paradise was planted in an earthenware pot set between the two sinks and a good sized peace plant sat on the floor in front of a frosted floor to ceiling window. I'd never seen one with so many flowers blooming. When I turned on the water in the shower stall, it came straight down from a flat round fixture jutting out from the back wall. Stepping underneath it, the water felt like warm rain and fell all around me. I tilted my head back and let it soak my hair and run down my back.

"Here you go, babe." Cole's arm reached into the shower handing me a glass of white wine. As I took it, his hand slid along my arm, my shoulder and then down around my breast, giving it a firm caress. I could see him in profile through the glass now steamed. His silhouette moved forward and he stuck his tongue out from behind the shower door, wiggling it back and forth suggestively.

"You silly man."

"Ha, ha. Just you wait. It won't seem so silly later on," he said, his long, low pitched laugh trailing him as he left the room.

The wine, the fish, the fucking. It was a good night and we were back in love.

☙☙☙☙☙

We became quickly and happily accustomed to our new home. I had to. I couldn't afford any frailty or worry. I clung to hope like a desperate woman in a cheesy romance novel.

I was glad for the maid, Pilar, who spoiled us and kept the apartment neat and clean. I needed some other woman to keep my life orderly and calm. I couldn't handle messiness let alone a household crisis, whatever that might be. Mold would have been an incapacitating challenge. I was feeling responsible for the house, responsible for our marriage and responsible for keeping myself together. I tried to show Pilar my appreciation. I imagined Patricia paid her well. I hoped so.

I also didn't know how to tell her what to do as having a servant embarrassed me a bit. But we got along with broken sentences and hand gestures, she speaking no English and me little Spanish. Cole was more comfortable with her as his family had a maid, his mother incapable of housework. He practiced his Spanish with her and Pilar treated him as master of the house. Of course he was almost two feet taller than she was so their relationship fell into place.

Cole got into his writing, establishing something of an office for himself in the living room, though usually taking his typewriter into the courtyard to work. I puttered around during the day without disturbing him unless he felt like talking. I brought him lunch and snacks and drinks, which he appreciated. I began to enjoy the regularity of our days.

Not sure of what to do with myself, I asked Cole what he thought of my trying to write, based on what he thought of the help I'd given him with the first book.

"If you want to write, the best thing to do is read. Read all the books you brought, read all the books in the living room and then get some more. Try to imagine the process of what they put down on paper. There are several good classics in the living room. Start with Hemingway."

And so I did. I ploughed through novels, plays and short stories. I queried Cole about writing styles and he'd suggest writing tasks to build my skills.

Some nights we'd lie back on the lounge chairs next to each other in the courtyard, looking up at the stars and talking about books and history and science. He'd tell me about philosophers and social theories or go into his universe talk about quantum mechanics and physics and how black holes were portals for energy streams. He'd say things like *Faith and science are like a Mobius strip*, and I'd nod, hungering agreement. We were getting excited together, like the old times. I was also getting more comfortable talking seriously with him and he took me seriously in return. I needed that. My days in New York had hardened me, but back with Cole I was mush. I wanted to be stronger, get my resilience back. And, yes, be more valuable to him.

"We're doing it, babe," he said one evening. "This is just the beginning. With the next advance I want us to go to Europe. We'll do the whole thing – England, France, Germany, Austria, Spain, Italy. It'll be like the honeymoon we never really took."

"I liked our honeymoon."

"Well, you for sure can't beat a moon liftoff, but it's not exactly traditional." He reached over and ran his fingers along my arm. "No, babe, I want to take you on an amazing trip. The Paris Opera, German theater, the Saltzburg Festival, Spanish flamenco, Italian art, all of it. We'll do it, babe. We will. Just you wait. For now, Mexico. How about a short trip to

Mazatlan, hmnn?"

"That'd be wonderful!

"Let's go next week then. It's not that far. I've almost got the first hundred pages of the book done and then we'll take off." He reached up to my cheek. "Just you and me, babe. You and me," he said softly. I leaned over to him for a long kiss.

The days lazed by. The Mazatlan trip came and went. I experimented with cooking local foods. When I wasn't doing that or reading I was at the beach or strolling around the central square. Some nights we'd walk together to the Malecòn and now and then hit the dance clubs.

Mostly, we stayed at the apartment. Cole was transfixed by his novel, deep into the middle of it where the action was intensifying. He was quite pensive, often spending hours reading through his research, wanting to get the details correct. I worried about his becoming morose, but he seemed leveled off. I'd ask him how his characters were coming, just to understand what was directing his mood.

"She's started a journal," he announced during our dinner one night, referring, I knew, to his main character, Marybeth.

"No kidding. That's pretty far out. What's she writing?"

"She's keeping track of what happens when she goes back in time. It's amazing. It's like I'm not writing it at all. She is. I'm just the scribe. The ideas for what she's seeing seem to come before I think of them. It just flows."

"That's fascinating," I said. "Like what is she seeing?"

"Well, you know how she travels back to the

Second French Empire to assume the identity of the woman named Celeste?

"Right."

"She's describing an affair Celeste is having, which means Marybeth's having it too as she's become Celeste through traveling back in time. Only it's complicated because the man is a business associate of Celeste's husband. Celeste's afraid they'll be found out. But she can't resist seeing him. They're having torrid sex, of course."

"Of course." I smiled. "Go on. What else?" I was genuinely interested.

"Well Marybeth is totally wrapped up in Celeste's life. Celeste's very upper class, so she's socializing with all sorts of people, some getting famous in their time, or later on. And Marybeth's writing all this down about where Celeste goes and who she meets. Then Celeste slips off to rendezvous with this guy and Marybeth of course experiences it too and then writes about it in her journal. It's great! It's like I'm a voyeur watching another voyeur. It's crazy but I'm really into it."

"I can see that," I said, pouring us more wine. "I'm really glad it's going so well."

"I'm telling you, babe, I'm becoming a real writer. I can do this."

"Of course you can. But I know you've doubted yourself. It's great you're seeing how good you really are."

"Yeah, I guess I'm okay at that."

I was glad. His insecurity was often mixed with exaggerated ego, but I always took that as his need to bolster himself up. Maybe he was feeling some satisfaction that would last.

Our days stayed peaceful and productive. We even took another side trip south to a bay just north of Manzanillo to go snorkeling and then went into the city for a couple days of shopping, eating and just hanging out watching the deep sea fishermen come in with catches of barracuda and marlin.

When we got home, there was a letter from Cole's agent letting him know how well the first pages of his book were received by the editors at the publishing house. The welcome news got Cole psyched for stepping up his writing pace. His energy increased so much he took brisk walks that still didn't alleviate his growing tension. He began drinking more to soothe physical complaints. He paced the courtyard biting his nails, and I worried he'd throw himself into one of his panic attacks.

Coming home from the beach one afternoon I found him talking to a young woman in the courtyard.

"Hey, babe, glad you're back," he said, waving me into to the courtyard. "Meet Carolyn, our new tenant. I ran into her at the newsstand where she was looking over the posted notices for a place to rent. I told her we had the little apartment downstairs that no one was staying in. So she took it."

"I see," I said. Or thought I did. I was too upset to hear myself.

She walked over to shake my hand. "This is just so amazing you have this great apartment downstairs. I can't believe my luck running into your husband. It's just so far out!"

"Carolyn's just come from school in San Diego. She's spending the summer here. And then in the fall you'll be what grade again?"

"A junior. Just two more years!"

"Isn't that something," I said. "Well, I'm sure you need to settle in so don't let us keep you."

"Yeah. I still have to unpack. Well, thanks again! See you later I guess." She walked across the courtyard, all bronze arms and legs in a short sundress, her lanky blond hair hanging to her waist, her many bracelets jangling as she hopped down the stairs.

"Nice girl, huh?" Cole said. I sank onto a stool by the bar.

"How could you do this, Cole?" I glared at him. "Didn't you think I might have some feeling about having someone here?"

"Gee, I didn't think you'd mind. It just seemed the thing to do. She needed a place to stay and we have the room. I don't know. I really didn't think about it."

"Obviously." And I was obviously pissed.

"It'll be okay. She's got her own entrance. We won't even see her."

"Yeah, right." I left for the kitchen to make myself a drink, then went into the bedroom and closed the door. My anger scared me. To keep from raging and killing him, I got drunk and stayed away from him. From the bathroom window I looked out into the courtyard and saw him sitting and staring at the stone wall, his glasses off and his fingers arched against the bridge of his nose. A familiar pose. Maybe he was actually thinking about how stupid he'd been. I didn't care.

I kept my distance from Cole over the next week. Carolyn only made one appearance and talked with Cole about garbage removal. She wasn't consciously seductive. She was just what Cole liked best. She looked like his favorite porn material. Young and luscious. I was only a few years ahead of her, but felt old. I wasn't even sure Cole knew what he was doing. His pursuits always started so innocently. She just needed a place to stay, that's all. Yeah. Our place.

I took to wandering, coming back to the apartment at odd times to see if there was something to interrupt. Nothing happened, it seemed.

I stopped in the Church of Our Lady of Guadalupe, the cathedral in the center of town, to try and center myself and stop the ruminations circulating unproductively in my head. The church's many windows filled the vaulted ceilings with light reflecting off the starkly white interior, its immense columns trimmed in dark wood. The pleasure of sitting quietly on one of the wooden benches contrasted well with my feeling of dread. I liked the echoing sounds of footsteps, the swishing fabric of women's skirts as they knelt in prayer, the occasional cough or whispered word. The sound of people was comforting.

Returning home from the cathedral one day, I kept going past our place and headed up the hill to see if I could find the old house with all the bougainvillea. It was there, just as the woman I'd met in the square had described, set into the steep side of the hill, the purple, white and red blossoms spilling over the stone wall surrounding the house except the street side where there was a tall white fence.

As I got closer I saw that the fence gate was open. More flowers hung in heavy boughs from window boxes and the small front yard was filled with short palms and other trees I couldn't name. A cat lay outstretched in the shade of a bush with huge dark green leaves thick enough to paddle a tennis ball. Hanging baskets lined the roof of the porch of the small house, blue and pink flowers on long green tendrils catching the breeze. A wind chime hung by the door, its song a friendly greeting.

I walked up the flagstone path and stopped before going up the stairs to the porch. I could see my friend through the open door into the house. She was holding another cat and talking animatedly to it. I didn't move, but something must have caught her eye because she turned as if to a sound and looked at me. Smiling, she waved and headed towards the door.

"Well hello, hello!" she said, stepping onto the porch. "You've come after all. I'm so glad. Please come in. And don't mind my mess," she added, dropping the cat to the floor. "It's always like this and I'm much too old to bother with it."

Newspapers were strewn on the padded porch swing, books perilously stacked on too small table tops, a teapot nestled against a basket filled with what looked like bound sage, its blunt end singed black. A third cat, a tabby, lay sprawled and dozing across the open leaf of a writing desk, its top covered with figurines. A nearby standing lamp had a deep red shade with strands of beads along its edges and hanging from its crook and also along a cord strung across the window were beautiful and unusual pieces of decorative glass.

"Do sit down," she said, raking the newspapers off the long swing. She took a wicker chair in the corner, propping her feet on a small woven footstool. "And tell me why you've come. I sense there's a story to hear."

I sat gingerly on the swing, settling my weight on it and pushing my feet against the floor to glide it back and forth a bit. I felt like the little girl I wanted to be.

"I don't think you ever told me your name. Mine's Grace," she said, seeing my hesitation.

"I'm Lily." I paused. "And you're right. There is a story and not a very happy one, I'm afraid." The long-haired grey cat from outside jumped up on the swing and flopped next to me.

"I see. I'm sorry to hear that. You'll need some tea then. I'll get us a fresh pot. I have water set to boil and it must be ready by now. Just relax and I'll get it." She picked up the teapot as she rose from her chair, patting me on the knee before heading inside.

I started crying as soon as she left the porch. I didn't even know this woman, but I was glad to be in her home. I needed to talk and she seemed to know that. And I knew she'd listen. I leaned back against the swing and breathed deeply. Out the side window I could see down the hill to the ocean, the afternoon sun glinting off the water, sailboats lazing along the coast.

"Here you are, Lily." She handed me the teacup and made space on the nearby table for me to rest it on. "I hope you like it. It's my own blend. A little of this, some of that. I don't even remember what all is in it at this point. I just keep adding new teas as I use it with friends. But it's all calming ingredients and I think the taste is holding up." She looked thoughtfully out the window, stirring her cup. I was still quiet. "The tea blend reminds me of a friend, a shamanic woman, who holds fire ceremonies during the winter and summer solstices. These are very ritualistic affairs where a gathering of people honor the spirits of the cardinal points and also Father Sky and Mother Earth. They make vows of intentions and pray for those they love as well as themselves. When they do this they toss bits of tobacco into the fire to kind of seal their intentions and wishes. She always keeps some of the ash from each ceremony and adds it to ash she's kept from fire ceremonies she's held over the past forty years. Then with each new fire, she adds some of the old ash to the blaze. Years of prayers and intentions all mixed together." Grace sighed. "My tea blend is like that to me, having shared this tea and its history with so many friends." She smiled and tilted her head. "But enough about that. Tell me what's troubling you, Lily. I can tell you're upset."

"Oh, some things have happened that make me sad and confused" I curled onto the swing and let it glide. "My husband came to find me and we ended up moving into an apartment that's actually just down the hill from here."

"Well that is news. The husband returns, does he? And you move into, well, into Pat Whalen's apartment I imagine.

"Yes, Patricia Whalen, that's the owner.

"Oh, I've known Pat for years. Quite the socialite. Has she thrown any of her wild parties lately?"

"She had one last month. The band played until really late and people were out on the veranda and wandering around the lawn sounding very drunk."

"Oh yes. She has quite the friends. She often invites celebrities who've come to town, a few of the local politicals, and the Hustons are usually there. At least Angelica goes. I'm not sure John does anymore.

He's as old as I am. I can't take all the frivolity and hilarity at this point, though I used to go. I stop by and say hello to Pat now and then or she'll stop in for tea." I was smiling. I loved listening to her talk. It helped me relax. "I'm glad to see a smile. So tell me what's happened between you and this husband."

"Well, we were having a good time once we moved back in together. But, well, Cole has these ups and downs and sometimes his attention wanders and I feel so uncared for and unwanted. I just don't know what to do and I'm feeling afraid."

"Hmnn, I see. His attention wanders you say. Wanders to, what, deep sea fishing? Golf? Or, I rather suspect, to other women?"

I paused, not sure of what to say, but the words tumbled out anyway. "He invited a girl to move into the studio apartment under ours."

"Ah, yes. The old maid's quarters when Pat's son lived where you are. Well, that's certainly unfortunate. And you have reason to believe he has intentions towards this woman?"

"If not now, it'll happen soon enough. There've been other women, other times."

"Well, then, it's more than time to get out. You've no reason to hang around with this cad. His attention's more than wandering. It sounds totally dissipated. He should be focusing on whatever the hell is eating at him that makes him feel he needs such devotion from multiple women, for heaven's sake. He sounds a bit narcissistic to me. I don't mean to jump into this and meddle, but I'm old and I've seen this sort of thing happen too often to too many women. And you say he has 'ups and downs'?"

"Yes. He's very excitable and then very depressed

sometimes. It seems to run in cycles."

"Is he in therapy?" She was pruning the dead blossoms from an African violet on the table near her, plucking their heads off with some gusto as if peeved at them.

"No, he isn't."

"Well he should be. And if you stay with him you'll need it yourself soon. I don't mean to condemn the man, Lily. And I know that marital relationships have two people in them and both play a role. But this fellow's out of bounds. If you want to save the marriage you'll need counseling for the both of you. But don't feel you have to continue living with him for that to happen. You left him before. What do you think you should do now?"

"I love him and I want it to work, but no matter what I do it always ends up the same way. I don't expect him to adore me alone. People have attractions to other people. But Cole acts rather impulsively towards other women or, well, even pictures of women, and starts to ignore me. I can't handle it anymore." I was beginning to rant and I knew it, but it was just coming out in a rush and I couldn't stop it. I felt the tears coming, too. "I want to leave him, but I don't know if I can live on my own. I never have. I'm terrified."

Grace's hand was on my arm. "My dear, slow down. You'll whip yourself into a frenzy over this. Take a very deep breath and let it out slowly." I did, and felt a little better. "That's better. Drink some more tea. Here's some tissue," she said, going to her writing desk for it and handing it to me.

You'll find your way, Lily," she said, returning to her chair. "We always do. But you have to start with yourself. Do what's best for you, not him. He'll have to find his own way. And that's alright. In the end, you might even be back together. But if not, then don't regret the past Just look at your own future."

She sat back on her chair, but kept looking at me. "I don't mean to be an old busy-body, but it sounds to me like the person you need to fall in love with is yourself, Lily. From there you can love others more freely. If we don't love ourselves we get desperate and don't make good decisions." She heaved a sigh. "I get upset about these things because I know. I w a s married to the wrong man for twenty-five years. Well, he was the right man in the beginning for the wrong reasons, but people grow and change and we're not always the best for each other down the road, even if we've travelled it together. Sometimes the road divides for a while or forever. It sounds to me, Lily, like it's time to step out on your own." She took another sip of her tea. "I'm afraid I do ramble a bit, but I've been where you are and I honestly don't think you have to suffer like this."

"Oh, I'm tired of it," I said uncurling myself. "I just don't know how I'll manage alone."

"You won't know until you try it. Do you have the resources to be on your own?"

"Yes, for a while, I suppose. I could go back to New York, but in time I'd be broke again and not know what to do about it."

"Those answers will come, Lily. Take it slowly. Of course it'll be unsettling at first, but things will change and you'll be fine. This life offers lots of solutions if you open yourself up enough to find them. We all need to try and enjoy the adventure. If we don't, we become resentful and then that turns to jealousy and greed. We'd all die feeling unfulfilled, and our spirits would become pretas. Do you know about pretas?"

"No, not at all."

"Well," she said, crossing her feet and pulling a shawl over her knees from the back of her chair. "It's not a good outcome. The word 'preta' is Sanskrit for 'gone forth.' In English we call them 'hungry ghosts.' The poor things depart from their miserable earthly form only to find themselves in a perpetual state of hunger and thirst, their jealousy and unmet needs leaving them terribly gaunt, with thin arms and legs, but hugely distended bellies and long thin necks with narrow throats. They constantly suffer as their throats are too small to swallow the food and water they need to satisfy their enormous appetites in their large stomachs." She took a long drink of her tea. "So they're always hungry and they also get cold or hot very easily. I've heard even the moon scorches them in summer. It's a terrible state to end up in. You don't want that to happen to you do you? I certainly don't. Just to be sure, I'm meeting my needs as best I can to banish even the chance of becoming a preta in my afterlife, especially now that I'm nearer the end of living for me. Sating the preta, I call it – finding affirmation and celebrating our authentic beings so our spirits don't take the path of the preta, turning to more angelic destinies instead. We need to care for ourselves and be able to speak of our needs to those who can share their health and happiness with us. The others, the greedy ones who only want to take from us, well, it's best to stay away from them," she said, waving her hand as if pushing something repugnant away.

"I'm sure you're right, Grace. I mean that. For

some reason I absolutely trust you, though I've just met you." I smiled at her.

"Oh, sometimes women just have an affinity for each other. It's our intuition thing working. I feel I've known you for a long time, Lily. You remind me of myself at your age. That's probably why. I was vulnerable, too. And now look at me! Living alone with more cats than I can count." Her laugh was loud and deep. It surprised me. "Not that you'll have the same fate. Not to worry. And actually I'm extremely happy. I've got enough friends to keep me company, but not too many to be a bother. I help out some of the young mothers in town by running errands for them or helping with their children. They have so many after all and I love every one of them. I have a million interests and hobbies. And whenever all else fails, I have my glassblowing."

"Glassblowing?" My contorted face showed my surprise.

"Why, yes. Would you like to see my shop? Oh, do come with me. It's such fun." Grace led me through her house, an obstacle course of unmatched things we were passing by almost too quickly for me to take in: A tall, free-standing wooden bookcase that swiveled when I grasped its corner for balance as we sped through the living room, a large model of an old sailing ship on the top of it with Christmas lights strung across the masts; a brass hat rack draped with dozens of colorful scarves and strings of glass beads, a captain's table covered with antique-looking knick-knacks, world maps pinned to the walls among old paintings in damaged frames of European-looking town squares with central fountains, and more standing lamps with fringed and fluted shades. The kitchen was filled with pottery and wooden bowls of fruit and vegetables, jars of grains and pastas, utensils of all sorts and sizes, more cats eating out of colorful ceramic dishes that might be locally made, a parrot perched on a dividing wall I wouldn't have even seen as real until it squawked. Out back of the house were rows of vegetables growing next to an avocado and a tamarind fruit tree. A few chickens clucked and pecked at the ground. Grace stopped suddenly and spun around to face me, almost throwing me off balance.

"Don't tell anyone about the chickens, by the way. I'm not supposed to have them so close to the town. It's against the rules," she whispered. She rotated again and stepped onto a crushed stone path that took us to a small shed next to the fence that bordered her property; open on one side to the yard. Outside the shed was a furnace and tables full of tools and pieces of glass in beautiful shapes and brilliant colors like the ones strung across her porch window.

"Of course I had to take classes to get good enough to do it on my own. It can be dangerous and I'm not an idiot. There's a studio in Guadalajara where I learned it." She hobbled around the area on her sturdy legs. "I've got my kiln over here," she gestured, "and this is my blowpipe," she said, handing it to me. "I blow the glass I've heated in the kiln through the pipe, obviously, making bubbles I can blow into objects. I started with beads and I've graduated to making small art objects using these little cylinders of colored glass they call 'cane' or these cross-sections of colored patterns called 'murrines.'" She held them up for me to see. I put down the pipe, afraid of breaking it, and took one of the cylinders from her. It had intricate patterns I recognized in the art pieces on the table, though in the objects the glass and the patterns were stretched and various pieces were somehow molded together. "I'm finding it challenging to do these. I don't know how far I'll get with this, but I'm loving what I've been able to create so far."

"This is amazing, Grace. I can't believe you're doing this. I'm really impressed."

"Well, nothing's holding me back." She gave me one of her soft smiles and handed me a beautifully crafted piece of glass she took off a shelf from the shed. It was a solid piece that had a large bubble in the middle of it that magnified the patterns of the glass around it. "This was an experiment," she chuckled. "I used an uncut murrine, heating it and blowing into the whole thing until it expanded into this shape and made that bubble inside. It took everything my lungs had. Good thing I walk up and down the hill every day. But it turned out well. I want you to have it, Lily."

"Grace I couldn't possibly accept this! It's too lovely."

"Oh yes you can, and will. Please have it. I want you to remember our chat today. I want you to remember to take care of yourself and tend to others later. You're what's most important – not what they think of you or how much they need you or you think you need them. You are like this glass – beautiful on your own, with a growing bubble of life inside of you – the goodness, beauty and truth you hold for others to discover. That's been your gift to me, Lily. And this is my gift to you."

Later, after I left Grace, I didn't know if I'd ever

see her again. But she'd come into my life for a reason and my memory of her would never leave me. She was so wonderfully casual and self-assured. Like one of her glass objects, she'd warmed and shaped herself over the years into this very solid and beautiful human being, colorful and patterned with intricate thoughts and feelings. I'd miss her, I knew.

I went home and found the living room dark though light came from the patio. Stepping outside I saw that Cole had set the table with candlelight for dinner, but there was only one plate of food.

"Where've you been?" His voice came out of the darkness by the bar and I could see the outline of him sitting on one of the tall stools.

"Just walking and thinking."

"All this time?" Dead silence. "I made dinner for us over an hour ago. I ate. Yours is cold by now."

"Well thanks for making it, Cole. That was nice." I sat down at the table. "It's a steak. I can eat that cold." I started cutting into it. "Sorry, I didn't realize how late it was getting." I wasn't feeling hungry and Cole keeping his distance in the darkness was making me uncomfortable.

"I thought you might've gone to Carlos O'Brien's so I stopped by to look for you."

"Oh, no," I mumbled, chewing the steak. "I didn't go there."

"Yes, I found that out from Alomar." I heard a glass clink a bottle and knew Cole had been drinking. "In fact he says he hasn't seen you in a while and that he misses seeing you."

"Well, that's sweet of him to say." It seemed I was endlessly chewing the same piece of steak and it was getting dry in my mouth.

"I didn't believe him. Something about the way he said it." Cole emerged from the darkness and sat down at the table opposite me. He'd brought his drink and the bottle of Jack Daniel's that was half empty. "Have you been seeing him?" He crossed his legs and stared at me quizzically and coldly.

"What? No, of course not!" My fork clattered on the glass top of the table. He was scaring me. "Why would you think that?"

"Just guessing." His lips twisted as he smiled. I knew he'd gone deep into convincing himself I was seeing this guy. "Did you fuck him?"

"Cole, listen, I'm not going to have this conversation. You've convinced yourself I've done something wrong and I haven't. I'm going to enjoy this dinner and let's please talk about something else. I went for a walk tonight and I'm not seeing anyone. Okay?" I looked at him as directly as I could, though his stone face made me look away. "Is there any wine, please?"

He got up and sauntered to the bar. He pulled a bottle out of the small wine rack and held it up. "Sure, there's some wine. Here," he said calmly, as he hurled it at my chair. The bottle smashed against it, shards of glass and red wine bursting all over me.

"Cole! Damn it!" I jumped up, brushing glass off with a thick cloth napkin. It looked like I was bleeding, but I didn't feel any cuts, just sticky warm wine dripping off my left side. I stepped away and stood by the wall, seeking its protection. "Cole, I can't do this anymore." I pressed against the wall, wanting to disappear into it. "I'm leaving." I let my head fall back, looking at the stars, knowing he could hit me if he wanted to, but I didn't care. I felt so tired.

"What do you mean you're leaving?"

"I'm leaving here, Cole." I turned to look at him. "I'm leaving you." He was quiet, and I heard him sitting down on a lounge chair.

"Why would you do that? We're just getting started. You wouldn't want to miss what's coming. I'm all you've got. You know that."

"No ... you're not." I left the wall, tossed the red stained napkin on the table, and started to walk inside. "You're not all I've got ... I've got me."

"Lily!" I pulled off my stained clothes, threw them on the floor and lay on the couch in my underwear, pulling a shawl over me, the darkness feeling close. "Lily!" A pause. "But what about me?!"

I woke in the middle of the night. Walking softly, I looked into the bedroom, but Cole wasn't there. I found him asleep on the lounge chair in the moonlight. Quietly, I once again threw most of my clothes in a suitcase, plus anything else I'd need. I rinsed my face, sponge washed myself, and dressed quickly in jeans and a tee-shirt. Grabbing my bag, I stealthily left the apartment, looked up at Grace's house and then started walking down the hill. In town I found a cab at the little square and asked for the airport. It was six o'clock. There'd be a flight at eight-thirty for New York by way of Miami. There always was.

Leaving the town behind me was hard. With everything that had gone wrong and maybe because of it, I'd had so many moments of enjoyment there. It was like leaving a friend – someone who smelled like frangipangi and sounded like waves, who tasted spicy and felt like warm stones and sand. But at that time in the morning there was little movement. At least I was leaving the town asleep. The cab rode quietly through, the road becoming dusty. By the side of the bigger road leading to the airport I saw two figures walking along in the distance, one tall, one short. As they came closer I recognized the necklace lady and her young protégé walking in from who knew where to begin their day on the Malecòn. As the cab drove by them I smiled and she smiled back, though I doubt she recognized just one of the many tourists passing through.

When the plane sped down the runway and took off from Vallarta, I reached into my bag and felt the elongated glass that fit so neatly in my palm. *Yes, Grace, I believe I'll be alright. Thank you,* I silently said to her, looking down at the hilltop, at Gringo Gulch, as the plane lifted higher and the town disappeared from view.

♋♋♋♋♋♋

When I got back to New York, I went underground. I didn't want anyone to know where I was, especially Cole. Anyone I knew thought I was still with him in Mexico. Eventually I'd give him my phone number for emergencies, pretending to my parents that I was still living with him when he moved from Mexico to Boston to continue work on his novel. When they called he'd always say I was busy or out, and I'd call them back when Cole let me know they'd asked for me.

I'd been so afraid of living alone, but what I discovered was an incredible freedom. Being without Cole was a level of relief I hadn't expected. It was hard for me to accept how frightened of him I'd often been, even when we were getting along. Scared of his not liking me and turning away. Scared of his sudden anger.

I did visit him when he came back and we reconciled to some civil extent, agreeing to stay married but continue our separation for a while. We phoned. We stayed in touch. But no one else knew where I was living. I liked it that way, feeling my resilience returning and enjoying having control over my days and nights.

Being somewhat underground didn't keep me from becoming suddenly aware of all that had happened in the world while I was gone, stuck away inside my own stuff. I knew major things like the fall of Saigon and the sentencing of Watergate scum, but being back in New York meant getting flooded with newsstand magazine covers, passing boom-boxes, cab radios, television screens in stores, bus advertising, and subway posters. I felt like I'd been off the planet. Everything felt so different through the time warp, as if it was a new start for me.

I got a room in a cheap hotel on Gramercy Park South where I paid by the week and no one asked questions. I loved it there. Spending time alone I didn't have to answer to anyone's assumptions about me. It was the only way to begin understanding who I was without being connected to someone else. Just experiencing the day on my own terms led to finding out what I liked to do and who I liked to be. My anonymity was a great cover as I changed from someone I'd made up to please Cole and other people to someone more authentically me. I could try out new roles and see what fit. I could also explore old feelings, understand and help rid myself of the bad ones and return to the good ones from happier times. At twenty-five, it was as if I was nine years old again – the explorer with maps of exciting places, testing my life like I'd tested my rock collection, seeing how my chemistry mixed with the world.

The hotel was very quiet. I could see a small park out my window. You couldn't go in it without a key for the one small gate, which was only given to owners of the very elegant townhouses in the intimate neighborhood surrounding this wrought-iron fenced greenery. Strangely, I never saw anyone there. But it was a lovely view, which I always remember as it was at dusk, or lit dimly on a rainy night. My life was like that then – somber and shadowy. I kept the lighting low in my room, a pink bulb in one lamp, and lived like a woman cast in a film noir, peering through the long, thin window drapes expecting to see a man on the corner, a gumshoe in a dark hat pulled slightly over his face to hide his surveillance of me in my delightfully seedy room. I'd toss him a sidelong glance, throw my head back in a cynical laugh and leave the window, pulling closed the drapes. It was one of the parts I auditioned for in my own head to see if I liked it, to test its validity within myself. *Yes, it's a nice fit,* I decided.

The room came furnished and a large double bed took up most of it. The bed was covered in a badly frayed crochet spread that had seen a lot of bleach in its time, the sheets stiff and a pillow I didn't trust. A writing desk sat between the two floor-to-ceiling windows and a dressing table was on the opposite side of the room with a huge round mirror on the wall behind it. On the table was a lamp with a stained and fringed shade, its gooseneck laden with my cheap necklaces. This was the pink bulb lamp, which cast a bordello effect to the whole room. Next to the lamp was an art deco blue glass vase full of white Chinese silver dollar flowers I'd bought in what was becoming SoHo, an artsy part of Manhattan below Gramercy Park. A straight-backed wooden ladder chair was in front of the dresser and I'd bought a plush red velvet cushion for it from a dingy thrift shop full of old theater props. Near the front window was an over-stuffed armchair of questionable cleanliness over which I'd draped one of my large shawls from Mexico, black with red and white hibiscus flowers. I'd lounge my body across it, imagining myself a character in a Raymond Chandler novel: *She was a blond. A blond to make a bishop kick a hole in a stained glass window.* The man could certainly write.

I'd taken to writing a novel myself, a psychological thriller about a female serial killer. Like Chandler's femme fatale, she was also a pretty young blond twisted by a painful past into killing women who resembled her, in the end thinking she's killing one more victim, but too late discovering she's killing herself while looking at her reflection in a pool, the knife having found its target in her own gut, bringing her sharply to consciousness from the trancelike state she'd been living in: A prolonged and treacherous suicide.

When I'd finished several of the chapters and an outline for the rest of the book I submitted it to Cole's agent, who gave it to an editor for review. The editor said it was an interesting premise, but oddly lacking in suspense, though she liked some of the flashback chapters I'd written about the woman's childhood. I was no Raymond Chandler. The manuscript sat untouched on the writing desk after that. Another nuance of my private fantasy life, a mystery half-told.

I spent all my time alone, venturing out to explore art galleries and bookstores, coffee shops and restaurants in SoHo and Tribeca in lower Manhattan. I thoroughly enjoyed the easy invisibility you can find living there. No one hassles you unless they're looking for something. You don't make eye contact for long and they don't bother you. You walk on.

After the warmth in Mexico, I liked the chill of fall in New York. I bought a thick, dark green turtle-neck sweater in a shop somewhere on Spring Street and wore it like a uniform over my most comfortable jeans and a pair of good fitting boots. I walked a lot. Only it was more like cruising without a destination. One set of footsteps. Mine.

I went through my share of Cole's book advance and then my savings started running out. It got colder. I had to decide what to do. I figured I should probably find some legitimate way to earn some money, but nothing seemed to fit. Besides, I knew my decision had been made before I even began thinking about it. The too easy money of escort work hung there like an old hat on a hook by the door, just waiting to be worn the next time I stepped out. I had to admit I missed the life, the personal power. Scoping out my options, I went by The Herald Agency only to find out from another tenant that the business closed down. A quick review of *Backstage*, one of Manhattan's theatrical rags, gave me the phone numbers of a few escort services to check out. I chose one near the theater district and started working right away.

Something else I missed was the comfortable

camaraderie I'd felt with the other girls I'd known before. In the theater district most of the girls in the escort service were non-working actresses trying for a break. We were like a troupe of thespians with strange parts, again with all of us sensing we'd come from similarly distressing backgrounds. Of course searching questions weren't asked. They weren't needed.

The choice to be an escort was only for some women.Other actresses became waitresses in Hell's Kitchen, a neighborhood nearby. Most other girls worked their way into secretarial, then business careers. This kind of work was for women needing to take back the night.

This escort service was a little different from those I'd known. Men were invited in to choose their girl. More than an apartment, this service was laid out like a small showroom with a center floor surrounded by two rows of slightly elevated platforms theater-style. Perhaps it'd been a cabaret at some point. Each platform held several tables where drinks were served. There was muted lighting and soft rock music was piped in. Guys would have a couple of drinks, make their selection, pay the desk and leave with their escort for whatever evening entertainment they'd scheduled.

Cocaine was the drug of choice or the girls would be high on pot or both. It could be a long evening sometimes. On slow nights some of the actresses would do scene studies together, practicing lines for auditions, using the room's center and platforms like staged areas. Now and then someone would get hired for a part and they'd vanish, to be soon replaced. I liked a lot of them. One in particular. She was obviously lovers with one of the other women, but that didn't bother me.

Elise was a siren as worthy of the title as any in Homer's *Odyssey*. I'd never met anyone as seductive. When she walked across the room, I watched her sultry stride so closely that the room seemed to move with her, molding itself to her shape as she passed, framing and ornamenting her body as if by her tacit command. When she spoke her tongue pulled you unresisting down her beautiful throat, fully consuming you. You had no choice.

Elise had exquisite and noble features from her Bulgarian Jewish heritage. Her russet brown hair coiled around her long neck, which she'd gracefully turn to look at you with her heavy-lidded dark eyes, something like the asp in Eden sensing innocence. She'd seduce me from across the room, and in another instant be at my side, her perfume swirling around my nose like mist off the Black Sea of her ancestry. Not one to be captured, she took you first and quickly, if she wanted you at all.

There was no question of my becoming her companion and then her lover. She tossed out her current lover without even a ritual parting. I felt bad for the woman, who was clearly hurt. It should have been a warning, but I was certainly too naïve then to suspect Elise changed companions like scarves.

Elise and I went everywhere and did everything together. She maintained a luxurious, near perfect existence. Her SoHo apartment reflected the best of her elegant taste. She groomed herself immaculately and wore impeccable clothing. We ate in good restaurants and drank the best wines. An after-dinner cognac would be had in the most intimate and classy bar only she could find, where we'd sit in glamorous antique chairs by a flickering fire, the light catching the playful gleam in her eye, her smile a slanted vixenish invitation. *Come here you sweet thing,* she'd say, pulling me to her and kissing me boldly in front of whoever was watching. She loved to shock people. She'd take me home to her stylish bed and we'd make love under the finest down comforter, an Ella Fitzgerald song playing softly while we kissed the softness of each other's most delicate places.

Elise taught me the womanly moves of a confident female. She dressed me to equal her, and we shopped for clothes that suited our moods and answered to no style. We were a show together, chic in cashmere sweaters and fine wool trousers or outlandish in matching white jumpsuits covered with brightly colored racing insignias, un-snapped to the mounds of our full breasts and worn over shiny red vinyl boots. We turned every head on the street and loved the stares. She was an inch taller than me, but I stood as straight as her and strode along with the same grace, balance and beauty. She was the dark one and I the light one and we played our parts as if it was always opening night.

During the day, Elise was all business and very motivated by the success that would clearly come to her. She took courses at New York University with thoughts of maybe going into science after getting her bachelor's. We'd often be up half the night drinking and drugging and she'd set off in the morning for her early Italian class. Ti amo, she'd say, professing her love as she left while grazing my ear with her lips. She amazed me.

We'd meet in the afternoon for drinks and often go to her apartment to get ready for work. In the elevator she'd press herself against me, run her hand over my ass and give it a squeeze, puckering her ruby lips and throwing me one of her heavy-lidded winks that she knew got to me. She was in control of me – her student of all things sensual.

I adored her and wanted her to want me. After feeling so dispensable to Cole, I was desperate for affection from someone who could make me feel desirable. Elise did just that, relishing the attention I returned to her. Everything about one of us seemed shaped to fit the other perfectly.

"Sweetie," she called from the bathroom. I pulled the door open and looked in. She was soaking in heaps of bubbles in her immense tub surrounded by candles, the light of the flames filling the gilt framed mirror on the wall that reflected her smoothly muscled torso as she leaned toward me, her nipples brushing the inside of the tub. "How about a brandy alexander?" she said, requesting one of her favorite drinks. "And some music? I think I left Nina Simone on the record player."

I'd never met anyone so capable of finding pleasure. It wasn't a talent I'd cultivated and as much as I enjoyed Elise, I could easily feel intimidated by her, challenged to rise to her level of womanly class.

Switching on the record, I carried the drinks into the bathroom. She blew a kiss at me that parted the bubbles, revealing her coy smile. The room was steamy and fragrant from the scented bath oil. She took her drink from me as I sat down on the edge of the tub, placing mine on the small marble table nearby.

I want a little sugar in my bowl, Nina sang. Elise took a long sip of her drink, and then set it next to mine. "I want a little sweetness down in my soul," she sang, accompanying Nina's lusty vocal. She lay back against the curved tub, the bubbles barely concealing her glistening breasts. Her fingers slid out of the water and she began playing with her hardening nipples, her other hand sliding down to stroke her pussy hidden in the warm water, her breasts heaving slightly, the nipples bobbing in and out of the bubbles as she became more and more aroused. Then she leaned forward and began unbuttoning my shirt, her steady gaze seducing me even more. *I want some steam on my clothes,* Nina continued. My shirt opened, she fingered the front clasp of my low cut bra, opening it and pushing the sheer cups aside, freeing my breasts which she fondled with her warm, wet hands, spreading bubbles over my nipples before taking them in her mouth, sucking and nibbling them teasingly. *Maybe I can fix things up so they'll go.* I pulled off my shirt and bra and stood up to unzip and remove my jeans. Stepping into the bath, I lowered myself onto her, our breasts sliding against each other in the scented bath oil, my thigh opening her legs and pressing against her, Elise turning so her pussy rode my thigh. *I ain't foolin'... I want some sugar in my bowl.* My tongue found hers, writhing and penetrating in rhythm with our pushing together, gaining tempo to her pleasured gasps. *I want some ...* and her little cry of delight ... *yeah ... in my bowl.*

Afterward, we got dry and dressed, rubbing each other with thick towels, powdering with large, ribboned puffs, drying and styling our hair and selecting the night's wardrobe, dressing each other slowly before heading out to Seventh Avenue to hail a cab to work, our boot heels clacking on the sidewalk, concluding another lesson for me in the art of femininity.

On nights we didn't work, a regular haunt was *Bonnie and Clyde's,* a women's gay bar in the Village, a few steps down into a smoke-filled, dark hole-in-the-wall full of women in pairs and a few singles. We'd get sloshy drunk, snort cocaine and dance ourselves into exhilaration with Elise breathing into my ear the words to Barry White's *You're the First, the Last, My Everything* without losing the momentum of our bump and grind.

Other nights we'd take in a music act like the Manhattan Transfer at Reno Sweeney's on Thirteenth Street or disco and female impersonators at Trude Heller's on Sixth Avenue. To recuperate from these nightly excursions we'd go to a women's bathhouse on the West Side in the forties block that had a distinctly art deco theme for its small swimming pool, steam room and sauna. Thick-armed masseuses would finish our indulgent routine and leave us to nap, swaddled in terrycloth robes, on lavender-scented pillows in white wicker lounge chairs. Strangely, we were often the only ones there as if it was our private club.

In time, I shed a lot of uncertainty about myself. Elise's brazenness gave me strength and she validated my self-esteem. She insisted I demand the best for myself and I learned from her example. I'd never been this close to a woman and it was the only really romantic affair I ever had. I trusted her with my feelings and grew fond of her. But I was also much too dependent on her. For all I gained from her, a lot of what I'd finally found of myself after leaving Cole got lost in the musky places of our affection. I now felt my strength mostly in her company. I'd become hidden in her, roaming around looking for a more comfortable identity for myself, one with more class, more sensuality, more pizzazz.

Elise was her own woman. She had other friends and, I learned one day, other lovers, including men. I caught up with her one afternoon heading out of her apartment wearing an almost sheer blouse fit snugly around her bare breasts. "Where are you going dressed like that?" I asked. She freely told me she was going to the apartment of two gay male friends, saying they used each other for sexual pleasure only, nothing more than that. Clearly, our romance had expired, or at least it did for me then.

I worked at convincing myself it didn't bother me if she had needs met with someone else or even fun-loving gay guys with hot dicks. But I couldn't hack it and competitively became lovers with the uptown bartender who'd made Cole jealous. I hoped to make Elise jealous, but it didn't work. She didn't need me like I needed her. So I sometimes let slip a little snide remark or inconsiderate gesture, nothing totally damaging, but I wanted to even the score while fighting to gain her attention. She tolerated my small insults, at the same time telling me once that I wasn't a nice person. I didn't argue with that. Then again, we weren't always nice women.

I began a slow cat fight with her in my head. Her sexual friends got me squirrely and insecure and even more dependent though I was frightened of her too, and what she might do with me if I was now the old scarf. I tried harder to ensnare her with the kind of bitchy charm she could exude like a spider's sticky webbing.

We started hooking together outside the escort service. I had a few excellent regulars and so did she. Between us we could skim off the best clients, a wealthy but seedy bunch. One ran an undisclosed business out of his penthouse garden apartment involving shady deals we assumed were Mafia-connected. There was a great deal of cash on hand at all times. We didn't ask. We were paid not to know. Another did business with Saudi Arabians staying on Fifth Avenue in suites at the Hotel Pierre and the Waldorf Astoria. One wanted me to return with him to his palace somewhere in the Eastern Province. Wisely, I didn't go. With another client pair, Elise and I'd be invited to Long Island for a weekend of drugs and drinking, Dean and Deluca's extravagant food and wine, and we'd partner in sex with the men. On a plane to a Florida getaway of another client, I foolishly agreed to bring a locked metal suitcase full of what I was told was a change of clothes and some toiletries that I knew to be large amounts of cocaine packaged probably as hand soaps or seltzer tablets. After losing touch with this client, I received greeting cards, illustrated with Vargas girls, sent from him in prison for murder. Yes, a seedy bunch.

Our drug intake escalated to each of us carrying vials of colored pills for different occasions demanding different states of mind. Amphetamines and sedatives regulated our days and nights, mostly black beauties and reds. For a bad cocaine crash in the early morning, there was always valium.

Regularly I'd return to my little rented hotel room for a hiatus from it all, a chance to detox and unwind, an evening in comfortable pajamas, my hair in a ponytail, a good book, and a bowl of hot wonton soup from the Chinese take-out two blocks away. During those times I'd pick up and hold Grace's glass gift to me and wonder what the fuck I was doing and how my chance at becoming whoever I was really supposed to be had gone so very awry. Or maybe this was the only way to get there.

♋♋♋♋♋

Another reprieve from intensive escapades with Elise came when I'd visit my client Jerry. I'd gotten past my initial discomfort with his advanced age and found his company calm and reassuring. Of course having the leased car didn't hurt.

His apartment never changed, everything always in the same place and nothing new added. It was always tidy and there was always food in the refrigerator and fresh towels in the bathroom.

I'd see him in the afternoon and we'd chat over one of his nicely made lunches. Then we'd have thirteen minutes of predictable, undemanding sex, after which I'd pose for his sculpture, a modest nude figure about a foot tall. It was coming along. Jerry wasn't a bad sculptor and although the statuette didn't entirely resemble me, it had pleasant features and he'd captured the pose very well. It was demure and delicate, like the young woman was resting after a swim in some secluded lake.

I'd scheduled an afternoon with Jerry for the same day that Cole suddenly announced he'd be visiting his agent in New York. He and I agreed to have dinner, and I asked Elise to entertain him in her apartment after he'd seen his agent until I could get there. Elise and Cole hadn't yet met each other, though each knew of the other. I thought we could all have dinner together.

I left Jerry's and called Elise from a phone booth on the corner. "Hi there. Everything okay?"

"Sure is, sugar," she answered.

"Cole get there alright? You taking care of him for me?"

"I sure am," she breathed into the phone. "I'm taking really good care of him," she said, the word *really* receiving elongated attention.

"I'm on my way."

I hung up the phone and strode to my car, my high heels stabbing the pavement. I had a good idea what Elise was doing and I was pissed. I had the ignition turned before I got the door closed. Screeching into the road, I shot down Riverside Drive to the Westside highway, maneuvering through the stream of traffic like a spawning salmon. I focused on the drive and the metal and concrete around me, pushing thought aside. I barely slowed down to manage the smaller West Village streets until I arrived at the parking lot in SoHo where I rented long term space. Swinging into the lot I hit and bent the entry gate. I didn't care. I'd pay for it. It felt great to slam into something.

I crossed the street to Elise's building and let myself in. Not waiting for the elevator, I pounded up the stairs to her floor and opened her door. My suspicion was confirmed as they were lying naked together on her white shag rug surrounded by decorative pillows, Elise giving Cole a blow job.

"Well that was fast," Elise said as she pulled her head off Cole.

"What the fuck are you doing, Elise?"

"That's kind of obvious, isn't it?" she said, pulling her silk Japanese print bathrobe over Cole's shrinking penis. She was smiling and her motions were slow. "Sorry, sweetie. We took some Quaaludes and this sort of just happened," she said, her tongue struggling to find her teeth as she talked. Cole was fumbling for his glasses, his head lolling about.

"I see. It just happened. Well I just happen to be really pissed. I'm going to the bar on the corner. I want you there in fifteen minutes."

"Sure, babe. We'll catch up with you," she said.

Cole looked groggily at me through his glasses, crooked on his nose. I left, slamming the door.

There was no way I could just be angry. I'd gone straight to rage after talking to her on the phone. I stood in the hallway with my forehead against the wall, breathing, or at least trying to, struggling against the constriction in my chest and the very familiar burning pressure in my gut. I took the stairs again, my weight heavy on each one.

Outside was like a silent movie, my rage demanding focus. People were talking on the corner with no sound. A car passed noiselessly by. I headed for the lights of the one neighborhood bar. I opened the door and all the bar sounds spewed out: Music, laughter, loud voices and clanking pitchers of beer. Someone offered a stool at the crowded bar and I took it gratefully. Ignoring everyone around me I started slamming Bacardi and tonics. A half hour and three drinks later, Elise and Cole shuffled in.

"I need to sit at a table," Elise said almost too softly to hear.

"Yes, I can see that," I barked loudly. "You look

like you better sit or you'll fall down." People were staring at us. I paid my tab and headed into the adjoining restaurant. One table was free and I sat down, followed by the two of them.

"We need to eat, too," Elise said, sliding carefully onto the chair.

"Oh, hungry are we?" I couldn't find a sarcastic enough tone.

The waitress left menus and they both ordered. I got drunk so fast I hardly remember what I said to them except it was a torrent of shaming accusations that flooded me so quickly I didn't have a chance to react differently. I was not nice, finding every insult I could throw at them. I was not graceful. I was ugly. I made fun of Elise and lashed at Cole. They picked at their food and worked at defending themselves. We got loud. The waitress told us to quiet down as other diners had complained. I was only aware of the three of us in the room. I do remember finishing my tirade by slamming my drink down on the table, shards of glass flying into their food. As I did this I was shouting "You never really even made love to me!" at Cole. That I remember. Then I left.

I know I went to at least one other bar that night, ending up in a drunken blackout, having no idea how I got back to my hotel room. Cole must have stayed with Elise. I never asked. He was gone the next day. Elise called to tell me that. I hung up on her after putting in a *Thanks, Bitch*.

Over the month, Cole made a few trips to meet with his agent and editor, his book well along towards being published. I didn't see him on these visits, though I knew he and Elise were seeing each other. They both assured me they'd fallen in love, Cole even telling me "their song" was *What I Did for Love* that they'd play on the jukebox of their favorite Village restaurant. I thought I'd puke on hearing that. I avoided Elise and ignored Cole's attempts at appeasement when he called. He seemed to feel there was some way I'd understand; some way I'd forgive him. They were, after all, helplessly in love. No fault of theirs.

I clutched at my rage as it slowly turned to the anguish I resisted and feared. Rage was so much easier. I couldn't bear the abandonment. I also couldn't manage the simplest things and stayed alone in my hotel room. Trying to cook for myself, an unusual effort, I cut a finger trying to slice an old, mushy onion. Holding it under cold water in the now unclean bathroom, it wouldn't stop bleeding and I let out a howl as I waved my finger back and forth, out of control, streaking the mirror and walls with blood. Finally wrapping it in a towel, I sat down on the toilet lid and cried, my head resting on the sink until I exhausted myself.

"I got another book advance, Lily," Cole announced to me over the phone. "It's a big one this time. There's even talk of selling the film rights. This is it, babe."

Babe. How dare he. I'd even started supporting him again a couple of months before when he ran out of money, though I hadn't sent him a dime since he'd fucked my lover.

He wanted to see me and suggested for old time's sake that we meet for a drink at the Sign of the Dove, our old bar on the Upper Eastside. I weakly agreed. I wanted his apology and I wanted an end of some sort to the drama.

"I know I've been a shit," he volunteered, when we met. "You may not want to forgive me, but I want to try putting all this behind us. I'm going to Los Angeles and I want you to come with me. This book publication is what we've been waiting for. This is the real thing. We're headed for the big time and you're the woman I want to have with me."

"Oh, really?" I said. "What about Elise?"

"Yes, well," he stumbled. "I do have strong feelings for her, but it's you I want to spend my life with. Honestly, Lily. I've always loved you more than I could anyone else. I need you with me. You're my muse. And you're my wife."

"I've heard this before, Cole. What's different now?"

"What's different is that I've made it, babe. My book will get published and it may become a movie. I'm going to Los Angeles to help make that happen. I'm signing on to William Morris, one of the top literary agencies. I've already talked to them about my next book idea and they like it. I'm being given more money and they're looking for an apartment for me – for us, in one of the nicest neighborhoods in Los Angeles. I have a meeting at William Morris in a month when the next chapters of my book are due." He stopped and looked hard at me. "You've got to come with me. I can't do this without you."

"I'll think about it."

"Don't think, just come."

I let the piano music play over me. Clinking glassware and the hum of conversation around me brought nostalgia of our earlier days living in the neighborhood, memories now softened by time. *I can't possibly agree to this move,* I thought. *Then again, what do I have going for myself? I've got no future and this could be a new chance at an old hope. I don't know what else to do, and I want this anguish to stop. Plus we'll be moving far away. We can try starting over – again."*

"Cole, if it doesn't work out this time, I'm not staying. You've got to promise me this is really what you want and that we'll be alone together. Just you and me this time and always. Or I'm gone for good."

"Yes, Lily. I do promise. Remember how we used to talk about all the things we can do together? We can do them now, babe. It's all happening. It's for real. Los Angeles is just the beginning. We'll get settled, I'll get the book finished and then we'll take that trip to Europe."

Within the month we were in Los Angeles. Cole's agent had found a large, nicely furnished apartment with wall-to-wall carpeting and a working fireplace. The apartment complex had an outdoor whirlpool that could fit a football team. But I found Los Angeles uncomfortable. The climate felt strange, though it was perfect for Cole, having grown up in Florida. It was all a little too "fern bar" for me. Drives into the hills or out to the ocean helped ease the transition.

We set up life again, my faith in a new chance holding firm. Cole busily settled in, working hard to get the new chapters done in time for the meeting with his agent. I spent my time getting to know the city, but finding it hard to assimilate into what felt like a foreign culture. I didn't like all the sun and great weather and flashy cars and too trim people. I missed the grit of New York. But I kept at it. I knew I needed to get myself started on something. Maybe I'd try dance again, or start writing. I needed an anchor, and I needed to stop the annoying voices in the back of my head whispering to each other about how pathetic I was for coming here with Cole.

I came back to the apartment from a day of exploring and was getting ready for the whirlpool when I heard Cole on the phone in the other bedroom he'd made into a writing den. In a few minutes it was quiet.

"Elise is in Los Angeles," he said from where he was. I slumped onto our bed, face first.

"And why is she here?" I mumbled through the covers.

"Visiting her father." I knew she'd grown up outside the city.

"I see." I flopped on my back and closed my eyes. "What are her plans?"

"They're not clear."

"Of course not. That's her way. She has the patience of a stalking lioness."

"I didn't know she was coming out," he said, and paused. "I couldn't have stopped it. She has a right to visit her own parent."

"Yes. I'm not questioning that. It's the rest of her intentions that concern me." Cole didn't respond and I sensed weight to the space between us that was more than the orange air of Los Angeles.

Within a week, Elise was moving in with us. She was subtle about it, starting by bringing us house warming gifts. Then she brought a change of clothes and used the whirlpool, throwing her wet things in the dryer in the apartment afterwards, which she and I argued about.

"When you're living here, you can do as you please," I said, angry about what we both knew she was doing. "But for now, I still live here and what I say goes. You're not using the fucking dryer."

She kept stopping by and began to leave clothes behind, finally arriving with a large duffle bag, groceries and a bottle of wine. That day she stayed late and stayed over, climbing into our bed. I chose to sleep on the living room floor in front of the fireplace. Cole's suggestion to me privately was that we all try living together. I said no, flatly no. In the morning, Elise was gone before I woke up. I made a plane reservation and packed my bags.

"Don't leave, babe. We can work this out."

"Cole, I'm out of here. This relationship isn't worth fighting for anymore. For some demented reason, I still love you, but I hate this marriage." The cab had come to take me to the airport. I opened the door to go. "She's going to fuck you over too someday, you know. I'm seeing now that's what she does. She uses people to advance herself and she used me. She wants your money and maybe your connections. And when she's done with that, she'll be off with the next person who's got something for her to take advantage of. I'll be sorry to see that happen to you, Cole."

It was almost my twenty-sixth birthday, and I was on my way back to New York. To what else, I had no idea. Sometimes it's good enough to just be leaving somewhere behind.

෧෧෧෧෧

Cole agreed to support me for a year. He owed me at least that much. It'd give me time to work my way into something. But I didn't start anything right away. I drank.

I got an apartment on Barrow Street in the West Village, a brick building once a firehouse stable in the 1850s. It was a small, triangular, two-floor apartment with a spiral staircase. It suited my angular mood.

I spent my afternoons at bars like the White Horse Tavern on Hudson Avenue and my nights at Seventh Avenue bars like Sweet Basil or nearer my apartment at Chumley's, an old speakeasy still with no outdoor sign. I hung out with other regulars and talked about anything that came up. I didn't care. As long as I was drinking, everything was funny or fascinating. I had an odd assortment of drinking buddies who also didn't much care about the topic, but enjoyed spending hours in conversations that escalated in fervor and decibel level as more of us gathered together and drank.

During the day I'd poke through alternative newspapers looking for things to do with my life. Ideas came and went and I decided on nothing at first. I'd never had to handle the degree of devastation I felt from Cole and Elise and didn't know where to begin finding the equilibrium I needed. I felt lousy and started to blame myself for what happened and for failing so thoroughly to become anyone worthwhile. So, around four o'clock it was easy enough to hit the bars again. Since I made no difference to anyone it didn't matter. It wasn't as if I was a world class violinist falling off the wagon and someone had noticed. I was just another asshole as far as I could tell.

I'd been out to New Jersey to visit my parents and let them know I'd left Cole and was living in the city. They were glad, never having really liked him, though they'd tried. He'd just seemed a bit egocentric to them. How little they knew. I spared them the details. They drove me back into the city with stuff Cole and I'd stashed at their house: the bear rugs, kitchenware, some books, a tape player and tapes. I didn't want anything I didn't need or that reminded me of Cole. My parents gave me a dresser and table, and I planned to buy at least a mattress and two chairs. I didn't know who might sit in the other chair. I was starting over, only I just hadn't managed to get very far yet.

Mom and Dad were supportive. Dad was quiet and focused on parking the car and doing the heavy lifting. I thanked him with a tight hug. He kissed my cheek. Mom was exuberant. "Oh, sweetie, you'll have this looking like home in no time. I'm so proud of you. I admire your resilience. You've been through so much, but you're handling it all so well. And it's all behind you now. You've got a fresh start and I know you'll be fine."

I cried when they left, the loneliness heavy in the apartment like a big piece of furniture, an overstuffed armchair I could sink into, weeping myself into a despair I could drag off to a bar like a big, dumb drinking buddy. I was pathetic.

I'd been a little concerned about my drinking and had bought a nice Italian-made Atala racing bicycle, which I loved. I figured if I rode the bike to the bars I couldn't get too drunk because I'd have to ride home. I even risked going out of the area to bars down in Tribeca because the distance would keep me sober. So would my having to be aware of the unpredictable street denizens I'd be vulnerable to and the strangers I'd drink with, or so I reasoned. But on the night after

Mom and Dad left, I found out how much fun it is to ride a bike drunk. I'd gotten used to riding it all over town during the daytime and felt comfortable cruising the streets. And being drunk relaxed me. It took Mom's *I know you'll be fine* out of my head, me terrified that no, I would not be fine. I was a doomed fuck-up and they'd learn that soon enough.

After leaving Chumley's that evening I decided to ride around awhile in the early spring weather, bar-hopping up Seventh Avenue until I was quite shit-faced. Meandering on my bike through a tangle of streets to get home, I rode over Waverly Place and across Bank Street, slowing down when I came to where Cole and I'd lived, musing over our history and missing even those times, blurred now so that only the better memories surfaced, the tenderness that had sustained us. "Shit!" I called out. I desperately wanted to go back in time to some happier era. *And when, exactly, was that?* I questioned myself, knowing the only way to go was forward into probably even more miserable crap. *Damn Cole!*

More pissed than sad now, I swung over to West Street, under what remained of the old elevated Westside highway. I found I could get up speed and time the traffic lights so I didn't have to stop. I shifted the Atala's gears and sailed down this very desolate stretch of Manhattan. The east side of the street was lined with warehouses and the west side led out to the abandoned piers left from the days of the ocean liners, weeds now growing between the rotting planks of wood. It'd rained earlier that day and under the elevated highway the afternoon sun hadn't reached the puddles, now reflecting the few streetlights, creating shiny yellow ovals in the black asphalt. Steel girders still carried the weight of the old highway and its long history, the abandoned road waiting while city planners decided what to do with it, a rusty carcass that groaned in high winds like an old giant in some Norse tale. It was silent now except for the dripping rainwater slowly channeling through the metal and splashing down onto the yellow pools that flashed as I sped by. A current of cool spring air rushed up the roadway, pushing my long hair back into a waving banner. It felt good on my face, flushed and hot from drinking. There was a mist in it reminding me how near I was to the Hudson River, snaking alongside Manhattan all the way up to Saugerties and Rhinecliff and the houses Cole and I'd lived and loved in back then, back in the beginning when we were still silly together and kept our promises. It'd been a long journey down the river over all those years until now. My anger shifted back to missing him, or my memory of him, and the miserable abandonment came again, of friendship and love feeling ripped from me like an animal skinned alive.

My bike bucked over a chunk of fallen highway debris, jerking me out of this dismal reverie. The light was switching from green to yellow ahead and I raced to beat it. But my game caught up with me at a particularly dark intersection where I had to stop and wait for the crossing of the only car I'd seen on the roadway. It was a dark blue car with a white convertible top and it cruised slowly by me, a brown face taking a long smiling look up at me from the driver's seat. I let it pass, staring straight ahead.

"Say, pretty lady," crooned a low voice out of absolutely nowhere. "You're lookin' mighty nice sitting up all perky on that little seat," a tall, muscular man said as he slid up beside me, his pocked and ruddy face coming close to mine. "I been watchin' you ride," he said, the long vowel sound blown into my ear, foul breath reaching my nose. I glanced away, seeing there was no one at all in the dark under the dripping elevated highway with only one street light and no more traffic; not even any gay guys heading for the backs of idle delivery trucks on the piers for an orgy of rough sex. I tried to cycle forward, but he gripped my back wheel with his left hand. "Where you goin', sweetness? I figured maybe you and I could get to know each other, what with our being out here alone together so late at night. What do you say?" He was sliding his right hand around my waist.

I froze and became very focused, the alchemy of booze and adrenaline surging through my blood, grabbing my deep sadness of a minute ago and picking up rage along the way that I'd stored in deep, secret places. It was all flooding through me with a force outdistancing any hope of rational thought or emotional control, my wolf soul unleashed, fangs bared.

"Get the fuck off me you bastard!" I screamed, digging my fingernails into his brawny forearm and pushing it away from me.

"Shit, babe. That's no way to be," he said, backing off a few feet and raising his arms in mock surrender, but moving to block my way forward.

"I am telling you … to get … the fuck … away … from me!" I could hear myself yelling louder and deeper, almost growling. I dropped my bike and strode toward the man, my hands reaching for his face, my rage streaming through my arms, inviting action.

"What the fu...." I'd grabbed his mouth with my right hand, a fingernail piercing his protruding lip. His hands clamped around my ribcage, trying to pull me free of him but my left hand found his neck, fingernails digging into its fleshy folds. My lungs compressed air and a guttural sound vibrated past my vocal chords and came screeching out my constricted throat. Grace's image of pretas flashed in my mind and I feared my own preta coming into its own, my rage reaching a threshold for its emergence out of my soul, the screeching sound the preta's scream in terror of my imminent death at this man's hands, my unfulfilled soul birthing it into an eternity of thirst and starvation. I was losing it completely. I felt a trickle of blood run down the man's chin. My left hand found his eye and as I began to dig a long red thumbnail into his eye socket, he jumped away, throwing me back.

I'd tempted danger many times on this city's streets before, daring someone to hurt me so badly I'd finally feel no pain. But here I was the aggressor and it felt triumphal. There in the dark with no one to intrude I wanted to kill this motherfucker and enjoy it immensely for the satisfaction I so wanted to get for all the bad times. Just one powerful kill; one moment of supreme control.

"Fuck you, bitch! You fuckin' crazy!" I lunged again, huffing a laugh at him. He turned and bolted away. I let out a victory howl and watched him meld with the darkness under the highway. *Maybe next time*, I thought, my wolf soul panting hard inside me.

I stood still for the longest time, hearing sounds arising out of the silence. Planks of the nearby pier moaned as they grated against the pylons, starlings nesting in the girders of the highway above fluttered and cooed, a door banged against a warehouse wall in the strengthening wind of oncoming rain. I was coming back into myself.

The familiar tightening in my chest began and breathing got hard. I was trembling and my head began to pound. I felt soldered to the ground when the panic came. My solar plexus pulled in suddenly with nausea. A tunnel seemed to open up in my body when the hot vomit came spewing out, splashing onto the pavement in heaves. It was as if I was ridding myself of the rage I'd drawn from so deep in my being. Remorse surged in its place bringing a calming humility and I imagined my preta, relieved, receding in gratitude.

I had to get out of there. In seeming slow motion, I wiped my blood-sticky hand on my jeans and spit the remaining vomit out my mouth. I went to my bike, picked it up and steered it as I walked in the direction of home.

Rain came pelting down. It streamed through my hair as I held my head back. Opening my mouth, I took in the rain, swilled it and rinsed out the rest of the puke, spitting it into the road. I came to Hudson Avenue and turned toward Barrow Street. A foursome of tough looking gay men hustled by, rubbing shoulders and laughing hard. Seeing them calmed me. I felt an odd kinship with these metal-studded late night revelers, with their raw muscularity.

Once home, I fell heavily into bed and a deep sleep. I had the dream again. But instead of sand, I was running along black pavement, the mackerel stripes of cirrus clouds above backlit by a full moon reflected in bright white pools of water on the road that splashed as my feet pounded down in front of me. The men and their torches were closing in, but I was gaining strength and confidence with every stride, my legs elongating into powerful haunches and I easily sprang, like a sleek animal, into the sky, rising at tremendous speed this time, my trajectory peaking and leveling off into the comfortable glide I knew so well, the feeling of freedom and safety as I grasped the even rows of the cirrus clouds like monkey bars in a child's jungle gym, the moon dancing playfully alongside.

The following day I woke up with the usual hangover and the familiar self-loathing always accompanying a drunk. I remembered the incident under the highway and pulled a pillow over my head as if to block out the self-punishment I knew was coming. I berated myself for again subjecting myself to the annoying death wish that my drunken self just loved to toy with. That *fuck it* state of mind was going to get me killed. I just couldn't do this to myself anymore. There was no good pay-off coming and I was risking more and more all the time.

I dosed my cotton mouth with a liquid protein vanilla shake, downed some vitamin B, brushed the little sweaters off my teeth with baking soda toothpaste and took a valium. Feeling marginally better, I sat with a cup of coffee on my spiral staircase overlooking the Blue Mill Tavern and the Cherry Lane Theatre on the very quaint adjoining street. This was my pondering place, and as I sat there it struck me again there was no question I was done. I'd crossed a line, with no urge to go back. It was that simple. I needed to start something new. I'd known that for a while, but hadn't been able to do anything about it. I'd needed to hit bottom and I'd found it the previous night. Reaching there changed me. Relieved, I sat back on the spiral steps and cried out all my tension, pressing my face into the thick bathrobe covering my knees until there was nothing left. I let go of a lot of fear, knowing my problems were inside me, not outside where I'd expected to find them, looked for them, wanting to confront evil and prove I could defend myself from its harm. Looking out at the quiet, sunny, undisturbed street, I realized the best protection might just be in taking care of myself for a change. What was most frightening was not potential harm but what was real – the harm that'd already happened to me and everything else I'd brought on myself. I thought maybe I could deal with that. I could try anyway.

I started by making eggs and toast with blackberry jam while listening to an old Joan Baez tape. She sang about strife with a courage I emulated. I sang along, me and Joan making breakfast and peace with ourselves. After a long shower I found a clean flannel shirt, jeans and my last clean underwear. I sat back in my window and thumbed through a catalogue I'd gotten weeks ago from a design school over on Fifth Avenue. I found a class in architectural design, a subject that always intrigued me. It started in two weeks. Tomorrow, on Monday, I'd sign up.

Then I headed for the Laundromat with the rest of my clothes. Everything in the washer, I bought a *Village Voice* down the street and settled on the window seat of the Laundromat to look through the want ads and people-watch out the window. The steady rhythm of the dryers and the smell of detergent were comforting and the sunshine through the window warmed me. I was feeling better about myself.

There was an ad for a film company that needed a production assistant. I had no real idea what that entailed, but I had a notion. Tomorrow, after I'd gone to the school, I'd check out the ad. I spent the rest of the day treating myself to good feeling things. I drank organic tea with organic honey. I gave myself a facial and rubbed lotion into my legs that were so dry the skin was cracked. I cut my toenails and put different colored nail polish on each one. Finding one of Dad's old poetry books among those in the box I'd brought in the day before, I wrapped myself in a blanket on the bear rugs reading Tennyson's poems and began to *faintly trust the larger hope.*

Feeling much stronger the next day, I challenged myself and succeeded in actually going to the school and signing up for a class. Then, having worn my best production assistant outfit of black jeans and a black turtleneck, I started out for the film company several blocks north in Chelsea, one of the more "in" neighborhoods.

It turned out to be a very small production company that shot interview shows for local television. I'd help spiffy up the guests for the show, making sure there was no lint on their clothes and their hair was neat. I'd learn to help with the equipment, maybe more. *We'll see how it goes,* they had said. The pay was dreadful, but I didn't care. I just wanted the experience and to see where it might lead. They hired me. I think they liked me.

So by day I went to the production studio and on Tuesday nights went to my architecture class and designed a space station out of cardboard rolls from toilet paper and paper towels, along with small squares of poster board. It was cool. The smaller rolls formed two circular tunnels around a longer roll where all the equipment, labs, dining and recreation facilities were, while small platforms connected the rolls and made the living quarters. Large windows gave everyone a great view of space.

I also learned drafting and drew floor plans of my apartment plus elevation drawings. Drafting a spiral staircase next to large windows in a triangular room wasn't easy. I loved it.

The job at the film company was fun and I ended up doing other production shoots. I was given more responsibility and helped scout outdoor locations, picked up at my apartment by a crew member at impossibly early morning hours.

I was gradually feeling better about myself and that maybe I had some talent that could take me somewhere, anywhere. I focused on what I was doing and tried to keep obsessive Cole-Elise thoughts to a minimum, though my dreams at night were full of self-hating excursions through scenes of abandonment and betrayal, dreams that continued for decades, though eventually became less frequent and finally faded away.

Knowing that Cole's contribution to my living expenses would eventually run out, I got more serious about earning money and started also working as a temporary secretary at various firms around the city, filling in for people out sick, on vacation or maternity leave. I ended up mostly in advertising firms and it led to a full-time job working at a boutique agency in mid-town that specialized in the film and television industry. It was run by a very short, very bright and delightful young man who became a lifelong friend. I started out writing press releases for him and he became my writing mentor, teaching me everything I would need to know about writing feature articles and ad copy. Working with freelance designers, we created publicity and advertising campaigns for film and video equipment and animation houses.

It was a busy year. Jimmy Carter became President, the World Trade Center got built, there was a twenty-five hour blackout in the July heat in New York, Apple computers went on sale, the Mid-East crisis loomed, punk music came in, kids got wrist radios and Farah Fawcett was pictured on bean bags in her famous red bathing suit and big blond hair.

I rode my bike everywhere and got healthier. I'd curtailed my drinking severely, was clean of all drugs and was eating fresh food cooked at home. Between having a job and my class, I was beginning to feel what I guessed was normal. I grocery-shopped and did laundry in seeming correlation with the schedules of average working people. I read the newspaper and got subscriptions to the *New Yorker* and *Newsweek*. I could keep a conversation going with sober people about everyday events which made me feel more visible and real than I had in a long time. I was part of the public crowd even if I didn't have any close friends. I didn't feel like a stranger in my own town when I hit the pavement. I was at home in myself and I was doing okay. At twenty-eight, I still had a lot of life to go.

ᖇᖇᖇᖇᖇ

I ripped the final page out of the typewriter and shuffled the article together neatly. It seemed I'd make the deadline for *Millimeter,* a film trade magazine. An economic recession had come and the marketing firm I'd worked for had folded. I was working freelance now, with help from my old boss and mentor friend. The work wasn't easy. I liked the writing, but the deadlines drove me nuts. The last interview I'd done had taken so long to arrange, but I couldn't do the article I was working on without it. But now it was done and I'd have time to get to my afternoon meeting uptown to negotiate a new assignment.

Calling the courier service, I was told that with the spring storm it'd take the messenger forty-five minutes to bike across mid-town and down to the West Village. At least he could get around. The blizzard that winter had shut down traffic altogether. *Fine,* I thought. I had time to take a shower.

I got the package ready for the messenger and laid it on the old card table that served as my desk. It, the dresser and the bed were the only pieces of furniture in the small studio apartment I'd rented in the same building on Barrow Street to save money. I could walk across the floor space in about five strides, but it was all I needed. I had places for what stuff I had and from my sprawling mattress on the floor I could look out the window over a tiny, tree-filled back yard. I liked to lie there watching the leaves dance, listening for birds.

Finishing my shower, I pulled on my long, hooded cotton robe. It was getting too warm for this heavy thing, but finances were low and a new bathrobe would have to wait. I started tackling my snarled wet hair with a brush when the doorbell rang.

It was the bell to my apartment door, not the buzzer from downstairs. It was the middle of the day and all the other tenants were usually at work. It was also too early for the bike messenger.

"Who's there?" I called out.

"Strand Messenger Service," a male voice answered.

"How did you get up to my floor?" I asked.

"The front door was open," he said.

Not the best maintained building, I wasn't surprised the lock was broken again. It bothered me that the messenger had just come up the stairs. I wondered what to do. I decided to just give him the addressed envelope and be done with it.

I opened the door and thrust out the envelope to the young man standing there.

"Do you have any Kleenex?" he asked. His snot was running down his face. *How disgusting.* "I just biked downtown in this rain, and I've got a cold." Feeling uncomfortable, but not wanting his mucous all over my envelope, I let him in and motioned to the nearby bathroom, not turning my back on him to get it myself.

"Grab some toilet paper," I said, moving closer to the rack of kitchen knives.

He did so, blew his nose and headed for the door, my envelope under his arm. But instead of leaving, he closed and locked the door from inside, turned around and rolled his knit hat down over his brown face, turning it into a ski mask. He let my envelope drop to the floor with a hard thud. I froze.

"Don't say nothing and you won't get hurt," he said slowly and deeply while shoving me toward the bed, throwing me down and landing heavily on my chest, the air forced out of my lungs.

I went into full blown rage mode, no preliminary emotions needed. I knew the rage route without feeling my way there and no thinking was involved, just an automatic reaction I'd been through so often before that it only seemed to quicken with time and experience.

I grabbed the lamp behind me and banged its brass base on his forehead, though it was cushioned by his mask. Pushing me down with one hand, he got his pants unzipped with the other and tried to dig out his cock. I kept ramming the edge of the lamp into his head and shouting, hoping one of my neighbors might be home for the day. Drool, or maybe blood, dropped onto my face.

He shoved off me angrily, tugging at his pants. But my lamp swung high and fast and gave a cracking blow to his forehead. Silently he got up and started dizzily to back away, blood seeping through his mask.

I grabbed over the end of the mattress and pulled up a rifle I kept there, a slender .22 caliber hunting rifle a fellow student's father had given her when she was ten years old that she'd left with me for temporary safekeeping while she was moving out of town. I rocked off the bed, lifted the rifle and aimed it at the boy's face, knowing it wasn't even loaded.

"Get ... the fuck ... out!" I screamed, stepping towards him, the gun barrel reaching closer to his blood-soaked ski mask. Without a sound, he bolted for the door, unlocked it and sped away, grabbing and taking my envelope with him.

I slammed and locked the door, threw the rifle on the bed, my hands flying to my face, sobbing and then sucking air in desperate gasps that coursed through my gut and back out my throat. Gasps became shrieks and fists found and pounded the wall. Falling to my pillows I howled and rolled fiercely back and forth, back and forth, holding myself tightly. Everything had been going so well. I thought I was done with this crap, this god-awful emotional flooding that brought back the panic and an urgent need to fight back, to snuff out the attacker.

I bolted upright, grabbed the phone and called my landlord. A nasty torrent spewed out of me at him, me not giving him a moment to respond. "The front door lock is broken – again! Someone just fucking tried to rape me, you big shit!" I slammed the receiver against the wall.

Next I called the messenger service, launching my wrath at the receptionist. "Your messenger just tried to rape me!" The manager got on the phone as I was screaming about the lock, the snot, the ski mask. "I'm calling the police!" And then did so. I was asked to come to the station immediately, once it was clear I wasn't injured and needing immediate medical help.

I stood dumbly in my room, my legs heavy, and my nails clawing at the terrycloth bathrobe. Oddly, I wondered about still making my afternoon meeting and what I should wear to the police station. I got myself somewhat dressed and headed to the station, foolishly clutching my briefcase, confusion whirling through my head.

The rain had stopped, but the streets were full of puddles. I stomped the three blocks, splashing water up my legs. I heard no sound as I marched into the station, where I'd never been before. I had no idea what to do so just stood there until spoken to.

"May I help you?" someone said, the noisy bustle of the station becoming suddenly audible.

"Yes," I said, my teeth clenched. An interview followed and notes were taken. I was asked to wait and was left on a bench next to several other miserable looking people.

The messenger service was called. The messenger had delivered my package and been asked to return to the service office. He did and was met by the police, who arrested him. He was brought to the station and questioned. They put him in a lineup.

I was called in and asked to identify my attacker through a one-way mirror. I stood in front of the window while a row of men entered the adjacent room, a row of black men, my attacker standing near the middle, looking down. They each were told to approach the mirror. When my attacker approached, I stepped back. He looked up placidly. "That's him," I said, and looked away.

What followed were days, then weeks and months of inquiry. I was questioned by lawyers, a grand jury and a forensic psychiatrist who prescribed medication I never took. He did warn me about startle reactions I might have and did later on; fearful moments triggered by anything that reminded me of the assault, even a sudden move by someone standing nearby.

I became unglued and said strange things. I accused a police officer of coming on to me and threatened to tell his wife. On the way to court one day, I swore I heard the cab driver invite me to ride with him out to Brooklyn for the afternoon and screamed at him until he stopped the cab so I could get out. I was constantly tense and suspicious. Routine tasks were hard. Nothing made sense.

I sued the messenger company and won the case, receiving fifteen thousand dollars in remuneration for the assault. My attacker went from Rikers Island to prison for three years. He was twenty-three, I was told. His criminal history was marginal. I often thought about him. He'd done a bad thing, made a stupid mistake. I wondered how much resentment he'd build up in prison, what friends he'd make, what crimes he'd learn, what angry plans he'd have. It was too bad. Things like this shouldn't happen. Then again, it took sexual assault to get the attention of the legal system. Up to that point, men were fairly free to do whatever they wanted to with women sexually. If women complained, they'd be blamed themselves. My resentment doubled.

Three years from the day of his imprisonment I also thought of my attacker. I feared him again knowing he'd be released, though I'd moved away. For many years I'd tremble when strange men came too near me – startle reactions. Of course I'd been startled enough times that it seemed those fearful moments had each exaggerated the next until any man within three feet of me was suspect. For a long time I carried a canister of pepper spray and always had my house keys in my pocket for quick access to at least a kind of sharp weapon. Over time my startle reactions went on automatic and I had no control over them. They compounded each other until I felt a constant low hum of fearful anticipation, often over-reacting to things people said or did that made me feel vulnerable to an attack.

After my assailant's arrest, I called my mother. I just wanted her to know what was going on. It felt like the right thing to do. "Hi Mom," I began.

"How're things?"

"Are you alright?" she asked, not hesitating.

"Well, yes, I'm fine."

"Something's happened, I can tell. Were you raped?"

I was twenty-eight years old and she was finally asking me if something bad had happened. She was showing surprising insight I'd so longed for in her. Perhaps her own growing independence had uncovered a deeply hidden perceptiveness unused until now in her adult life; self-will and expression finding new light.

Of course, after all these years I'd finally learned how to take care of myself, or so I thought at the time. I didn't think I needed her help, but her empathy was much appreciated and I admired her for it.

"Well not technically, but I was sexually attacked," I said. "But really, I'm fine and I'll be fine. There's no need for you to worry now. I just wanted you to know."

But I had called her. Maybe I did really need her help. And she'd been there for me. I resisted my very stubborn independence and admitted I'd received help from many people over the last months: The police; the considerate people at the messenger service; the smart and caring lawyer; and the people on the grand jury who'd listened intently to my story as I told all the details from the little box I sat in next to the concerned looking judge. Maybe I couldn't protect myself all the time. Maybe front door locks get broken and people do fucked up things that can hurt. Just maybe it was alright to let other people in and to know that justice could be found without my having to shoot someone for it. It struck me that maybe there were forces larger than myself that I wasn't giving credence to and I didn't have to rely on myself all the time. It was possible there were some people I could trust. Maybe I'd have to have faith in that for a while and see what happened.

I closed my eyes and thought of Mom again and an old image came to mind. I was standing in front of her as she sat reading a book in her blue-padded swivel rocking chair. Dad was nearby in his worn leather armchair, reading the newspaper. I'd just come home from the birthday party so long ago – from the back of the closet. Mom lowered her book and looked at me kindly. It was as though I, as an adult, was looking right through my child's eyes into hers. I reached my arms towards her, bending over to press my head onto her lap and put my arms around her waist, hugging her tightly. She placed her long-fingered hand on the side of my face and slowly stroked my cheek over and over crooning *Looly, looly, loo,* with a tune of hers I'd long forgotten. My child's eyes opened and I saw Dad looking over at us and smiling. Giving Mom another tight hug, I left her lap and went over to Dad, pressing myself to his chest and throwing my arms around his neck. He hugged me softly, patting my shoulders. *My beautiful,"* he said. And my child and I both cried, great gushing sobs of love and forgiveness. They hadn't known what had happened to me. They couldn't have, but for so long I'd blamed them for not knowing.

☙☙☙☙☙

I quit working and began subsisting frugally on

the insurance money awarded to me from the messenger service. Summer came and I took a vacation from my life for a while. With everything I did to recover, I slowly began feeling whole again instead of the shaky, startle-prone mess I'd become. I walked or rode my bike for miles, going to places like the Morgan Library and Museum on Madison Avenue, where I'd look through its collection of Medieval and Renaissance illuminated manuscripts, autographed works by Edgar Allan Poe, Henry David Thoreau, and Jean-Jacques Rousseau, a score from one of Brahms's symphonies, and even a letter written by a thirteen-year-old Mozart. That summer the library had a special show of Michelangelo and His World which brought me way out of myself and into another time, place and very exquisite mind.

Or I'd go to St. Patrick's Cathedral on Fifth Avenue and relax in the somber quiet of its massive interior, feeling gratefully small among the huge statues and colorful images of honored people from ancient times. I relished the easy feeling of humility in that towering space – an old feeling from so many years ago in Dad's church, but one that had become strange to me in the intervening time. I now eagerly accepted the spirituality I sensed flowing freely in that sanctuary. New hopes seemed available there, ones I could create from calmer stuff than the defensiveness I'd honed with my anger and self-righteousness, sharpening my iron will to a fine point. It tired me just thinking about it.

The Frick Collection further up Fifth Avenue was another good place for slowing down. Being there was like walking through someone's elegant home when they weren't there. Beautiful furnishings filled the rooms, and long windows with yards of drapes let in a nice amount of light for viewing paintings of incredibly bucolic scenes of sunny days, mounds of clouds, trees heavy with foliage and landscapes so soft looking you could feel yourself lying down in the long grass, the hayfields and wildflowers. Sweet faces peopled these scenes, a young boy tenderly putting flowers in a girl's hair, romantic boaters idling downstream.

All I wanted to do was slow down and rest, cruising along on my bike and stopping for frequent respites in these quiet places. I let the harsher sounds of the city engulf, but not bother me. The sounds were from other people doing other things. I had no responsibility for it and no need to react to it. I could just let it pass by. I practiced creating a pleasant detachment from things around me. Unless compelled, I didn't have to interact with anyone. Or I could choose to have a quick, safe conversation with a street vendor or newsstand seller. I liked to make people laugh at light, silly remarks I'd make about ordinary things. I needed the superficiality.

I learned about Buddhism and practiced mindfulness and meditation. I read works by Thich Nhat Hanh and listened to guided meditations he gave at Plum Village. I explored the Dharma, the teachings of the Buddhist tradition. I found great solace in its concepts and began using short meditations on my own to keep myself calm and centered in the present. I read about how Buddhas give alms to pretas and felt Grace's presence.

I even dressed differently and consciously, wanting to blend in. I wore only three pairs of jeans in blue, gray and black. I wore five long-sleeved tee-shirts in various muted colors under an old jeans jacket. I wore a cap with my hair tucked inside and used no makeup. A sturdy pair of old hiking boots completed my ensemble, good for walking, good for running away if I had to. I carried only essential things in a leather shoulder bag I wore comfortably while riding my bike. I had a small bag of bike tools attached to the rear carrier in case I broke down. I was bland, anonymous and self-protected.

Sometimes I'd still get shaky. Waiting at a street light in heavy pedestrian traffic, I'd be aware of people standing close to me or I'd get jostled by someone. I'd practice imagining a barrier between us, trying to trust that nothing harmful would happen, trying to have faith. If someone made a rude gesture or said something nasty, I'd practice separating myself from them emotionally. It was their bad day, not mine, and I didn't have to react by saying or doing something in return. It wasn't about me. When tensions arose, I worked at breathing deeply and letting them go, relying on larger forces I knew were there to take care of things. It wasn't all up to me. I found my own responsibilities were small and manageable. I didn't have to fight my way through everything all the time. I just wasn't that important. I was valuable to myself and maybe to some others at some times. That was enough. I was learning that respect mainly came from myself on the inside, not from others on the outside. So simple, really, but so hard to learn.

Cole called one day to let me know that Elise had left him. Not only had she left, she'd emptied out a shared bank account, taken all the furniture she'd made him buy, and driven away in the car she'd insisted on jointly owning. He was devastated. I gave him my sympathies, feeling genuinely sorry for him.

"And another thing I feel bad about," he said "is that I took Elise to Europe, Lily." I said nothing. "That was our trip, and I know it."

"I see," I finally responded. "Where'd you go?"

"Everywhere." He paused. "We did it all." I took *it all* in and then let it go in one long breath.

"That's okay, Cole. I'll have my own Europe trip someday. It'll be for me and it'll be fine."

We kept in touch a few times over the years. He continued writing successfully and even sold the film rights to one of his books. Then I got a call from his childhood friend who'd been the best man at our wedding. Cole was dead. He had a heart attack. He'd finally been diagnosed with manic depression and gotten treatment, but it wasn't enough and it was too late. I learned then about how manic depression caused not only mood swings, but compulsive and sometimes bizarre sexual cravings and behavior. Our marriage, or lack of one, began to make sense to me, at least his contribution to it. Understanding mine would take more time.

Apparently Cole spent his earnings on long manic trips to Russia, China and other places that showed up in his books, intermixed with periods of reclusiveness at home. And then the heart attack. He was so young. I grieved his passing. He once asked me to move back to California to be friends again. I'd said no. I was an easterner. His last call to me was soon before he died to see how I was doing. I think he knew he wasn't doing so well.

୬୬୬୬୬୬

When fall came that year, I started thinking I was maybe ready to handle a job again. I bought professional clothes for interviewing including two nice suits, one light grey and one dark blue. I got my hair cut and styled for a real job and bought two inexpensive necklace chains, one silver and one gold. I buffed up my resume and filled a portfolio with good work samples.

Looking for public relations jobs in Manhattan, I found one at a human services agency serving abused women and children. I'd suspected for a long time that I'd find this work. It just took a while to get there. By the time I did, I understood these women and children pretty well and felt compelled to tell the story of their lives and create more public awareness of their plight. It was part of my getting help as well.

It was a small agency and I thought I'd fit in pretty well. I was excited about the work and thrilled when I got hired. I'd work for the executive director.

In the beginning, she liked me. I worked hard and produced results. She even hugged me once, saying how pleased she was with my performance and how glad she was that I was on staff. And I liked her. She was tall, walked with a regal gait, had brilliant red hair and wore bright blue, green and pink jackets. She was English; I was Scottish. We were a team.

It didn't last. A board member had wanted my job before I was hired. The executive director had spent fifteen unsuccessful months interviewing candidates to fill the position and the board member finally *threw her hat in the ring*, I was told she said, graciously offering her services, having worked in the field before. She was turned down.

When I was hired, this board member became my nemesis, making every effort to discredit me. In time, it worked. No matter what earnest successes I had, attention was drawn to some work area not yet fulfilled or some detail not to her liking. I began to work more feverishly to take on the additional challenges, to leave no goals unmet, to assure my credibility.

I honed, made efficient, made effective, streamlined, enhanced, augmented, increased, sharpened and elaborated upon. But no matter what I did, it wasn't enough or I wasn't doing what my detractor thought should happen or in the way she felt it should be done. She freely communicated her opinion to the rest of the board, who had no context for the information and so had no idea what to think, except to believe her.

I invited her for lunch at a nice Italian restaurant I knew she liked. I arrived early and chose a good, quiet table under the hanging garlics and cheeses. We ordered a nice meal. Hoping to gently reduce our differences, I calmly approached issues of mutual interest trying to gain some common ground. All I got were her opinions without any consideration of my point of view. She just shrugged her shoulders and tensed her lips until the color drained away. The lunch ended without dessert.

I came to realize that what my boss had initially most liked about me was how I made her look good. But when my nemesis stalked my success with misrepresentations and became increasingly vocal to the board, my boss was afraid of getting tangled in my bad reputation and turned cold towards me. She increased her demands. Her supervision of me became a closed-door trial of my intentions.

Stepping into my office one day, her red hair blazing out of her head, she interrupted me by stating, "I want you to prepare weekly reports detailing what work you've done and what work you have scheduled." She was sounding more and more like the Queen of Hearts, and I felt increasingly like Alice.

I met her demands, answered her questions. And yes, I began to defend myself. Without realizing it, I'd dragged my armor out of my closet, polished its metal and put it on, finding its contours snug and familiar. My self-righteousness returned full force. Any faith I'd held in protective outer forces left me as did my fledgling ability to let things go. The more autocratic my boss got, the more defensive I became. I rocked her boat so forcefully I hoped it'd capsize and she'd drown. I wanted to force her to see things my way.

I stood up for my decisions, explaining my reasoning. I created spreadsheets to demonstrate my progress, shared my well documented achievements and charted my plans for the department's future. I mounted a huge, three-month work plan on the wall for passers-by to see. I was well liked by the staff and my work was good. But that didn't matter.

I began to understand even better how domestic violence victims must feel: no matter how clean the house, the dinner was too cold; no matter how well dressed the children, the lawn needed mowing.

It also began to dawn on me that I was someone from another class than the social club on the board that was eyeing me. My rival made the most of this distinction as she sidled up to these wealthy crones, the women who never worked but always volunteered for the less fortunate. It made them feel so much better, though their labors might have to be occasionally delayed by an art buying holiday in Italy or being dropped by helicopter onto the French Alps for a skiing adventure.

I became increasingly excluded from conversations, especially when they turned to the shortcomings of an expensive car, the convenience of having children away at boarding schools, or the annoyances of working with tedious interior decorators. My rival turned them from me. Unable to totally disparage my good work, she cast innuendos my way as might a woman of class to a servant in the room awaiting instructions.

I had my hair cut in a shorter, more executive style. I lost weight, bought a couple of very sleek suits: one was power red, the other a black pin-stripe, and wore them with higher-heeled shoes that hurt my feet. I smiled more. I used my hands professionally. I worked on controlling my defensiveness and my escalating temper.

At board meetings my boss and my nemesis began to glare at me, exchanging nods and bits of conversation. Afterwards I'd be scolded because my report to the board was too long or too short, too strongly worded or too weak.

My boss began to berate me in our supervision meetings. She'd sit stiffly in her chair across from me, her shoulders square in her glen green jacket, mouthing the impressions of my detractor, writing notes in her large black binder about whatever I said, slapping the book closed when our time was up.

Her attacks brought hurt quickly transforming into rage finding its smoothly worn path to my mouth. For a while, I could stop it there, taking no action, keeping my teeth clenched and saying nothing. But she'd have succeeded in making me cry, a smile curling across her upper lip. You'd better go wash your face," she said in one meeting. "Use the bathroom in the basement, going down the back stairs. Then no one will see you," she urged. "You don't want anyone to know your business," hissing this last phrase to give it heavy meaning.

To those outside the organization she led, she was irreproachable, the word "saint" used frequently in reference to her. She had, after all, been a nun. She seemed to depend on being held in high regard by others and especially liked to advertise her penchant for self-flagellating acts. To achieve this she'd perform submissive tasks such as kneeling down to wash the baseboards in the office, even making a point of once cleaning the toilets in the bathrooms in a local church after an agency event, letting it be known she was not too good or too important to avoid suffering by shining a floodlight on her humility and penitence.

Her behavior toward me grew demonic. She seemed to delight in our weekly meetings, always held, she insisted, in my office with the door closed. The darkness of her soul contrasted with my efforts to humanize my work space through plants, soft lighting, art, classical music and a very small, plug-in trickling fountain that she complained spit water onto the file cabinet.

I became increasingly sensitive. My pride dug in its heels. I voiced my opinions and held my ground stubbornly. My behavior only hastened the inevitable. Backing down and conceding to her executive position would preserve my job, but my dignity demanded I stand up to her. Any truth was threatening to her as it revealed her weaknesses as an administrator, which had become apparent to me over many months and through discussions with fellow staff who loathed her, but found ways to tolerate her including their dedication to work with those we served. But I totally lost it. During one especially painful supervision session, the rage was not stopped by clenched teeth, but came spewing out in razor-tongued allusions to her inept leadership and weakness in the presence of the board. I'd found my depth of vicious insinuation. You'd think I'd learn, but controlling my temper was not to be mastered, the rage stronger than any internal rationality.

I began seeing a psychiatrist. I'd become so depressed and frightened I couldn't sleep and spent non-work time ruminating and crying uncontrollably.

"Abuse is not okay," he said one day. He spoke slowly and quietly. The words stopped me. I watched his gentle, serious face and a long time seemed to pass before I could respond.

No one had ever acknowledged what was happening as abuse. People tend to be squeamish about such things, talking around the subject like it's a bag of debris to be quickly discarded. No one wants it around. No one wants to deal with it. Or the topic is dismissed in denial of is existence. *Oh, don't be so sensitive,* one person might say. *Why not just be more positive?* another might recommend. The abuse becomes a non-episode, passed over as just being your imagination. It's talked of as in the past, where it belongs, a dusty thing to be swept away. *Just give in and it'll pass.*

With my psychiatrist I prattled on about my anger

and frustrations, trying hard to understand what I'd done wrong, how to correct things. I'd been pondering what I needed to change to avoid the tension. Obviously some new, more acceptable behavior on my part was required.

Abuse is not okay. His words seemed to spread into the air, his empathy nourishing the many plants in the room, healthier than any I'd ever seen, their thick tendrils stretching into all corners. Healing took place here. Maybe I had a chance.

He meant his words and he silently gave me time to absorb them. And at almost thirty years old, I was perhaps finally ready to hear them. I felt lighter, decades of shame lifting from me. We talked comfortably, like old souls, about how our shame makes us vulnerable to those who take advantage of our weakness for their own needs.

He also told me about complex trauma and how repeated abuse over time causes a complex post-traumatic stress disorder that, without therapy, compounds on itself. Gradually, the least triggering stimulus produces instant rage with no chance for any controlled response without therapy to help regulate your emotions again.

He also explained that my need to control, to have my will triumph, was my way of making sense of the trauma, of trying to make things right again, to fix it. Of course it never worked so I'd find more blame for myself, making me vulnerable, which just began the cycle again.

His recommendation was that I confront her. He said perhaps my honestly expressing my feelings about her supervision of me would open up some understanding and we could strive towards a better relationship.

Confronting her was not easy and I was sure she'd fire me. But eventually, it seemed an unavoidable gamble. I could be miserable or I could work up the courage to try and change something, spark a profound realization in her, induce an alteration in my or her universe. I made notes, rehearsed my script, sucked the air of positivism into my lungs and threw on a thick vest of personal affirmations. I also asked the human resources manager to come with me to meet with my boss to discourage further assault and be witness to the outcome.

I confronted the saint. I was professional and calm as I shared my feelings and gave specific examples of her abusive behavior towards me and, as I'd learned in the process, similar behavior towards co-workers past and present. I made amends for any actions of mine that had perhaps impaired and exacerbated our relationship. I tried to be understanding towards her and openly hopeful we could resolve our differences, but firm in my conclusions.

"I've never been accused of abuse before," she said. "I'll have to think about this," she offered and then left the room. I left on a vacation, feeling hugely relieved. The tightness in my chest gave way to deep and restful breathing. I slept through the night for the first time in months. My mood brightened.

On my return, I was fired. "Bad chemistry," she said.

Yes, bad chemistry. I've found there's a toxicity in some troubled people, damaging personality disorders that attach themselves to those more vulnerable for the pleasure of manipulating and dominating them -- previously traumatized people like me, who seem to broadcast their vulnerability and who, when abused, become toxic themselves in time.

I went on unemployment and stayed home, alternating between rocking myself into a comfort zone and seeing my psychiatrist who helped me begin to understand and accept what all had happened and how I could empower myself to find a healthier and saner way of living.

In time I lost track of the small details of my experience, the mental turbulence eventually subsiding, the devastation giving way to anticipating better times. I even managed to forgive the saint. Holding the resentment only sickened me more. I wondered if something very sad had happened to her. A mother superior or a priest had maybe hurt her early on, her incubating malevolence nurtured by anger and resentment. I didn't want that happening to me. I was doing everything I could to sate my preta, as Grace had suggested. No spirit of mine was going ungratified to spend eternity tortured by hunger and thirst. By taking care of myself I'd find the fulfillment that leads to enjoyable giving of self to others and a sharing of life's blessings.

One day I went to the Morton Street pier near my apartment that jutted out into the Hudson River. I spent a long time watching the seagulls as I had many times before, trying to learn from their patience as they circled, searching for their next meal. Learning patience and also acceptance of events and people beyond my control, and the smarts to know what I have to do to make things better, not worse. Then I used a frayed piece of rope from the pylon to tie a shell onto a broken plank of the pier. Imagining the shell to be the saint, I dropped the plank into the current and watched it wash away downstream and out of sight, heading to the Atlantic.

Sometimes I think I live in a parallel universe to what most people collectively agree is normal. It's maybe just a few steps away. But I'm there, fully accepting that I'm a little off the beaten track, the road most travelled.

I've always loved the quote from Vincent Van Gogh printed on my morning coffee cup: "As for me, you must know I shouldn't precisely have chosen madness if there had been any choice. What consoles me is I am beginning to consider madness as an illness like any other, and that I accept it as such."

While not madness, my rage has at times driven me to states of mind where I wouldn't have gone had there been a choice. I'm certain this is true for more of us than we'd like to think – that being normal is an elusive goal and we must become kinder to each other as we struggle in our various ways to get there, hopefully finding acceptance of ourselves along the way and the discovery of choices.

1980

To celebrate my thirtieth birthday, I took my Europe trip. I had money saved and unused vacation pay from my old job. I found a travel agency offering cultural tours outside the usual tourist itinerary, using local hotels and transportation and family-owned restaurants. I didn't want to go alone and this suited me fine. It was abysmally hot in New York and I was glad to leave its heat-trapping metal walls of tall buildings, the air simmering with the smell of rotting garbage and dank sewers.

At the end of June I was flying to Madrid where I'd meet up with my group to tour through Spain, Portugal and Morocco. I carried a backpack with nothing in it but essentials. I chose light, practical travel clothes for their comfort, not for how I looked in them, my external persona a reflection of my truer self. How refreshing to show up in public as just me in loose cotton and sensible shoes with the occasional swirl of color.

I had no idea who I'd be travelling with except that I was one of twelve and to expect few Americans and more Europeans. As it turned out, they were mostly Australians, those lucky folk with six week winter vacations and a healthy economy.

They were young, athletic and good-looking. Two older women joined us, the last Aussie of the group and a German. I was one of four Americans, the others from Tennessee, Texas and California. We gathered one by one, none of us in couples, on the roof of a small, inexpensive hotel in the center of Madrid. The tentative, banal murmurings we made as we introduced ourselves were a poor forecast of the rich, lusty characters we revealed ourselves to be by the end of the trip through reveling in our travel experiences together and spicing up anecdotal tales of our lives back at home.

Only the Teutonic temperament of the elderly German woman caused me irritation through assuming my companionship and providing endless suggestions for how I should do things and what I should think. Of course, she thrust herself impatiently on others from time to time as well. When a cabdriver couldn't open his dented trunk at the train station to remove our baggage, she harshly berated the poor man in German while pulling out the back seats of the cab so as to gain access to the trunk's interior. She hadn't finished with him as we timidly retrieved our bags and headed towards the train, leaving the bewildered man beside his torn apart cab while she threw insults at him over her shoulder.

The woman's behavior was oppressive, but I managed to keep from being sucked into her insatiable need to conquer and intimidate. I was proud of myself for seeing this predator coming, of previewing the slow dance of entanglement I'd gotten caught up in before. Without defensiveness or sarcasm I was able to assertively, but still politely, draw a boundary between us that served to dismantle her intentions and shrink her domineering manner to a manageable size. I also asked the tour guide to relieve me of rooming with her as she had apparently requested. She didn't bother me after that and I was patient and accepting of her. It'd been surprisingly simple to intuitively accomplish something I'd been incapable of for so long.

The group had a terrific time on the tour, all of us knowing it was unlikely we'd ever meet again. There was a respectful but free spirited camaraderie between us that escalated from the sexy, cosmopolitan city of Madrid to the magical plazas and winding streets of the ancient town of Salamanca in the north of Spain, to the very romantic village of Coimbra in Portugal, hosting one of the oldest universities with its fragile library of science and philosophy authored by the originators of these fields of thought.

On a walk by myself up the increasingly steep cobblestone streets spiraling up the immense hill to the university, I left the busy center of shops and restaurants of Coimbra and came into a quiet residential area of small homes, each with a different muted shade of ochre and brown, with tiled roofs and balconies laden with flower pots gorged with red, pink and blue blossoms and vines winding around wrought iron balustrades.

Halfway up the hill I came to a little square with a small café and market, a shop selling hand-painted, beautifully decorative Portuguese tiles, and the Old Cathedral. I bought a few tiles, a lunch of bread, cheese and olives and then sat on the church steps to eat. I hadn't been there long when a Portuguese woman and her five children appeared and sat on the steps lower down to have their lunch. She held the baby while the two boys and two girls quickly ate and began playing on the steps. The boys ran up and down and up again, jumping off the higher steps onto the ground below, challenging each other to jump from a higher, and then a higher step until I thought they might break their ankles. I watched them, laughing and clapping at their wilder feats. They came and sat by me, smiling and chattering and offered me some of their gum, which I thanked them for. When they left to chase each other around the square, the girls came over and shyly stood watching me. The little one flopped down on the step beside me. I showed her the lovely blue and white ceramic tiles I'd bought in the shop and she fingered them happily. The older girl bent over to look, her dark eyes searching mine, her already rough hands reaching out to hold a tile. The mother abruptly called her children to her, and the girls ran back down the steps. I watched the family gather and then got up to go into the church.

An amazingly designed cathedral, it was built solidly on the hill beginning around 1100 A.D. I couldn't imagine how they'd done it, its foundation embedded in the surrounding rock. Plainsong chanting of monks filled the sanctuary – a recording, I realized, but with great effect. I examined every sculpture, icon and painting, infatuated with the detail of the works and the subtlety of expression in the ancient art. I found a row of small carved panels made in the soft stone of the outer wall. They were at eye level and as I stood there I felt the presence of the carver working quietly at his craft, his chisel very precisely etching figures in little scenes of everyday life. There were five-inch tall men in sack clothes hoeing and planting in one panel, sitting together at a long table filled with dishes of fish and fowl in another, and rows of what seemed to be learned men in long robes carrying out a religious ritual in still another. I stepped from one panel to the next, completely absorbed in the intricate detail, looking keenly at the fine-lined expressions on the tiny faces of these little men carved almost a thousand years ago.

Tears began streaming down my face as I took into myself the mystery of the place and the profound spiritual meaning it had for so many people over the centuries. I felt incredibly humbled and blessed to be there; to have wandered into what has been a communal home for the troubled and weary and to find myself so moved by their spirit that infused the space with gentility and grace. I thought of the Picts and Gaels of my own medieval ancestry and felt a connection to the august history of the place as if I'd laid my hand on a cord joining all humanity through which you could feel the vibration of eternal life.

I knew then I was not alone and that I was safe and always would be. I'd tapped into an essence I felt privileged to discover, a human connectedness so deep I experienced a surging forgiveness of myself, of my trespasses, as it were, and of those who'd trespassed against me. In the place of anger, even long held rage, I felt humility and kindness. I felt kindness for others and surprisingly for myself. I respected my dignity and had an appreciation of myself that had eluded me until then. A spiritual ease rose in me and my compulsiveness loosened, my hurt and fear drifting away, carried from me as if by a trusted friend and advisor.

I gradually moved away from the carvings, retaining their serenity, and slowly walked down the aisle and out of the stillness of the church into the dazzling brightness outside. Standing at the top of the steps, I was approached by the older of the two girls I'd met earlier. She held out her hand to me. I could also see one of her brothers approaching another woman down in the plaza, also holding out his hand. They were begging, I realized. I took her hand and motioned for her to come with me. We worked our way down the steps, and I brought her to her mother who was still seated on the lowest step, still holding the baby.

I felt in my pocket and found several large coins. "Para o bebê," I said, handing them to her and stroking the baby's head.

"Obrigado," she said, thanking me.

I turned to the girl and smiled, squeezing her hand before letting it go. If I could have told her to search for a life without begging, I'd have done so. I would have told her to become strong and centered in herself and not seek survival or approval through anyone else. I would have told her that for much of our lives we're not responsible for what happens to us or who we are, but we are responsible for who we later become because as we grow we have choices. Then again, perhaps it wasn't for me to say. It was up to her and to me to each find our way.

ABOUT THE AUTHOR

Now sixty-three years old, Lily Scot has lived in various parts of the United States, though mostly in the Northeast, with some time lived in London and Puerto Vallarta, Mexico, along with various travels to Europe and the Caribbean. Her professional life has been spent working more than thirty years in public relations and fundraising for non-profit human service organizations. In the past few years Lily has taken up political activism, applying her skills to the promotion of several causes she finds critical to restoring true democracy in her home country. Having just attained her bachelor's degree in Human Services, she hopes to find work for a non-governmental organization serving women and children in the Caribbean, where she plans to eventually retire. Though again divorced, Lily says her second husband is her "best friend forever," and they have a son she loves "more than all the stars in the universe." She now lives in Upstate New York with two elderly female cats. She's considering taking up glassblowing. *Sating the Preta* is her first book.

www.ingramcontent.com/pod-product-compliance
Lightning Source LLC
LaVergne TN
LVHW051620080426
835511LV00016B/2089